D1559454

TECHNOLOGY TRANSFER IN INTERNATIONAL BUSINESS

International Business Education and Research Programs

Technology Transfer in International Business

Edited by

TAMIR AGMON

and

MARY ANN VON GLINOW

New York · Oxford
OXFORD UNIVERSITY PRESS
1991

Oxford University Press

Oxford New York Toronto
Delhi Bombay Calcutta Madras Karachi
Petaling Jaya Singapore Hong Kong Tokyo
Nairobi Dar es Salaam Cape Town
Melbourne Auckland

and associated companies in
Berlin Ibadan

Library of Congress Cataloging-in-Publication Data
Technology transfer in international business
edited by Tamir Agmon and Mary Ann Von Glinow.
p. cm. Includes bibliographical references and index.
ISBN 0-19-506235-3
1. Technology transfer.
2. International business enterprises.
I. Agmon, Tamir. II. Von Glinow, Mary Ann Young
T174.3.T387 1991
338.9'26—dc20 90-39540

9 8 7 6 5 4 3 2 1

Printed in the United States of America
on acid-free paper

To Ora Agmon and Steven Kerr,
who help us create
much of what we transfer.

Preface

Technology Transfer in International Business is a book about the parallels that occur (both at a microorganizational level and at a broader macroeconomic level) between actions and transactions commonly thought to be the realm of international business; and the products, processes, and people comprising technology transfer. We have brought together a diverse group of scholars in this edited volume, who are extremely interested in, and puzzled by, the overlaps between international business and technology transfer.

Historically, international business has not been coupled with technology transfer, simply because researchers and practitioners have found each of the two phenomena to be sufficiently complex so as not to widen the net to encompass both. We take a somewhat different approach in this book, following the trend in both the practitioner as well as the research literature toward globalization of the economy; as well as the globalization of business organizations, people, and technologies. We view international technology transfer as an integral part of international business. Accordingly, we have amassed a group of scholars who have thought seriously about both international business and technology transfer. Their contributions are myriad and weave a pattern of considerable complexity, yet the general picture is simple. For we believe that put together, these studies show that international technology transfer and international business are synonymous. Toward that end, we take a quick glance at the authors and their topics, which reveals a highly integrated picture. In Chapter 1, Denis Simon discusses the changing global environment for international technology transfer. This is followed by Chapter 2, contributed by Steven Kobrin, who writes on global integration and its implications for technology development. Chapter 3 is Alexander Good's analysis of the role that governments play in technology transfer and international business. Chapter 4 is contributed by Raj Aggarwal, who discusses the historical roots of technology transfer and economic growth patterns. These three chapters comprise the first part of the book.

Chapter 5 begins the second part, by which we specify the conditions that allow technology transfer to occur. Yair Aharoni discusses education and technology transfer. Chapter 6 is Everett Rogers and Tom Valente's contribution that focuses on technology transfer in high-technology industries. Chapter 7 is offered by Vladimir Pucik, who concentrates on the organizational implications of international strategic alliances in high-technology organizations.

The third and the last part of the book deals with specific cases of technology transfer. Chapter 8 begins the discussion of particular country/corporation issues. Martha Harris discusses technology transfer and Sino–Japanese relationships. This chapter is followed by Chapter 9, contributed by William Fischer, which looks critically at China as a target for future opportunities as compared with other countries. Chapter 10 follows, with an analysis of key success factors in United States–China technology transfer projects offered by Mary Ann Von Glinow, Otto Schnepp, and Arvind Bhambri. Chapter 11 is Roy Grow's analysis of how Japanese and American firms interact with Chinese enterprises in the process of technology transfer. Chapter 12 is a contribution by Linsu Kim on the pros and cons of international technology transfer from a developing country's perspective.

Chapter 13 is by Bela Gold, who discusses recent changes in the pattern of technology transfers between the United States and Japan. Chapter 14 is Wesley Johnston's observations of industrial buying patterns in China. The book concludes with comments, whereby synthesis occurs.

This research effort was a part of a multiyear research program in international business sponsored by USC's International Business Education and Research (IBEAR) Program, directed by Tamir Agmon. We would like to thank the IBEAR Program and its director, Richard Drobnick, for sponsoring this research effort. In addition, key individuals helped in the compilation of the material for this publication. They include Jack Lewis, Maggie Hunt, and other IBEAR staff members at USC. To them, we owe an enormous debt of gratitude. Also, we thank the anonymous reviewer at Oxford University Press, and the editorial efforts of Herb Addison. And finally, we wish to thank our respective spouses for their patience during our technology transfer process. It is to them that we dedicate this book.

June 1990 T.A.
M.A.V.G.

Contributors

Tamir Agmon
University of Southern California and Tel-Aviv University

Mary Ann Von Glinow
University of Southern California

Denis F. Simon
Tufts University

Stephen J. Kobrin
University of Pennsylvania

Alexander Good
President, MTEL International

Raj Aggarwal
John Carroll University

Yair Aharoni
Duke University

Everett M. Rogers
University of Southern California

Thomas W. Valente
University of Southern California

Vladimir Pucik
University of Michigan

Martha Caldwell Harris
National Research Council

William A. Fischer
University of North Carolina

Otto Schnepp
University of Southern California

Arvind Bhambri
University of Southern California

Roy F. Grow
Carleton College

Linsu Kim
Korea University

Bela Gold
Claremont Graduate School

Wesley J. Johnston
University of Southern California

Contents

TECHNOLOGY TRANSFER IN INTERNATIONAL BUSINESS

I
THE ENVIRONMENT OF TECHNOLOGY TRANSFER

International business is usually defined as the transfer of factors of production owned by organizations across national borders, or the transfer of parts of that organization across national borders (Agmon, 1989). Technology transfer, on the other hand, refers to the application of technology to a new use, or to a new user for economic gain (Gee, 1981). Technology transfer is generally thought of as being product-embodied, process-embodied, or person-embodied. That is, technology transfer can be said to occur through the specific transfer of products, processes, or people. Most of the emphasis in the research and practitioner literature has been on the latter two types of technology transfer—process-embodied and person-embodied. To the careful reader, however, technology transfer, which occurs by process or person transfer, never occurs without some overarching organizational framework. Thus, if we augment this basic taxonomy of technology transfer by including organization-embodied factors, the processes of international business and those of technology transfer become virtually inseparable.

Technology transfer, as conceptualized above, then appears to be the core, or the heart, of international business. We can, and do, have processes of technology transfer within national borders. However, when it comes to international business, technology transfer is fundamental to the accomplishment of international business. Moreover, the success of the international business transaction under consideration frequently depends on the effectiveness of the technology transfer embodied in that transaction.

This basic argument is held throughout this book—that international business and technology transfer are highly intertwined. Throughout this book, we explore the different processes of international business, illustrating that in any one of them, technology transfer plays a critical role. We also analyze the various methods by which technology transfer occurs across national borders and show how these transfers are congruent with international business.

The twin concepts of international business and technology transfer share some additional important overlaps. Both are crucial to the business community, yet they are extremely complex issues involving economic, political, social, and cultural factors. When issues of complexity emerge, as is the case with international business and technology transfer, simplifying assumptions and frameworks are usually sought to help explain the complexity. From a simplified model, implications can then be derived for research or practice. Very often those implications are derived using mathematical techniques, and later those implications are related to some observed reality. This represents the inductive approach in science.

An alternative approach, the deductive approach, begins with an observation, and then additional observations are sought to help confirm or reject initial hypotheses. Sometimes that initial observation is a case study of one particular phenomenon. From that case, we seek to generalize findings to a whole group of cases. Thus, learning occurs through a step-by-step process. The literature on technology transfer and international business relies heavily on the second approach, or the deductive approach.

Both approaches have their strengths and weaknesses, however, and in this book, we seek to combine these two methods for ascertaining knowledge about technology transfer and international business. We begin with a conceptual framework rooted in economics and behavioral sciences. The use of case studies and vehicle studies (e.g., the "macro" vehicles used in technology transfer such as educational systems) allows us to ground the conceptual underpinnings in specific facts. To the extent that these facts are then generalizable, greater depth and completeness occur. The end result is a greater understanding of both technology transfer and international business.

Broadly interpreted, technology transfer is an integral part of the process of international business. To be successful in international business, the firm must initially possess some specific comparative advantage, which it then seeks to transfer across national borders. In navigating this terrain, the firm concerns itself with the overall effectiveness of its products, people, processes, and indeed, its organization. All of this occurs through technology transfer. To illustrate just how this process works, we begin by establishing a somewhat "abstract" model fo the competitive market as an initial benchmark. We then introduce some major "imperfections" that, in reality, are all noneconomic factors, to determine whether technology transfer is desirable from the corporate point of view.

In our abstract competitive market, usually referred to in economic theory as the "perfect market," technology is traded between nations like any other good or service. Prices are said to reflect complete and equal information, and everyone possesses perfect information. Thus, all transactions are carried out at "arms length," and international trade is accomplished through this process of exchange of goods and services. Factors of production need not be transferred across national borders for international trade to occur. In such a "hypothetical" world, technology transfer—the trades that occur involving technology—will be done directly. In other words, technology will be transferred separately from other products, processes, people, or organizations. The price of the "technology package" will reflect its marginal value. Put differently, in the perfect market scenario depicted earlier, there is no international business, and there is no unique problem of technology transfer. The two are isomorphic with one another. What we do have is international trade in a fully competitive market for all goods and services that include technology.

International business activities stem from the fact that in the real world there are factors other than those few we specified in the abstract perfect market model. In general, there are political, social, cultural, and organizational factors, in addition to the economic ones. When viewed in its complexity, these components combine to create the environment in which international business and technology transfer commonly occur. Specifically, when we discuss technology transfer in an international setting, we attempt to clarify this complex picture by distinguishing between (1) the macrovehicles for international technology transfer and (2) the microorganizational channels for technology transfer. The macrovehicles are factors more closely related to the perfectly competitive market approach discussed previously. These vehicles range from very broad topics, such as the general education system, to more specific topics, such as the technopolis (defined as a special purpose, organized technology environment), and together represent the infrastructure for effective technology transfer to occur. In the perfectly competitive market model and given the appropriate infrastructure, technology transfer is supposed to happen without further incentives.

The microorganizational channels deals with the question of how to effect technology transfer within a specific organization or a number of organizations. The focus here is on the transaction itself, not the environment in which technology transfer is said to take place in general. Thus, a key distinction emerges: macrovehicles are more broad-based, environmental issues, whereas microchannels refer to the specific technology transaction. Furthermore, the macrovehicles belong in the domain of economics, whereas the microchannels refer more to organizational theory and behavior. By definition, however, international business spans both macro and micro topics. So does international technology transfer. We, therefore, contend that the two are inseparable.

The book chapters are arrayed according to our macro and micro topics. We begin with the environmental, or macrofocused chapters. Denis Simon, Steven Kobrin, Alexander Good, and Raj Aggarwal contribute the first four chapters, respectively, on macro topics. We begin with the changing global environment for international technology transfer. Two chapters highlight global issues inherent in technology transfer, followed by two chapters highlighting historical and governmental concerns relevant to technology transfer. These four chapters set the stage. Part II commences with the macrovehicle discussion. Yair Aharoni discusses education as the vehicle for technology transfer; followed by Rogers and Valente who discuss the locational vehicle for technology transfer. The final chapter in this part, by Vladimir Pucik, focuses on the corporation as it influences technology transfer. Part III then commences with specific cases of technology transfer. Martha Harris and Bill Fischer both focus on international trade. The Von Glinow, Schnepp, and Bhambri chapter focuses on the case of China, and how key success factors inherent to that country play a role. Roy Grow follows with a cogent analysis of how Japanese, American, and

Chinese firms bridge the gap in their efforts to accomplish technology transfer.

Kim Linsu elucidates the Korean developmental policies typical of many less developed countries. Bela Gold discusses the changing patterns of technology transfer between the United States and Japan. Finally, Wesley Johnston discusses corporate buying behavior in China. In conclusion, we attempt to bring these diverse efforts together and synthesize the key learnings.

REFERENCES

Agmon, T. (1989). "The Process of Corporate Internationalization," USC Working Paper (August).

Gee, S. (1981). *Technology Transfer, Innovation and International Competitiveness*, New York: John Wiley and Sons.

1

International Business and the Transborder Movement of Technology: A Dialectic Perspective

DENIS SIMON

It has now become quite common to see daily in *The New York Times*, the *Financial Times*, or *Nihon Keizai Shimbun* at least one, if not several, prominent articles addressing the topic of global competition. And, as one reads through these pieces more closely, it is also usually the case that the respective articles are generally focused on the central role of technology in defining the nature and outcome of this competition. Even more important, the competitive dynamics within the international market for technology seem to have captured not only the headlines in the world's most reputable tabloids, but also the attention of chief executives in the boardrooms of the largest multinational corporations and key policymakers in the corridors of power among the world's major political entities. Irrespective of whether the issue is defined in economic or national security terms, the quest for global technological leadership has become so intense and the rivalry so strong that one recent book has referred to the pulling and tugging among companies and their home countries as a "technology war."[1] The authors go so far as to suggest that the outcome of this "war" will force dramatic revisions in the political and social systems that are in place around the world today.

Therefore, it is not surprising to recognize that, more so than ever before, developments in the realm of science and technology continue to have a pervasive impact on the conduct of international affairs in both the economic and political–military spheres. The emergence of new technologies such as superconductors and related special materials, informatics, microelectronics, and biotechnology have not simply expanded the existing frontiers of human knowledge, but have also provided the wherewithal for enhanced capabilities in the commercial and defense sectors.[2] Advances in manufacturing techniques, for exmaple, are transforming the nature of the production process and changing the role of labor in terms of cost and overall contribution.[3] More important, it is now essential to view these developments in a broader international context. Accordingly, it is appropriate to speak about the "globalization of science and technology" in much the same way as economists talk about the emergence of global markets and corporate executives speak about the need for global managers.[4]

Simply stated, the globalization of science and technology describes a process involving the development and diffusion of critical scientific knowledge and technological capabilities beyond the borders of a limited number of so-called advanced nations.[5] Globalization is primarily the result of the proliferation of technology transfer mechanisms, ranging from the increasing number of international conferences to the expanded numbers of students going abroad (or coming to the United States) for advanced study. It is also the result of concerted efforts on the part of some countries to "create competitive advantage," through the use of industrial policy and the targeting of specific technologies and industrial sectors.[6] At issue is more than just the emergence of Western Europe and Japan as a technological counterbalance to the United States. Bill Davidson's book, *The Amazing Race: Winning the Technorivalry with Japan,* in which he describes the massive Japanese effort to establish a commanding position in the global information industry, may have been provocative when it was written in the early 1980s, but actually only touched the surface in terms of the continuing evolution of the world economy. In particular, the appearance of the East Asia newly industrialized countries (*NIC*s: South Korea, Taiwan, Singapore, and Hong Kong), coupled with the growing economic power of countries such as Brazil and India, has created multiple loci of technological prowess.

In essence, the rapid spread of technology across the globe has *altered* the ways in which various global actors relate to each other as well as many of the prevailing patterns of international trade, commerce, and cooperation. Traditional forms of interaction are giving way to new types of cooperation and collaboration. The character of this interaction has also changed as such relationships shift away from their previous hierarchical character toward somewhat more mutually advantageous and equitable forms of association. The impacts can be felt at three distinct levels: the international and regional level; the level of the nation–state; and the level of the firm.

Interestingly, however, the globalization process itself has induced a sort of complex dialectic to appear, one centered around the tensions between two sets of seemingly contradictory forces, that is, the forces of collaboration and interdependence *and* the forces of competition, protectionism, and fragmentation. In other words, the same process, namely the expanded interest in and demand for transborder flows and sharing of scientific information and technical know-how, has fostered more cooperative postures, while at the same time giving birth to new forms of economic and technological protectionism. In some cases, the gradual playing out of this science and technology-induced dialectic has had the effect of mediating the impact of the globalization of science and technology in ways that at times reinforce as well as undermine the integrity of the nation–state and its ability to control events within its defined areas of interest.

WHAT IS TECHNOLOGY TRANSFER?

The issue of technology transfer is made complex by the fact that neither the process itself nor the package being transferred are homogeneous. Technology moves across national borders in many different ways. The most important of these can be placed into five generic categories: (1) the international technology market, which is made up of independent buyers and suppliers; (2) intrafirm transfer, whereby resort to the market is avoided and the transfer takes place through either a joint venture or wholly owned subsidiary; (3) government-directed agreements or exchanges, where the counterparts can be either public or private actors; (4) education, training, and conferences, where the dissemination of information is made public for common consumption by either a general or specialized audience; and (5) pirating or reverse-engineering, whereby access to the technology is obtained while resort to the market is avoided but at the expense of the proprietary rights of the owner(s) of technology. For purposes of this chapter, the two most critical are (1) and (2). This is not to deny the relative importance of the three other channels noted, especially the role of education and training. In fact, some persons would say that "people" constitute the most valuable source of technology transfer.[7]

This acknowledged, the reality is that most of the world's commercially based transactions involving the international movement of technology are linked to the multinational corporation (MNC), which is considered to be the most prolific purveyor of technology transfer.[8] It is, therefore, the MNC that typically decides whether to depend on the market to determine price and the contents of the package, as in the case of a licensing agreement, or whether to "internationalize" the transfer process in its entirety, as in the case of setting up a wholly owned foreign invested enterprise abroad.[9] Because of the continued pervasiveness of the MNC in structuring the scope and extent of global technology transactions, the result is that the international market for technology is usually considered to be an imperfect one. The imperfect nature of the market derives from the fact that (1) not all technologies in actual or potential use are available for sale in the market—even though theoretically there would seem to be some price where both seller and buyer could conceivably come to terms; and (2) the seller and the buyer do not possess equal information about the technology or its application. Vaitsos has categorized this latter problem as the "irony of knowledge," in that the technology that one wants to purchase is at the same time the information that is needed to make a rational decision whether or not to buy it.[10]

Technology itself falls into multiple categories. First, there are these technologies that are explicitly related to purely civilian *commodities* or the harvesting and production of these commodities such as textiles and agricultural products. Second, there are those technologies that are directly linked to *military* items such as weapons systems. Prohibitions regarding the sale or licensing of this type of know-how are fairly clear-cut in most countries, requiring special government permission and at times even its participation. The third type of "technology" is not really technology at all, but is best labeled *"scientific or basic research."* The projected applications of this type of information are highly uncertain even as the gap between basic and applied research has begun to narrow; it is usually freely disseminated through academic journals and scholarly papers. The last type of technology, and perhaps the most controversial is what is called *"dual-use" technology*. Dual-use technologies are those whose development and application are ostensibly intended for civilian purposes, but could have potential application in the defense sector. Much of what we call "high-technology" items today such as very large-scale integrated circuits (VLSI) and supercomputers would fall into this category. It is the control of dual-use technology around which a good deal of the disagreement centers as far as the utility of unilateral and multilateral export controls are concerned.[11]

Finally, technology transfer can be thought of in terms of the objectives for which it is being sought. Three classes of technology transfer can be distinguished.[12] First, there is *material-transfer,* which consists of the transfer of materials, final products, components, equipment, and even turnkey plants. Some would suggest that this is not actually a form of "technology" transfer since the important ingredient is not "know-how" but "show-how" and the core technologies are embodied within the physical items. In other words, the main objective is either to supply the physical capacity to produce or the desired products themselves. Second, there is *design-transfer,* which basically involves the movement of designs, blueprints, and the know-how to manufacture previously designed products or equipment. The major objective here is to provide the basic information, data, and guidelines needed to create a desired capability. Third, there is *capacity-transfer,* perhaps the most troublesome to define and evaluate. In its crudest form, capacity-transfers include provision of the know-how and "software" not simple to manufacture existing products but, more important, to innovate and adapt existing technologies and products, and ultimately design new products. Acquisition as well as development of this "capacity" is the most difficult of the three, yet it is also the most coveted.[13] These distinctions are important because they help define the parameters within which both the potential suppliers and recipients cooperate and collaborate.

FACILITATORS OF EXPANDED TECHNOLOGY TRANSFER

On one side of the technology transfer dialectic described exists a range of imperatives pushing for expanded international and regional cooperation and collaboration. These imperatives derive from the appearance of a series of new and complex global problems ranging from global warming to the management of space. At the international level, these problems have coalesced to form a principal driving force behind the rise in transnational interdependence as more and more nations have chosen to manage these pressing global problems from a collective perspective, and therefore, to share information and pursue various forms of cooperation as a means to better understand and deal with them. At the regional and national levels, the globalization of technology has given rise to relatively unique forms of cross-border collaboration such as JESSI, ESPRIT, and EUREKA, all associated with the coming together of the European Economic Community in Western Europe in 1992.[14] They also have fostered cooperation within the Western alliance in areas such as space, where NASA and the European Space Agency will pursue a joint mission to Saturn known as the Cassini project.[15] In the Pacific Rim nations, they have given rise to increased collaboration where political differences had heretofore seemed to present insurmountable barriers.[16] More specifically, as fears about the breakup of the world system into regional economic and trading blocs have spread throughout East Asia, we see Japan, South Korea, Taiwan, Singapore, and Hong Kong all expanding their cooperation with the People's Republic of China (PRC) in the technology and/or research and development (R&D) spheres.[17] For example, PRC and Singapore firms have begun cooperation in multiple aspects of the computer industry, including software design and R&D.[18] Moreover, at the level of the firm, they have found expression in the emergence of new forms of international business cooperation such as strategic alliances between American, European, and Japanese companies.

From an international business perspective, a number of factors can be seen as facilitating the expanded transborder movement of technology. Most important among these is apparently the evolution of a shorter product life cycle. Simply stated, in the original formulation of the product life cycle thesis, it was suggested that the manufacturing process for various products generally moved overseas only after product exporting opportunities became limited and the core product technologies reached a mature stage in their development and application. The theory describes how these technologies and production methods moved overseas and eventually ended up first in other developed nations and later in developing nations through the processes of foreign investment or technology licensing, or both.[19] In most cases, multinational firms were reluctant to export their newest technologies abroad because of concerns about competition and the security of the technology, that is, no well-developed patent system, as well as the different operating conditions overseas (especially in the Third World), as many technologies in the West were designed to be labor saving.

The theory was modified and used by several authors to explain the emergence and potential upward mobility of aspiring entrants into the international division of labor. James Kurth, for example, in an analysis of the Latin American experience, suggested that the key to the modernization of these economies is their ability to take advantage of the product cycle by relying on mature technologies to manufacture products that have been developed elsewhere—but on a more cost-effective basis.[20] As Vernon indicates, it is essentially through the activities of transnational corporations that these manufacturing technologies are both directly and indirectly diffused on to local firms.[21] Westphal and Dahlman, in an analysis of the Korean case, went one step further. Noting that the overall extent of foreign equity-based investment in South Korea had been limited, they suggested that through the process of export expansion, local Korean firms acquired substantial amounts of intangible technology and know-how by informal channels, such as exchanges with marketing agents from the advanced nations who have constant contact with product end users.[22] These information flows, while mainly containing already proven and fairly standardized manufacturing techniques and related know-how, still resulted in improved efficiency, diversified product designs, improved quality, and upgraded management practices. Nonetheless, the nature of the flows was often haphazard, indirect, and frequently nothing more than an unintended spillover from what the foreign buyer generally considered an arms-length transaction.

The framework for explaining the global diffusion process for technology was further developed by Magee using what he called the "industry technology cycle."[23] Magee's analysis suggests that industries, in a simlar fashion to Vernon's analysis of products, proceed through a development cycle composed of three stages: invention, innovation, and standardization. In general, once an industry reaches a mature stage, the entry requirements lessen in terms of managerial and technological competence. This helps explain the ability over time of NIC firms to enter and successfully compete in industries such as textiles and consumer electronics. However, as certain industries experience periods of rapid technological change where there is a growing demand for innovation-related skills in organization and management as well as in technology, most firms falling in the categories described have not been able to stay in the market, except perhaps at a very low end.

In the 1970s, if not somewhat earlier, owing to a number of fundamental structural changes in the world economy and technology system, the international diffusion processes, described by Vernon and Magee, respectively, underwent a process of truncation, with the result being that some newer technologies began finding their way overseas at an earlier point in time.[24] Mansfield, in an analysis of R&D and innovation with respect to international technology transfer at the macrolevel, identified three reasons to account for the more rapid diffusion of technology overseas: (1) the general growth of foreign direct investment (by existing sources of capital as well as newcomers), which tends to move technology abroad at a faster pace than exports; (2) the increasing tendency among firms to take a global view of their operations; and (3) the increased "internationalization" of the technology development process, with more and more components of the innovation process being located outside the advanced nations.[25] Mansfield should have also added a fourth factor, namely, the increased capacity of local firms in several developing nations to play a productive role in the value-added chain, either as a part of a multinational network or as independent actors.[26]

More recently, these changes have been reinforced and exacerbated, in some important cases, by a number of additional factors at both the macro and micro level. First, there has been a general acceleration in the pace of technological development spurred on by the growing intensity of technology-based competition in the international market. While there are some obvious exceptions, such as in the case of petrochemicals, for most part technological advance sesems to be occurring at previously unequalled velocity.[27] In addition, there is now less time between the recognition of a new technology in the innovation and design phases and its eventual commercialization. Similarly, in industries such as semiconductors, new ideas are so quickly imitated that specific methods of customization, such as application specific integrated circuits (ASICs), have to be introduced to slow down copying.[28] Fewer and fewer companies can afford the luxury of operating a "scientific sandbox" for basic research such as the type that existed at Bell Labs for a number of years. It is even true that a larger proportion of the monies being supplied by the corporate world for purposes of assisting university-based research are being funnelled in the direction of applied as opposed to basic research.[29]

Moreover, for firms that are truly global in strategic terms as well as in their decision-making processes, there is now a greater tendency to disengage overseas production (commercialization) from the product life cycle. In trying to optimize the positioning of their firm with respect to what Kogut has called "the value-added chain," many corporate executives have found it both necessary and desirable to structure their company's operations on a global basis.[30] The simple distinction between "domestic" operations and "foreign" operations is no longer realistic for a host of companies engaged in appreciable levels of international business activities.[31] This has frequently meant that "younger," higher potential technologies are being increasingly used as a form of economic and political leverage overseas to obtain market access or to woo potential partners to access complementary functional assets.

A second factor facilitating the more rapid movement of technology overseas has been the convergence of international capital and factor markets. In general, over the last decade or so, there has been a standardization of capital costs as far as most large, internationally oriented firms are concerned. This has allowed MNCs to access needed investment capital for overseas projects at relatively competitive rates irrespective of plant location. It also helps to explain, in part, the rapid rise of Japanese foreign direct investment in the United States as well as the increase, albeit relatively more gradual, in investment by Taiwanese and South Korean firms. Moreover, as a result of the energy crisis and related concerns, a shift has occurred away from labor-savings toward materials-savings technologies. This has altered the thinking of firms that seek the most "appropriate" site to employ their production techniques and know-how, thereby allowing them greater diversity in their choice of manufacturing location. While it may be true that in some cases firms may now be able to forgo the costly act of pursuing an overseas venture and "bring" the manufacture of their product back home, the reality is that this situation has merely enhanced rather than diminished the potential role of technology transfer.

A third factor that has also fostered the expanded transfer of technology overseas is related to recent advances in international communication and transportation. Whether we are talking about the Concords or the widely heralded "Asian" hypersonic jet, the fact is that time and distance are no longer major obstacles to the mobility of people or the movement of ideas and technical know-how. It is easier for executives, technicians, and scientists to move about than ever before as most major airlines have expanded their international routes and travel services. The truly global company now operates 24 hours a day; whether it be through the telex or the FAX machine, companies must communicate internally as well as externally on real-time basis. Communications satellites have improved the quality of information transfer as well as created new opportunities for sustained contact with logistically difficult to reach areas. Transport barriers have also diminished, especially in terms of previous capacity limitations. International cargo and courier services, such as Federal Express, have expanded as demand has grown. Under such circumstances, the decision of the MNC to locate overseas is no longer simply a defensive action, that is, an attempt to protect a threatened export market. Rather, a firm that wants to think and act strategically must use the globe as the drawing board upon which to base its key marketing, distribution, production, and R&D decisions.

With such an expanding focus for formulating and implementing business decisions, the requirements for information hhave increased exponentially. Some firms have established so-called "global scanning units" or environmental scanning units to assess international trends, perform competitor analysis (foreign and domestic), and provide risk assessments regarding various potential investment sites. Firms based in Taiwan and South Korea have set up "technological listening posts" in places such as Silicon Valley in California and Route 128 in Boston to ensure access to the latest ideas.[32] The ability to carry out these activities has been facilitated by the onset of the information revolution. Firms adept at effectively managing their information technologies can put in place a corporate infrastructure capable of storing critical data, accessing multiple data bases, and transmitting the needed information to key decision makers at home and in the field.[33]

In essence, corporations have been forced to develop a new approach to technology, one that places the management of technology at the center of corporate strategy.[34] The increasing global understanding of the sources of innovation, combined with the growing intensity of global competition, have made the management of technology evolve into something more than just the simple management of the R&D function or the choice of manufacturing technique. Technology has now become a driver itself; in all areas of corporate activity, ranging from human resources and procurement to operations and marketing, the efficacy of technology is shaping corporate thinking and behavior. Obviously, the pervasiveness of the so-called technology factor is more critical in some industries than in others. Biotechnology, optoelectronics, computers, and microelectronics are all prime examples where technology is king. Nonetheless, it is important not to confuse technology-based industries from technology-based strategies. Even in such industries as textiles, shoes, toys and plastics, the role of technology remains paramount and central to achieving competitiveness.

THE BARRIERS TO EXPANDED TECHNOLOGY TRANSFER

On the other hand, within the context of the dialectic noted above, there also exist a range of forces, some of which are not very different from those associated with greater cooperation, that are responsible for generating more intense competition and fragmentation within and across the three levels previously mentioned. At the international and regional levels, recent achievements in science and technology have contributed to a redefinition of traditional notions of national power. No longer is a nation's capability and influence measured simply in terms of its military might. Economic power, supported and advanced by scientific and technological progress, has become a growing source of global influence. The momentous rise of Japan and the East Asian newly industrialized countries as global powers has underscored the increasingly critical role of science and technology development.[35]

As suggested earlier, because possession of adequate science and technology capabilities promises to be such an important source of wealth and power in the years ahead, it has fostered what Robert Reich has labeled the rise of "techno-nationalism."[36] In retreating from their past adherence to a policy of "techno-globalism," some nations, such as the U.S., now covet technology more than ever before, and in an effort to protect and nurture domestic science and technological assets, new controls have appeared on the export and sharing of scientific and technical resources. Concerns about economic competitiveness as well as national security have been important considerations underlying the various attempts to gain a better grip on what one leading American official described in the context of the United States as the "hemorrhage of technology." Robert Gilpin's suggestions that we have entered a more neomercantilist period in world history may be an appropriate characterization except that the prize being sought and nurtured is technology.[37] Thus, while some nations are aggressively pursuing greater access to foreign technology and expanded forms of scientific cooperation, other nations are taking a more careful look at the degree to which they want to allow others unencumbered access to the full range of existing technologies. Even in countries such as Japan, there continues to be a fear of the so-called boomerang effect with respect to its willingness to transfer technology to other countries in East Asia. South Korean officials, for example, have begun to complain that one of the negative consequences of their rapid success is that they have begun to create serious apprehensions among potential technology suppliers who fear the creation of "another Japan!"[38]

At the level of the firm, national policies have complicated the process of transferring technology. Since the days of detente with the Soviet Union in the mid-1970s, major changes have taken place with respect to prevailing attitudes about export controls both within the United States and among the members of the Western alliance and Japan.[39] Still, the reality is that great concerns continue to exist among many Western and Japanese leaders, particularly within the defense community, about the possible closing of the technological gap between the U.S.S.R. and the West. While the number of technology areas covered by export controls and COCOM—the multilateral regime created to control the sale of dual-use technologies to the socialist bloc nations—have been appreciably narrowed since the beginning of the 1980s, those areas that remain covered by controls are being treated with even greater care and even tighter restrictions than perhaps was true in the past. Periodically, as relations between the West and the socialist bloc (including China) have improved, the idea of abolishing multilateral controls has emerged. Nonetheless, it remains true that despite the onset of "perestroika" in the U.S.S.R. and the "open policy" in China, the Western alliance and Japan still seem committed to preserving some facets of the technology transfer regime established at the height of the Cold War. Of course, countries such as China have complained vociferously about the continued imposition of so-called "national security" controls regarding technology transfers. Yet, few countries within COCOM appear prepared, either in public or in private, to totally relax existing restrictions in areas that might be related to Chinese nuclear weapons development, nuclear delivery systems, and so on.

Over the past few years, five key examples stand out as manifestations of the emerging concerns in the United States, in particular, regarding too much openness with respect to technology transfer. The example of the Fairchild–Fujitsu case in the United States related to the intended purchase by the Japanese firm of this once leading American microelectronics corporation highlights the extent to which governments are willing to intervene in the market to prevent the "globalization" process from proceeding.[40] While many in the U.S. government cited national security considerations as the underlying reason for opposition to the merger, American government opposition was also strongly fueled by a host of competitive concerns—all of which were exacerbated by the emotionalism surrounding United States–Japan trade frictions. When in the final analysis the Japanese firm decided not to pursue the acquisition, it was clear that its decision was specifically designed to avoid pushing the American government to take a firm stand on what would clearly portend additional trouble for future United States–Japan economic relations.

The revelation that the Toshiba Corporation of Japan was involved in the illegal sale of unauthorized technologies to the U.S.S.R. represents the second major example of tightening alluded to above. The subsequent prosecution of Toshiba, for selling controlled machine tools to the Soviet Union, including the strong penalties attached to the convictions both within its own country and the United States, further illustrates the extent to which the emotional aspects of the technology transfer issue can assume paramout importance. Perhaps just as important, the ramifications of the Toshiba case carried beyond the Soviet Union when the Japanese government placed strict limits on the completion of existing contracts as well as the sale of additional Toshiba products to the People's Republic of China and several other so-called communist countries. For Chinese officials in Beijing, this represented further evidence of the reluctance of Japan to transfer any technology to China as well as a further reaffirmation that COCOM was still being used to prevent their country from gaining unencumbered access to advanced technologies and equipment.

We can add to this list a third item, namely the concerted efforts made by the United States over the last few years, first, to have South Korea adopt a more judicious approach to technology transfer vis-à-vis its expanding relationship with China and second, to encourage Taiwan to accept a more cautious policy with respect to its expanding computers sales to Eastern Europe.[41] Ironically, the American pressure on these governments occurred within the midst of extensive trade friction that both have been having with the U.S. regarding their consistent trade surpluses. The attempt by Seoul and Taipei to expand into the China and East European markets, respectively, represents an effort to diversify trade partners and thereby reduce not just trade dependency, but also trade conflict with the United States. In both cases, the United States argued that some of the key technology embodied within items such as computers originated in the United States and was, therefore, subject to American jurisdiction. Rumors in South Korea also suggested that American officials forced Seoul's unilateral acceptance of the basic provisions of COCOM by threatening possible denial of U.S. military technology and offset provisions if sufficient evidence of noncompliance was discovered.[42]

The fourth example is drawn from United States–China relations, and involves the American decision to halt further relaxation of technology transfer restrictions vis-a-vis the PRC in response to evidence that the Chinese allegedly were actively engaged in the sale of "Silkworm" missiles to Iran and ballistic missiles (CSS-2) to Saudi Arabia.[43] In spite of initial Chinese denials that such transactions had indeed taken place, the American intelligence community apparently turned up evidence indicating PRC involvement through one of its military foreign trade companies known as "Poly-Technologies," which represents the Chinese defense establishment.[44] While debates raged on within Washington as to whether Beijing had significant foreign policy objectives in mind or was just anxious to generate substantial foreign exchange earnings, the fact remained that these PRC actions were deemed irresponsible in view of the extreme volatility of the situation in the Middle East. The U.S. response, which was immediately and unequivocally condemned by the Chinese leadership, was to curtail on-going negotiations in COCOM aimed to expanding the level of technology and equipment acceptable for sale to China. While the two sides were able to resolve their differences only after Beijing made a commitment to halt further sales, the willingness of policymakers in Washington to use technology transfer as leverage against Beijing highlights another example of the types of factors that can inhibit the free flow of technology.[45]

Constraints on technology transfer have also emerged in a fifth area, namely at the level of the firm. In some respects, what is most interesting in examining the international technology marketplace is not the firms that are willing to engage in technology transfer, but rather the instances of firms who are not. Just as some countries have chosen to adopt a more cautious approach to technology sharing, so have some major companies around the world. In an era of growing competition, while there appears to be less emphasis on political risk analysis, there is evidence that the corporate intelligence function seems to be growing in importance. At the same time, corporate protection against industrial espionage and spying has increased as the dynamics of competition seem to be driving a need among some firms to gain access to selected technical information at all costs. Perhaps the most explicit expression of this attitude was Kodak's 1987 attempt to prevent a Japanese executive from Fuji, a major Kodak competitor, from studying at the business school at the University of Rochester for fear that the visitor would use the opportunity to "spy" on Kodak managers in attendance at the school.[46] And, while the university ultimately reversed its decision, the Fuji manager ended up accepting an offer to study at the Sloan School at MIT.[47] Today, efforts by foreigners to visit U.S. industrial facilities are no longer simple requests; visitors are now more closely monitored and controlled than ever before from both a national security and competitiveness standpoint.

In contrast to those firms that are expanding their global operations and engaging in more extensive technological sharing, there are those firms that are taking advantage of recent technological developments to bring manufacturing back to their home countries. Frustrated by the difficulties of doing business overseas and confronted with the possibility that the initial advantages of off-shore manufacturing may quickly dissipate, they are looking to design new equipment and production processes that make manufacturing at home profitable once again. Moreover, as a result of recent trends in production technology and systems, the labor component has become a decreasingly important part of the production process, both in terms of cost and contribution. Rather than globalize and employ overseas labor, these firms want to confine themselves to the security of home.[48]

THE STRATEGIC OPTIONS: NEW FORMS OF CROSS-NATIONAL COLLABORATION

Major questions exist as to whether a strategy of "circling the wagons" and trying to limit the outflow of technology can really serve as an effective instrument for guaranteeing economic competitiveness or protecting national security. Such an approach would represent nothing less than an attempt to deny the present and future efficacy of the globalization process. In fact, one could argue that it is counterproductive for any country, especially the United States, to spend the energy to close its borders and to try to shut off the multiplicity of technology transfer mechanisms that have proliferated over the last decade or so. After all, from the American perspective, a good argument could be made that it has in fact been the contribution of foreigners, studying and conducting research in the U.S. in both science and engineering, that has been a primary source of American technological advance.[49] Moreover, while it might not be impossible to contain "technology loss" through controls on the export of products and related "hardware," the same cannot be said about the "software" side of the equation. In fact, since it is the "software" that is primarily being sought, it would be almost futile, short of barring foreigners from entering our country and buying our periodicals and journals, to actually tightly regulate, let alone completely halt, foreign access to American know-how.

Recognizing the difficulty as well as the potential costs of trying to constrain the transnational flow of technology, many firms have decided that a better way to approach their competitive problems is to join forces with actual or potential competitors. Those multinational corporations that have developed a sense of internal confidence from gaining a mastery of the overall international business environment have come to appreciate that globalization is a process that must be managed and addressed head on. Efforts to thwart the consequences of technological globalization might meet with some short-term success but, from a long-term perspective, the reality is that the imperatives of the globalization drive cannot be denied or ignored.

In essence, the more rapid movement of technology overseas has contributed to a new kind of international business venture, namely the strategic alliance. Technology-based joint ventures among firms that have been or may become strong competitors are assuming an increasingly important role in a firm's global business strategy. For U.S. firms, in particular, this presents a marked departure from the general tendency to shy away from joint ventures. In some cases, firms are looking for partners to offset the high costs and risks associated with undertaking a new, expensive venture. In other cases, the convergence of technologies, such as in electronics and informatics, offers opportunities for obtaining needed complementary skills not present in one company. Other benefits could include access to patents and licenses, access to materials and equipment supply, and a reduction of competition that could divert resources away from needed areas.

Strategic alliances and partnerships in the informatics sector, such as the semiconductor industry, have been the most numerous so far.[50] Since 1981, for example, there has been a significant rise in the number of accords signed. West European companies have tended to be in the lead, forging alliances with Japan, the United States, and more recently with several of the Asian NICs, such as South Korea. Several of the European companies, such as Phillips (Holland), have extended their activities to places such as Taiwan and the recent VLSI project.[51] Interestingly, while much of the attention regarding strategic alliances has focused on United States–Japan collaboration, the reality, as suggested, is that the EEC has been both the major target and participant. Based on results of a study of 839 cases conducted at the INSEAD management school in France, approximately three-quarters of all collaborative ventures involved at least one partner from Europe.[52]

In the majority of these cases, the dominant pattern of activity is the exchange of technology for technology. In a study of 189 of these new cooperative ventures among Japanese and United States firms by Osborn and Baugh, the authors found that accessing technology either in the form of R&D or manufacturing capability was the primary objective of the alliance.[53] In line with this finding, there is growing reason to believe that Japanese firms have now altered their technology acquisition strategy for the 1990s to focus on strategic alliances rather than licensing. In most instances, strategic alliances emphasize a *bilateral* flow of technology, while traditional forms of technology transfer and joint ventures have tended to emphasize a *unilateral* flow of technology. Obviously, this new emphasis on greater symmetry within the relationship represents a significant change in approach.[54] With the increased attraction of strategic alliances, technologies are moving overseas much sooner while their full market value has not yet been fully exploited. What remains to be seen, however, is whether this shift in approach and technology content actually will add to the long-term survivability of these ventures or whether they will also succumb to what several scholars have seen as the inherent obsolescence of many "co-operative" international business agreements.[55]

One particularly noteworthy case involves the relatively unique collaborative relationship established between Motorola of the United States and Toshiba of Japan.[56] The agreement between the two companies apparently involves one of the most complex technology transfer and sharing arrangements to date between American and Japanese firms. It is even more remarkable because Motorola has been considered to be one of the more caustic firms in terms of its position regarding Japanese penetration of the U.S. electronics industry. Moreover, it has generally held extremely conservative and restrictive views regarding the transfer of its key technologies.[57] According to the *Financial Times,* the agreement involves three main components: (1) Motorola will transfer its microprocessor technology to Toshiba, (2) Toshiba will pass on its memory technology to Motorola, and (3) Toshiba will assist Motorola in expanding its sales into the Japanese electronics market.[58] The quid pro quo here is clearly Motorola's willingness to leverage its technological advantage and leadership position in the 32-bit microprocessor field in return for access to Japan's growing industrial electronics customers.[59] The progression of the reciprocal transfers is closely tied to the build-up of Motorola sales in Japan. According to provisions of the agreement, Motorola must have an established market presence before it will be required to surrender its most critical technology.[60]

Few would disagree that these noted changes in the nature of international business management have important implications for long-term transnational technology transfer and the nature of international competition.[61] They have already begun to transform industries such as the global construction industry.[62] They are also significant, however, because they may represent little more than a short-term response to a more deep-seated long-term problem, that is the decline in American competitiveness. There are numerous risks associated with strategic alliances in which technology is the main focus.[63] First, in the case of U.S. firms, they will be sharing some of their unique skills and capabilities with an actual or potential foreign competitor. If the alliance fails to meet expectations or the U.S. side does not properly manage its interaction, it may give away more than it gets. Clearly, a firm does not want to get locked into an alliance in which it is benefiting less than its partner. One of the major criticisms voiced against American companies about their past international business behavior, particularly with respect to their relations with Japan, is that they were ineffective at managing and leveraging their technology for maximum advantage; some would even go so far as to suggest that they gave away their technology too cheaply!

Second, there is always the possibility that an inappropriate partner might be selected, one that does not have the capabilities desired or one that proves difficult to cooperate with under the intimate terms required. Cultural and organizational incompatibility may be difficult to overcome. Partner selection, therefore, becomes an important factor in determining the value of the alliance both in the short and long term. Roehl and Truitt, in their study of the experience of Boeing and its cooperative relationship with a consortium of Japanese firms (JADC) for commercial aircraft production, provide an excellent case of how cultural factors as well as uncertainty regarding motives can result in apprehension and dissatisfaction on both sides.[64]

The critical international business issue raised by the emergence of the strategic alliance and its proliferation in global industries including automobiles and microelectronics is whether they represent a "Trojan horse" of sorts by which foreign firms can infiltrate U.S. industry and gain access to American technology and markets, or whether they are indeed the wave of the future in terms of transborder business cooperation and interaction. Moreover, there remains the fundamental issue of whether the totality of strategic alliance-related technology transfers results in a net outflow or inflow of technology to the home country. In a series of case studies within the manufacturing industry, Mowery et al. show that within certain industries, such as steel and automobiles, the U.S. balance has tended to be favorable; in other industries, such as microelectronics and telecommunications, the American position is generally unfavorable.[65] The most provocative finding of the Mowery study, however, is the perhaps worrisome conclusion that the net inflows are occurring in industries where strategic alliances and/or the industries themselves are of decreasing strategic importance to the U.S. competitive position, while net outflows are occurring in industries that are growing in importance in the world economy, particularly in terms of current competitive advantages possessed by the United States.[66]

Five specific issues seem to be of paramount importance in determining the balance of benefits within the strategic alliance: (1) valuation of the technological contribution, (2) the perception of the reciprocal technological benefits of the interaction, (3) the selection of management and technical personnel, (4) the differences in management techniques used in the respective parents versus the strategic alliance, and (5) termination arrangements, especially concerning disposition of any new technology. While some research has been done in the area of strategic alliances, it has tended to be more macropolicy-oriented rather than management-oriented. Answers to three questions will be necessary to evaluate the implications of the growing number of strategic alliances as far as the technology transfer issue is concerned: (1) What types of alliances are being pursued in terms of their management structure, general operating characteristics, and mechanisms of cooperation; (2) What corporate policy adjustments must be made to handle the managerial challenges posed by these alliances; and (3) How has (or will) the growth in terms of the number of such alliances as well as changes in the quality and depth of these alliances affect the nature of international competition?

While global competition has been the major driving factor behind the increasing numbers of technology-based strategic alliances, there have also been a number of new alliances brewing that are focused primarily on defense cooperation. With growing competition confronting the United States in the international defense industry, there are a number of important changes taking place in the nature of the relations between the partners that are relevant from the perspective of technology transfer. As a *The New York Times* article suggested, American military firms are finding it increasingly necessary to share their technology as a way to secure business abroad.[67] At issue are more than just the typical offset agreements that have accompanied arms and military equipment sales in the past to places such as Canada or Saudi Arabia. Due to the enhanced technological capabilities of Japan and the Western Europeans, strategic business collaboration seems to have become the main issue. Within the aerospace industry, an agreement was concluded in November 1988 between the U.S. and Japan whereby the Japanese will manufacture their own jet fighter based on the design of the F-16 built by General Dynamics. In return for Japan's agreement to adhere basically to American designs and standards, and not design its own plane, the United States agreed to collaborate by providing much of the key technology and know-how, thus possibly setting the stage for a strong Japanese presence in the aircraft industry at a much earlier point in time.[68] Similarly, American defense officials appear to have relaxed their opposition to extensive United States–European military collaboration. Texas Instruments of the United States and Thomson CSF of France have apparently been given permission to share know-how regarding advanced radar technology.[69] United States intentions are to discourage development of a more independent, self-sufficient European defense aerospace capability or, failing that, to secure access for the U.S. defense industry to a number of on-going European projects, such as the Rafale advanced combat aircraft program.

PROSPECTS AND CONCLUSION

Concerns about the rapid globalization of science and technology and its implications for economic competitiveness and national security will occupy an increasingly important place on the agenda of political leaders, scholars, and the multinational corporate executives. Simply stated, just as America's position of economic hegemony has eroded, so has its position of technological dominance. The challenges to American technological superiority have gone beyond Japan and Western Europe; new sources of technological capability are emerging in places such as Brazil, India, South Korea, Taiwan, and Singapore. South Korea's recent entry into the one-megabyte memory chip market exemplifies what can be accomplished in a relatively short period of time.[70] Yet, out of the fears about new competitors as well as the desire to reduce risk and share some of the financial burdens have come greater opportunities for expanded cooperation. The more critical question to be addressed is whether or not the increased salience of the technology variable will lead to long-term collaborative arrangements among nations or produce the ingredients for more significant conflicts over time.

Perhaps the clearest insight into the future direction and thrust of international technology transfers and collaboration can be obtained by looking at the development of high-definition television (HDTV). HDTV represents the wave of the future in terms of picture quality, reliability, and set mannufacturing. Japan began developing HDTV approximately 20 years ago with the explicit aim of making present day conventional televisions obsolete.[71] The main questions surrounding the introduction and adoption of HDTV revolve around three issues. First, what is or will be the role of the U.S. electronics industry with respect to HDTV, especially since American television manufacturers have almost all dropped out of the market? Without an existing foundation for production or distribution, the United States would have to recreate an entire infrastructure to support entry into the industry.[72] The only remaining U.S. firm, Zenith, has only 13 percent of the domestic market. Moreover, only 6 percent of America's semiconductor chips go to consumer products compared with 50 percent for Japan.[73]

Second, which HDTV standards will be adopted across Japan, Western Europe, and the United States? The standards question is critical because it will help determine how the HDTV market gets divided in the future. Initially, the Japanese had tried to install their system as the world standard, only to be thwarted by the West Europeans. Unlike the Japanese who wish to make a complete break from existing conventional television standards, the Europeans foresee a more gradual transition in terms of technology and programming. In September 1988, the United States decided to adopt a set of standards more consistent with its own existing television system, possibly as a way to curtail the seemingly insurmountable Japanese lead. No one in the United States or Europe is willing to concede the HDTV battle to Japan because at stake is more than just the television market; widespread HDTV use would entail replacement or adaptation of nearly all production and broadcast equipment. It is also likely that the core technology behind HDTV will drive other electronics segments such as semiconductors, telecommunications, and software.[74]

Third, what is the potential for collaboration in what some estimate will be a $50 billion industry in the United States in the next 20 years? So far, it appears that all three actual or potential players in the HDTV industry have decided to pursue separate, independent strategies. Thomson of France, for example, through its acquisition of RCA as well as through a series of deliberate business decisions, has decided to confront the Japanese challenge head-on—along with any related challenges that might eventually come from South Korea or Taiwan.[75] The American Electronics Association is trying to mobilize a number of major domestic electronics firms along with government financial support to ensure a U.S. presence. Japan has decided not to retreat from its approach, which has been to attack the HDTV problem first from the perspective of programming, to ensure demand for its HDTV sets once they enter the market.

The HDTV scenario suggests that a great deal of reticence remains on the part of many firms and their home governments to venture beyond their respective national borders in the formulation and implementation of major technology decisions. Whether or not new forms of collaboration or consultation will occur remains to be seen. A similar argument could be made about the consequences of Europe 1992 as well, which from one perspective may seem like an excellent example of regional collaboration but from the perspective of North America and East Asia seems a potential problem in the making. Ironically, it is highly unlikely that a "fortress Europe" type of situation will easily emerge; within the context of this chapter one could argue effectively that the regionalism begin pushed in Western Europe is actually nothing more than an enhanced form of extended technological nationalism. Primarily because many of the historical obstacles to cooperation remain ever present, Europe 1992 will never truly materialize into the coherent, consensus-oriented entity that some would like to see. Some of these obstacles recently came into play when the French, West Germans, and Italians tried to launch the JESSI microelectronics program but met with serious difficulties on the part of Siemens and SGS-Thomson.[76] A similar argument could be made about two other initiatives in the biotechnology arena, ECLAIR (European Collaborative Linkage of Agriculture and Industry through Research) and FLAIR (Food Linked Agro-Industrial Research), both of which have had their successes but have also encountered obstacles.[77] It should be added that Europe is not alone in confronting these problems; major obstacles also exist to more formal collaboration in East Asia.

The main conclusion to be drawn from this analysis, therefore, seems to be that while both conflict and collaboration will emerge out of the globalization dialectic, the sources of the conflict will grow while the foundation upon which the cooperation rests will continue to be fragile and uncertain. There appears to be no reason why the global movement of technology will not increase, but with these increases it is likely that a host of new and complex issues will emerge. For example, in the case of strategic alliances, what role will home governments play with respect to antitrust as well as the application and disposition of the technology as far as various regulatory and export control regimes are concerned? Even more critical, how will some of the new efforts to tighten up on pirating through stricter enforcement of intellectual property laws affect innovation and the nature of competition? Will disagreements over intellectual property lead to actual "technology wars"? Finally, how will the established players in an industry such as the space industry react in response to efforts by countries such as China to offer launch and related support services to prospective customers at comparatively cheaper rates?

Unfortunately, the answers to many of these questions cannot be answered at this time. Suffice to say, these and other issues will be with us a long time. It is a sobering thought to realize that the appearance of new programs such as Strategic Defense Initiative (SDI) promise to generate even greater cross-border controversy—even if we focus solely on the technology-related aspects of the initiative. Fears about the possible success of this program have been largely instrumental in helping to globalize some of the research activities associated with SDI; few countries want to be in the position of not having been associated with SDI if indeed it ultimately proves itself even modestly successful. Moreover, the possibility of appropriating the benefits of SDI research for civilian purposes has not gone unnoticed by the respective countries involved. The fact of life we must accept is that the global spread of technology, however fast or slow, may be doing more to strengthen the viability and justification of the nation–state than anything that might be done to bypass it or raise questions about its utility in the twenty-first century.

NOTES

1. David Brandin and Michael Harrison, *The Technology War: A Case for Competitiveness* (New York: John Wiley & Sons, 1987).
2. Tom Forester, *High-Tech Society* (Cambridge: MIT Press, 1987).
3. Bruce Guile and Harvey Brooks (eds.), *Technology and Global Industry* (Washington, D.C.: National Academy Press, 1987).
4. Michael Porter (ed.), *Competition in Global Industries* (Cambridge: Harvard Business School Press, 1986).
5. Janet Muroyama and H. Guyford Stever (eds.), *Globalization of Technology: International Perspectives* (Washington, D.C.: National Academy Press, 1988).
6. Francis Rushing and C. G. Brown (eds.), *National Policies for Developing High Technology Industries* (Westview Press, 1986).
7. Charles Stewart and Yasumitsu Nihei, *Technology Transfer and Human Factors* (Lexington, Lexington Books, 1987).
8. Jack Baranson, *Technology and the Multinational: Corporate Strategies in a Changing World Economy* (Lexington, MA: Lexington Books, 1978).
9. Piero Telesio, *Technology Licensing and Multinational Enterprises* (New York: Praeger, 1979).
10. Constantine Vaitsos, "Bargaining and the Distribution of Returns in the Purchase of Technology by Developing Countries," in Henry Bernstein, ed., *Underdevelopment and Development: The Third World Today* (New York: Penguin Books, 1973), pp. 315–322.
11. J. Fred Bucy, "Technology Transfer and East-West Trade: A Reappraisal," *International Security,* Winter 1980/81. See also Michael Czinkota (ed.), *Export Controls* (New York: Praeger 1985). see also U.S. Department of Defense, "Soviet Acquisition of Western Technology" (Washington, D.C.: Government Printing Office, 1982).
12. Edwin Mansfield, et al., *Technology Transfer, Productivity and Economic Policy* (New York: Norton, 1982).
13. Edwin Mansfield, "Inter. Technology Transfer: Forms, Resource Requirements & Policies," *American Economic Review,* Vol. 65, May 1975.
14. The JESSI project (Joint European Semiconductor Silicon) is aimed at achieving United States and Japanese technology levels for the 1990s. See "European Chips plan Clouded by Siemens, SGS-Thomson Dispute," *Financial Times,* April 5, 1988, p. 1. For a broader overview, see Margaret Sharpe, et al., *European Technological Collaboration* (London: Royal Institute of International Affairs, 1986).

15. "Europeans Decide on a Trip to Saturn," *Science,* December 90, 1988, pp. 1375–1376.
16. Tomio Shida, "Powerful Asian Economic Bloc Emerging," *Japan Economic Journal,* November 12, 1988, p. 5.
17. For a discussion about the feasibility of creating a "Pacific Community" see Michael Yahuda, "The Pacific Community: Not Yet," *The Pacific Review,* Volume 1, Number 2, 1988, pp. 119–127.
18. "Singapore Aiding Chinese Computer Firms," *Japan Economic Journal,* September 24, 1988, p. 7.
19. For a coherent discussion of the product cycle model, see Richard Caves, *Multinational Enterprises and Economic Analysis* (Cambridge: Cambridge University Press, 1982).
20. James Kurth, "Industrial Change and Political Change: A European Perspective," in David Collier (ed.), *The New Authoritarianism in Latin America* (Princeton: Princeton University Press, 1979), pp. 319–362.
21. During the author's own research on Taiwan, for example, it was discovered that one of the major vehicles for the diffusion of technology is the mobility of technical personnel, who after several years of working in a foreign-invested firm may start-up their own firm using technologies, information, and other forms of know-how acquired while in the employ of a multinational company. See Denis Fred Simon, *Taiwan, Technology Transfer and Transnationalism: The Political Management of Dependency* (Boulder: Westview Press, forthcoming).
22. Larry Westphal and Carl Dahlman, "The Meaning of Technological Mastery in Relation to the Transfer of Technology," *Annals of the American Academy of Political and Social Science* (November 1981), pp. 12–26.
23. Stephen Magee, "Multinational Corporations, the Industry Technology Cycle and Development," *Journal of World Trade Law* (July–August 1977), pp. 297–312.
24. Raymond Vernon, "The Product Cycle Hypothesis in a New International Environment," *Oxford Bulletin of Economics and Statistics,* November, 1979.
25. Edwin Mansfield, "R&D and Innovation: Some Empirical Findings," in Zvi Griliches (ed.), *R&D, Patents and Productivity* (Chicago: University of Chicago Press, 1984), pp. 127–154.
26. Hood and Young refer to the ability of multinational firms in Taiwan to exploit their "ownership" advantages, i.e., marketing channels, management, and financial system and the island's "location" advantages, i.e., low labor costs, investment incentives and, at present, increasing technological skills, as one reason for their widespread participation in this economy. See Neil Hood and Stephen Young, *The Economics of the Multinational Enterprise* (New York: Longman Publishing, 1979).
27. For a discussion of the general slowdown in the rate of innovation in the petrochemicals industry, see Robert Stobaugh, *Innovation and Competition: The Global Management of Petrochemical Products* (Cambridge: Harvard Business School Press, 1988).
28. "Leaping Ahead on a Surface of Silicon," *Financial Times,* January 26, 1988, p. 20.
29. A good example is the R&D consortia that are being established at many American universities with the help of U.S. industry. The proliferation of these

university-industry consortia has raised such questions as "who sets the agenda for research?" and "how will the university and its traditional mission be shaped by these new forms of cooperation and sources of funding?" See Dan Dimancescu and James Botkin, *The New Alliance: America's R&D Consortia* (Cambridge: Ballinger Publishers, 1986).

30. Bruce Kogut, "Designinig Global Strategies: Comparative & Competitive Value-added Chains," *Slogan Management Review,* Summer 1985. See also Bruce Kogut, "Normative Observations on the Inter Value-added Chain & Strategic Groups," *Journal of International Business Studies,* Fall 1984.
31. Thomas Hout, et al., "How Global Companies Win Out," *Harvard Business Review,* September/October 1982.
32. Taiwan and South Korea have also greaetly benefited from a reversal of the "brain drain" that plagued them as recently as 10 years ago. Many Korean and Chinese scientists, a large percentage who have had successful careers in U.S. high-technology firms, are returning home to set up new ventures.
33. Stuart Madnick (ed.), *The Strategic Use of Information Technology* (New York: Oxford University Press, 1987).
34. See Mel Horowich (ed.), *Technology in the Modern Corporation,* Special Issue, *Technology in Society,* Volume 7, Number 2/3, 1985.
35. In a recent article, one author suggests that in the U.S. the demands of the military compete with and impede productive economic growth, while in Japan this problem does not exist—thereby freeing up extensive amounts of capital for new investment, especially in areas such as R&D. While the argument is a powerful one, however, it does not account for the Taiwanese and South Korean cases, where rapid technological progress and large military expenditures have occurred simultaneously. See Joshua Goldstein, "How Military Might Robs an Economy," *The New York Times,* October 16, 1988, p. F3.
36. Robert Reich, "The Rise of Techno-nationalism," *Atlantic Monthly,* May 1987, pp. 63–69.
37. See Robert Gilpin, *U.S. Power and the Multinational Corporation* (New York: Basic Books, 1975).
38. Interviews by the author in Seoul, August and November 1988.
39. For a critique of some of the most recent changes see "How Export Controls Defend the National Interest," Heritage Foundation *Backgrounder,* Number 589, June 30, 1987.
40. "Fairchild Semiconductor Pact's Link to United States–Japan Dispute Chagrins Firms," *Wall Street Journal,* March 13, 1987, p. 5. See also *Electronics,* "Is the Fairchild-Fujitsu Deal a Vision of the Future?", November 13, 1986.
41. "Taiwan Introduces Computer Ban," *American Wall Street Journal,* March 29, 1988, p. 3. This effort by the United States is especially ironic in view of the fact that Taiwan's attempt to diversify its trade and enter markets outside the United States represents a response to American pressure to ease its trade problems with the island.
42. These two cases also reminded the United States that alternative centers of indigenous technological capability had emerged outside of the COCOM regime in places such as Sweden, Brazil, and India as well as in Taiwan, South Korea, and Singapore.
43. "U.S. to Boost High-Tech Exports to China," *Financial Times,* March 10, 1988, p. 20.
44. Michael R. Gordon, "War in Gulf Spurs China Arms Export Role," *The New*

York Times, May 19, 1987, p. 9. Background on the Silkworm crisis is provided in Robert S. Greenberger, "U.S. Retaliates Against Chinese for Sales to Iran," *Wall Street Journal,* October 22, 1987; Don Shannon and Sara Fritz, "U.S. Punishes China for Iran Silkworm Sales," *Los Angeles Times,* October 23, 1987, pp. 1, 11; David Holley, "U.S. Angered by New Chinese Arms Shipments to Iran," *Los Angeles Times,* October 28, 1987, p. 1.

45. Chinese statements refuting Washington's accusations but pledging to curb further Iranian access to the Silkworm are found in Holley, "China Pledges to Prevent Silkworm Delivery to Iran," *Los Angeles Times,* November 4, 1987, pp. 1, 9.
46. "Rochester U. President Troubled by Fuji Case," *The New York Times,* September 2, 1987, p. 27.
47. "Fuji Employee is Accepted as University Shifts Stance," *Wall Street Journal,* September 14, 1987, p. 16.
48. C. C. Markides and N. Berg, "Manufacturing Offshore is Bad Business," *Harvard Business Review,* September/October 1988, pp. 113–120.
49. More than one-half the number of engineering doctorates in the United States have gone to foreign students since 1981. And, if the number of foreigners in engineering doctorate programs grows by about 2 percent a year, foreign students will outnumber Americans by 3 to 2 by 1995. Nonetheless, more than 1/2 in 1985 as compared to less than 1/3 in 1972 indicate an intention to remain in the U.S. See "Foreigners in Science," *Science,* August 28, 1987, p. 970.
50. Carmela Haklisch. *Technical Alliances in the Semiconductor Industry* (New York: NYU School of Business Administration Press, 1986).
51. Free China Journal, "VLSI: A Booster to Information Industry," *Free China Journal,* February 3, 1986, p. 4.
52. Deigan Morris and Michael Hergert, "Trends in International Collaborative Agreements," *Columbia Journal of World Business,* Spring 1987, pp. 15–21.
53. Richard Osborn and C. Christopher Baughn, "New Patterns in the Formation of U.S.–Japanese Cooperative Ventures: The Role of Technology," *Columbia Journal of World Business,* Spring 1987, pp. 57–66.
54. For a variety of views on strategic alliances see Farok J. Contractor and Peter Lorange (eds.), *Cooperative Strategies in International Business* (Lexington, MA: Lexington Books, 1988).
55. Michael Reich and E. Mankin, "Joint Ventures with Japan Give Away Our Future," *Harvard Business Review,* Vol. 64, #2, 1986, pp. 78–86.
56. *Motorola, Inc.—Annual Report 1987* (Schaumburg, IL: Motorola, 1988).
57. In the early 1980s, Motorola licensed its 8-bit and 16-bit microprocessor technology to Hitachi only to discover that Hitachi's progress on the learning curve was faster than anticipated. Subsequently, Motorola declined Hitachi's request for acccess to its 32-bit technology. See "Japanese Firms Challenge Dominance of U.S. Microprocessor Manufacturers," *Asian Waall Street Journal Weekly,* July 11, 1988, pp. 9 & 24.
58. "Microprocessors: Japanese Link Crucial to Motorola Strategy," *Financial Times,* November 16, 1987, p. 7.
59. Motorola's decision, in all likelihood, reflects the realization that the only way to succeed in the Japanese market, especially in the semiconductor industry, is to be tied in with a Japanese firm. See "Japan Hangs on to Its Cutting Edge," *Financial Times,* November 6, 1987, p. 6.

60. *Financial Times,* November 16, 1987, p. 7.
61. Kathryn Harrigan, *Strategies for Joint Ventures* (Lexington, MA: Lexington Books, 1985).
62. "Why It's Buy Out or Fall Out," *Financial Times,* February 11, 1988, p. 12. Past competitors such as Komatsu and Dresser, Mitsubishi and Caterpillar, Hitachi and Fiat, Hitachi and John Deere, Clark Equipment and Volvo, and Kawasaki and Aveling Barford (UK), respectively, have chosen collaboration as a means to hedge against overcapacity and poor sales.
63. See Marjorie Lyles, "Common Mistakes of Joint Venture Experienced Firms," *Columbia Journal of World Business,* Spring 1987, pp. 79–86. See also Benjamin Gomes-Casseres, "Joint Venture Instability: Is It a Problem?" *Columbia Journal of World Business,* Spring 1987, pp. 97–101.
64. Thomas Roehl and J. Frederick Truitt, "Stormy Open Marriages are Better: Evidence from U.S., Japanese, and French Cooperative Ventures in Commercial Aircraft," *Columbia Journal of World Business,* Spring 1987, pp. 87–96.
65. David Mowery (ed.), *International Collaborative Ventures in U.S. Manufacturing* (Cambridge: Ballinger Publishers, 1988).
66. David Mowery (ed.), *International Collaborative Ventures in U.S. Manufacturing* (Cambridge: Ballinger Publishers, 1988).
67. "No Longer the Only Game in Town," *The New York Times,* December 4, 1988, Section 3, pp. 1, 7.
68. *The New York Times,* December 4, 1988, Section 3, p. 1.
69. "U.S. Set to Soften Line on Technology Transfers," *Financial Times,* January 29, 1988, p. 2.
70. "South Korea's High-Tech Miracle," *The New York Times,* December 9, 1988, p. D1, 4.
71. "Do Not Adjust Your Set," *The Economist,* October 1, 1988, pp. 80–82.
72. "HDTV: Will U.S. Be in the Picture?," *The New York Times,* September 21, 1988, pp. D1, 7.
73. "Do Not Adjust Your Set," *The Economist,* October 1, 1988, pp. 80–82.
74. "HDTV: Will U.S. Be in the Picture?," *The New York Times,* September 21, 1988, pp. D1, 7.
75. "Overnight, Thomson Has the Stuff to Take on the Titans," *Business Week,* August 10, 1987, p. 36.
76. *Financial Times,* April 5, 1988, p. 1.
77. "New Projects and Policies Planned for Biotechnology," *International Herald Tribune,* Special Section: 1992—the World's Rendezvous with Europe, November 4, 1988, p. IV.

2

The Implications of Global Integration for the National Control of Technology

STEPHEN J. KOBRIN

> Modern industry has established the world market . . . All old established national industries have been destroyed or are daily being destroyed . . . In place of the old local and national seclusion and self-sufficiency, we have . . . universal inter-dependence of nations. As in material, so also in intellectual production. The intellectual creations of individual nations become common property.[1]

Despite the current wave of interest in the topic, the idea of world markets, of global competition, and global industries is not new. However, when Karl Marx and Friedrich Engles wrote these words in 1848, they could not even begin to imagine jet aircraft, satellite communication, large scale computer networks, or the modern, integrated multinational corporation. Nor could they imagine the central role modern technology plays in the life of nations and the impact on states—and the state system—of intellectual creations becoming "common property."

The importance of national control of—or at the least, access to—technology has increased over time. In the twentieth century, the development and control of technology have become requisites of national security and economic competitiveness. Modern weapons systems are technologically intensive and nations such as the United States go to great lengths to prevent technologies that have potential military applications from falling into enemy hands. This includes attempts to exert direct control over the use of these technologies by allies.

More fundamentally, technology is an important element in national industrial competitiveness and the newer technologies, such as information processing, play a central role in a large number of industrial sectors. As John Zysman and Stephen Cohen have noted, these critical industries are the modern equivalent of roads and bridges during the industrial revolution; they are a form of "industrial infrastructure" and are seen as an appropriate concern of governments even in free-market-oriented economies.[2] Control over technology is a requisite of national security in a political and economic sense.

Questions were raised about the impact of international trade and foreign direct investment on national economic and technological independence well before global competition became a focus of discussion. As numerous authors have noted, free flows of trade and investment make national control over technology more difficult as specialization and interdependence increase the costs of policy autonomy.

Global competition, however, implies something beyond interdependence resulting from trade and investment. It is a manifestation of the underlying cross-border integration of the world economy. As Rober Gilpin points out, however, there is a fundamental difference between the integration of national markets that began toward the end of the nineteenth century and the transnational integration of markets.[3] The latter is taking place in a world divided politically among competing nation states and, as noted, those states increasingly recognize that technology is a, if not the, critical element in that competition.

In this chapter, I argue that the increased importance of global competition or global industries, or both, makes national control over technology more problematic. Integrated multinational operations increase the permeability of national borders and make it more difficult to erect barriers to information flows. More significantly, to the extent global industries—in the sense of the transnational integration of markets—are a reality, uninational development of, and thus control over, technology may be beyond the reach of all but the largest countries.

Until recently, there has been a general symmetry between political and economic geography; the territory encompassed by most nation-states has provided an ample market for efficient business operations. In a number of critical industries, that may no longer be true. The minimal geographic territory required for achieving production economies of scale or supporting the development of competitive technology may be larger than that of most nation-states. Efficient production or large-scale technological development may demand transnationally integrated markets.

I will first discuss global competition and global industries conceptually, then draw some conclusions about the impact of global industries on national control of technology, and lastly suggest implications for the multinational firm.

GLOBAL COMPETITION AND GLOBAL INDUSTRIES

Michael Porter has defined a global industry as one where there is ". . . some competitive advantage to integrating activities on a worldwide basis."[4] As a number of authors note, the concept of global competition is ambiguous: global competition and industries are often tautologically defined in terms of one another.[5]

If global competition (or a global industry) is to have meaning, it must imply more than internationalization. The idea of competitive advantage can serve to order the concept in the sense that a global industry is one in which the advantages of international investment or operations reach a critical threshold where the domestic or uninational firm can no longer compete. As Bruce Kogut observes, "the question is then . . . how international activity augments or creates strategic advantages."[6] I suggest a threefold typology:[7]

Exploitation of Differences in Factor Prices/Resource Allocation

International firms gain competitive advantage from access to more abundant/cheaper factors of production abroad: they can exploit differences in national comparative advantage. For example, a firm can produce components where labor is relatively cheap and productive, local energy intensive refining operations where hydroelectric power is abundant, or technology intensive operations in countries with high levels of education.[8]

Multinational Operations

Integrated, centrally controlled multinational operations provide sources of competitive advantage such as the ability to transfer learning across markets, increased returns to basic research and development, exploitation of ambiguous national jurisdiction, subsidization across markets, diversification in terms of adverse economic or political conditions in individual countries, and the ability to scan for new technologies or market opportunities worldwide. Although it is rarely articulated precisely in the literature, the concept of global competition assumes that firms gain operational advantages from a presence in all, or most, significant markets worldwide.

Transnational Economies of Scale

In a number of critical industries many (if not most) national markets are too small to support efficient business acitivity. In some, plant level economies of scale cannot be achieved with volume generated by a reasonable market share in a single country (automobiles are an example). In others (mainframe computers), most firms' sales in a single market are insufficient to generate the absolute level of research and development expenditures needed to remain competitive.

In both situations, firms must integrate transnationally to compete: they must sell relatively standardized products in a number of markets to generate the volume necessary for efficient production or competitive research and development (R&D) expenditures. In these cases, transnationally integrated firms gain an advantage over domestic competitors. It is important to note that the critical point is reached when domestic firms can no longer compete; when the competitive advantages of international operations are such that a uninational firm is forced from the industry.

There is reason to suggest that technological intensity may be a more important cause of transnational integration than manufacturing scale economies. First, there have been indications that the tendency toward larger minimum efficient scale plants may be reversed through the application of computer processing to manufacturing. Smaller runs may allow for both flexibility and efficiency. It appears, for example, that the average size of model runs in automobile manufacturing has declined in recent years.[9]

On the other hand, there is every reason to believe that the major international industries are getting more technologically intense. When R&D expenditures as a percentage of sales in a sample of 239 large firms in 17 industries are compared for 1977 and 1982, all of the industries but one show an increase in technological intensity, with the average increase 22 percent.[10] Even though computer-assisted manufacturing may decrease the minimum efficient scale of manufacturing plants, it increases the technological intensity of the manufacturing process.

GLOBAL COMPETITION AND THE CONTROL OF TECHNOLOGY

International competition—at all three levels—can affect the technological capability of states directly, in both an absolute and relative sense. International competition makes it more difficult to contain technology—to restrict access to it by nonnationals—for reason of economic competitiveness or military-political security. It also can increase the costs of independent or autonomous technology policy, possibly to the point where it is no longer a viable option. Last, and most fundamentally, many national markets may be too small to allow independent development—or even control—of technology on a uninational basis.

By *expoiting differences in national comparative advantage*—whether through trade or foreign investment—multinational corporations (MNCs) tie national economies together through direct intrafirm links and markedly increase the costs of independence or autonomy. At the macroeconomic level this has led to a significant change in the nature of international trade, with an increasing proportion of flows accounted for by intrafirm rather than "open market" interactions.[11] By facilitating flows of trade and capital, MNCs contribute to shifts in national comparative advantage making it considerably more difficult to contain technology. Perhaps more important, greater specialization and interdependence increase the cost of formulating and implementing independent technology policy.

Integrated multinational operations affect national technological capabilities and control more significantly. First, the establishment of subsidiaries in a large number of countries facilitates the transfer of resources between countries. Foreign direct investment *is* a flow of resources, primarily technology and management. Although the flows are intrafirm, they are also interstate and, despite the strongest efforts to contain proprietary technology, considerable diffusion is bound to occur. One does not have to go as far as Robert Gilpin, who argues the U.S. "traded away" its comparative advantage in technology through reliance on foreign direct investment (FDI) rather than trade, to accept the point.[12]

One of the primary competitive advantages attributed to integrated worldwide operations is the capacity to "scan" globally for new technologies and market opportunities. For example, although the large size of the U.S. market makes it attractive to foreign firms, one of the more common arguments for FDI in the U.S. has been access to technological development; both product/process and marketing. The presence of multinationals in most of the major markets makes it increasingly less likely that any given state will be able to restrict access to a new technology to its own (i.e., national) firms.

In discussing the applicability of the product life cycle hypothesis to the new international environment, Raymond Vernon argues that one of its basic assumptions—the considerable barriers to the flow of technological and market information across national borders—is now questionable. He concludes that given the spread of MNCs, it can no longer be assumed that innovating firms are uninformed about conditions abroad.[13]

There is evidence for the increased international flow of technology through MNCs. Raymond Vernon and William Davidson found that the percentage of new products transferred abroad within one year after U.S. introduction increased from 7.5 in 1951–1955 to 35.4 in 1971–1975. Although this reflects convergence among the major markets, it also reflects the internationalization of U.S. firms.[14]

Integrated multinational operations also reduce the control exercised by any given state over its economic actors and its economy, making it more difficult to contain technology, for either economic or security reasons, through regulation of enterprise. Multinational corporations have operations in a large number of countries and are subject to multiple policies and legal jurisdictions that hold very different opinions on issues of trade and the transfer of technology.

In 1982, for example, the U.S. government attempted to prevent the transfer of oil transmission technology to the Soviets for use in a pipeline to Western Europe. Although it could successfully impose sanctions on exports from the United States, despite its strongest efforts the Reagan administration was unable to prevent European subsidiaries of American firms from exporting components for the pipeline.[15]

The most fundamental effects of international competition on national control of technology are found in industries whose structure is such that they are inherently transnational: where national markets are too small to support either efficient production or competitive levels of technological development. Although individual firms may gain competitive advantages from international, or even global, operations, it is important to note that in this case *transnational integration* is structural; it is a function of the economics of the product or process technology.

As discussed earlier, international firms who seek competitive advantage through exploiting either factor price differences or integrated multinational operations can have significant impacts on the national control of technology. In these cases the problems arise from either limits on, or increases in, the cost of national control. Given the spread of multinational enterprise and the direct transnational social, technical, and political linkages they entail, national borders have become increasingly permeable.

The impacts of structural transnational integration mandated by increases in the scale of production or R&D are changes of degree rather than kind. As noted, an isomorphism between political and economic geography—between efficiently sized markets and state borders—can no longer be assumed.

If firms cannot generate competitive R&D budgets on a uninational basis, they must integrate across markets to survive. While it is possible to centralize research and development in the home country and simply sell the product in other markets, it is unlikely that host country governments will long tolerate that state of affairs. Local production and technological development are likely requisites of entry, especially for "leading edge" technologies that are considered critical for industrial competitiveness.

Put simply, all but the largest national markets—and even that is questionable—may be too small to support development or control of technology in major industries. The dramatic increase in international strategic alliances between firms from advanced industrial countries is one manifestation of this trend. Michael Hergert and Diegan Morris found that the vast majority of these new alliances were among advanced country firms and concentrated in a few industries characterized by intense technology or scale economies. Fifty percent were in aerospace, telecommunications, and computers, and an additional 24 percent in motor vehicles.[16]

The discussion of global strategic alliances has been restricted to firms to this point. However, these alliances are simply a manifestation of underlying structural changes; they reflect the need to link markets through alliances between states to allow the development of technology. Even the resources of relatively large states may be insufficient to support development of a "national champion."

The result of well over a decade of effort by France to develop a national computer firm was Groupe Bull's acquisition of Honeywell's computer operations in an alliance with NEC. The demands for research and development expenditures in that industry may require this sort of transnational alliance among all but the largest firms in the largest markets.

The question at hand is much more general than that of a given firm's competitive advantage. It is the technologies or production processes themselves that may no longer be viable on a uninational basis. National technological independence may be beyond the reach of governments in many countries, industrialized as well as developing. Transnational integration—either within a single MNC or through alliances between firms—may become the norm. That has implications both for the national control of technology and a state system based on absolute control, both political and economic, over discrete geographic territory.

IMPLICATIONS FOR THE FIRM

Although the focus of this chapter is on national control over technology, there are obvious implications for the multinational firm. Multinational corporations are the most visible manifestation of interdependence and global integration and, as such, are often the target of attempts by nation–states to maintain autonomy and target of attempts by nation–states to maintain autonomy and independence.

There have been a number of instances of firms caught between conflicting state policies in the past. One of the most publicized was Dresser Industries' French subsidiary, which was caught between the diametrically opposed orders of the U.S. and French governments over shipping compressors for use in constructing the Siberian–European gas pipeline in 1982.[17]

As national control over technology becomes both more important and more difficult, MNCs are likely to find themselves the targets of state concern with increasing frequency. Firms engaged in strategic alliances may well fade conflicting directives from each of the parent governments or even concern on the part of each government over the transnational sharing of technology. Subsidiaries abroad may face hostility from host states if they transfer locally acquired technology out of the country. (One of the arguments raised by proponents of controls over foreign investment in the United States is that investors are here simply to acquire American technology and reduce American competitiveness.)

Managers of MNCs should thus expect increasing sensitivity over these sorts of issues in the future and the strong probability of increasing conflict with governments. Although these tensions reflect underlying changes in the structure of the world economy, they are manifest as MNC-government conflict. An awareness of political factors will become even more important than it has been in the past and the need for an explicit political strategy even greater.

NOTES

1. Karl Marx and Friedrich Engles, *The Communist Manifesto* (Middlesex, England: Penguin Books, 1967), pps. 81, 83, 84.
2. John Zysman and Stephen S. Cohen, "Double or Nothing: Open Trade and Competitive Industry." *Foreign Affairs,* Summer 1983, pp. 1113–1139.

3. Rober Gilpin, *The Political Economy of International Relations* (Princeton: Princeton University Press, 1987), pp. 176–177.
4. Michael E. Porter, "Competition in Global Industries: A Conceptual Framework" in Michael E. Porter (ed.), *Competition in Global Industries* (Boston: Harvard Business School Press, 1986), p. 19.
5. See Sumantra Goshal, "Global Strategies: An Organizing Framework" *Strategic Management Journal* (8) 1987, pp. 425–440 and Gary Hammel and C. K. Prahald, "Do You Really Have a Global Strategy" *Harvard Business Review,* July–August 1985, pp. 139–148.
6. Bruce Kogut, "Normative Observations on the Value Added Chain and Strategic Groups," *Journal of International Business Studies* (XV) Fall 1984, p. 156.
7. The typology is not original and reflects arguments in Kogut, "Normative Observations . . ." It is similar to that of Porter (exploiting differences in markets across countries, economies of scale, or economies of scope) which is reflected in Goshal. See Michael Porter, *Competitive Advantage* (New York: The Free Press, 1985) and Goshal, "Global Strategy . . ."
8. See Bruce Kogut, "Designing Global Strategies: Comparative and Competitive Value-Added Chains" *Slogan Management Review,* Summer 1985, pp. 15–28, for a more complete discussion of this topic.
9. See John Holusha, "Detroit Bets on More Models for Smaller Markets," *The New York Times,* July 13, 1987, p. 6.
10. Calculated from data reported in John H. Dunning and R. Pearce, *The World's Largest Industrial Enterprises: 1962–1983* (New York: St. Martin's Press, 1985), p. 166.
11. For a discussion of the changing nature of international trade see, Paul R. Krugman (ed.), *Strategic Trade and the New International Economics* (Cambridge: MIT Press, 1986).
12. Robert Gilpin, *U.S. Power and the Multinational Corporation,* (Princeton: Princeton University Press, 1975).
13. Raymond Vernon, "The Product Life Cycle in a New International Environment," *Oxford Bulletin of Economic Statistics,* (41) 1979, pp. 255–267.
14. Cited in Vernon, "The Product Life Cycle Hypothesis in a New . . ."
15. See Stefanie Ann Lenway and Beverly Crawford, "When Business Becomes Politics: Risk and Uncertainty East–West Trade." *Working Paper,* The Strategic Management Research Center, University of Minnesota, Minneapolis, May, 1986.
16. See Michael Hergert and Deigan Morris, "Trends in International Collaborative Agreements" in Farok J. Contractor and Peter Lorange (eds.), *Cooperative Strategies in International Business* (Lexington, MA: Lexington Books, 1988), pp. 99–109.
17. See Lenway and Crawford, "When Business Becomes Politics . . ." (op cit.)

3

The Changing Nature of United States Government Policy on the Transfer of Strategic Technology: An Overview

ALEXANDER GOOD

The basic premise for controlling the export of strategic commodities and technology is clear and few question it. Yet, the implementation of that premise generates intense debate among the Free World countries. To understand the changing nature of U.S. government policy, a review of some of the major driving forces is appropriate. This chapter briefly traces the development of export control policy since 1949, examines the current state of affairs, and considers the direction technology transfer policy may take in 1990 and beyond. Since the scope of this subject is broad, this chapter is necessarily limited in its coverage of any particular issue.

The Basic Premise

The defense of the nation and its people is, of course, one of the primary functions of any government. In today's world, the ability of a nation to defend itself and its allies is heavily dependent on technology to provide sophisticated and effective weaponry, strategic information processing capabilities, surveillance of the enemy, and so forth. In the case of Western nations, this dependence on technological superiority is particularly significant. The Warsaw Pact forces today have a massive quantitative superiority in troops and conventional weapons.[1] The North Atlantic Treaty Organization (NATO) hopes to offset this numerical advantage in large part with technically superior weapons. Accordingly, the security of the Free World largely depends on maintaining our superiority in strategic technologies. Since much of the technology used to enhance military capability is developed by the private sector for commercial applications, certain strategic "dual-use" (i.e., commercial and military) technologies must be controlled.

While there is wide acceptance of the need to control technology, the implementation of export controls raises complex questions. The debate centers around two fundamentally different approaches, albeit with many variations. One approach would use trade controls to hinder the overall technical development of our adversaries by controlling virtually any dual-use item that would improve their existing technology. The other approach would control only truly strategic items that would directly and significantly engage military capability. To illustrate, advocates of the former position would argue that concrete hardness testers should be controlled because—apart from many civil applications—they can be used to test the wall hardness in missile silos. Advocates of the latter position might contend that even though it may be somewhat desirable, it is not feasible or economically appropriate to control these commodities. Their argument is based on the practical difficulties of the control of such technologies combined with the economic cost domestic businesses.

Stated succintly, these commodities are available from other sources and the economic costs (lost markets) outweigh the (marginal) strategic benefits. In such a debate, the distinction between foreign policy controls and strategic trade controls becomes blurred.[2]

The forces that drive the Soviet Union to seek Western technology, and the forces that frame the American response, go to the heart of two competing philosophies of government. Both governments find themselves caught in dilemmas—dilemmas that are mirror images of each other and that express the strengths and weaknesses of their respective societies.

The Soviet Dilemma

While it is an obvious generalization, most agree that technical innovation and creative risk-taking do not flourish in the Warsaw Pact nations. The Communist hierarchy restricts the flow of knowledge and ideas and the centrally planned economy stifles market incentives.

Although the Soviets have scored some major military and scientific successes by concentrating resources in designated fields, the lack of innovation in the rest of the economy constrains even these high priority projects. As a consequence, the Warsaw Pact nations devote a relatively high proportion of their hard currency to acquiring foreign technology.

While they have been able to steal many Western products, they have generally failed to improve on them, much less "leapfrog" into the next generation. Thus, there is an on-going need to pirate products in an attempt to reduce the technological superiority of the West.[3]

The Warsaw Pact nations are thus trapped in a circle of dependency on foreign technology, seemingly unable to generate their own or even fully utilize what they acquire.[4] As the pace and complexity of technical advance increases, it becomes harder to reverse engineer and assimilate foreign products before the next generation appears.[5] The Warsaw Pact dilemma thus intensifies. Even Secretary General Mikhail Gorbachev admits that the Soviet Union has fallen far behind. In part, "Perestroika" is aimed at overcoming the inability of the Soviet Union to keep pace with the West. Gorbachev states that ". . . unless we take into consideration the diverse interests of people . . . and draw them into active, constructive endeavors, it will be impossible for us to change the situation of the country."[6]

The American Dilemma

The strength of the United States burgeons from its open, free enterprise society—a society that encourages the free movement of ideas and rewards its inventors, entrepreneurs, and producers. While imposing controls on technology, it is necessary to maintain or expand the technological lead over the Warsaw Pact. This is a difficult challenge for Western nations.

First, the openness of our society makes it difficult to control the export of technology without the support of the private sector. While most in the private sector are committed without qualification, unfortunately, a small number of individuals will ignore the nation's security if the profit is large enough.

Second, as controls limit exports, sales opportunities are lost, thus hurting our "high tech" sector and reducing the incentive to develop new technology. At worst, the pace of technological change may be retarded, thereby potentially impacting security. Export controls also divert resources from productive (R&D) to nonproductive (administering controls) activities.

Third, technology has become so diffused that U.S. firms must compete in a global marketplace against foreign businessmen whose governments often impose less stringent controls. This competitive disadvantage undercuts U.S. vitality in some key technical fields.

National security is a complex combination of economic, technical, and strategic factors. More and more, the United States is obliged to act in concert with our allies, both to ensure economic vitality and effective controls.

The American dilemma boils down to this: How do we restrict the flow of strategic technology to our adversaries without slowing the pace of technological change, damaging alliances, and losing the overseas markets, all of which are necessary to sustain our technological edge?

THE EVOLUTION OF UNITED STATES GOVERNMENT POLICY ON EXPORT CONTROLS FROM 1949 TO 1979

The 1949 Act and the Founding of the Coordinating Committee for Multilateral Export Controls

During the first decade after the close of World War II, certain trends became evident in the domain of export controls. Many of these trends remain with us today. In the Export Control Act of 1949, Congress consolidated and extended wartime powers that authorized the president to regulate exports for reasons of national security, foreign policy, or short supply. Congress was motivated partly by postwar economic conditions, but also by concern over the military power of the Soviet Union and the People's Republic of China.[7] NATO was also formed in 1949 to assure the defense of Western Europe. Concern increased when the Soviets exploded an atomic bomb in 1949, using secrets stolen from the United States. Clearly the Soviets had an active program of espionage that targeted Western technology.[8]

The dangers of uncontrolled technology transfer were not lost on other Western nations. Six European nations joined the United States to create the Coordinating Committee for Multilateral Export Control (COCOM).[9] Designed to facilitate cooperation on strategic embargoes, the COCOM member governments drew up the first embargo lists in 1950. This informal arrangement functioned reasonably well through the Korean Conflict. In peacetime, however, cracks began to appear as some of the European governments sought to increase trade with both China and the Soviet Union.

The Truman Administration, which took a tough line on selling to the Soviets, quickly discovered the disadvantages of an informal, nontreaty organization. COCOM rules required unanimous consent and each member government was entirely responsible for implementing those decisions. Since all matters within COCOM were confidential, including the COCOM embargo lists themselves, exporters had to rely on their separate governments to find out what could be sold to embargoed countries. Inevitably this led to different interpretations of the rules and varying degrees of compliance. Evasions of the multilaterally agreed controls had already caused serious gaps in national enforcement practices.[10]

Partly in response to the perceived weakness of the COCOM system, the United States increasingly relied on its licensing system as the principal constraint to illegal technology acquisition. The 1949 Act had authorized the administering agencies to attach conditions to export licenses. From the outset, the United States used this unilateral authority to exert jurisdiction over U.S. origin products and technology even after they had left American shores. Allied and neutral countries disliked reexport controls, but, since the United States dominated many areas of technology, they had little recourse.[11]

In 1953, Congress extended the Export Control Act, not only due to continued tension with the Soviet Bloc, but also because NATO doctrine had already begun to rely on superior military technology to offset growing Warsaw Pact numerical strength.[12]

Changes were later made in the regulatory mechanisms. Congress had given the Department of Commerce primary regulatory authority for export controls but, over time, other agencies accumulated various review and enforcement functions.[13] Eventually, most departments within the Executive Branch became involved with export controls. While the involvement of so many agencies permits the Executive Branch to draw on a broad range of expertise, it also causes delays, uncertainty, and a lack of accountability.[14]

The Rise and Fall of Detente

The blossoming of detente under President Nixon cast trade with the Warsaw Pact in a somewhat different light. Many believed that the Soviets could be drawn into an interdependent relationship with the Free World through expanded trade. The Export Administration Act of 1969 reflected this optimistic view by significantly facilitating East–West trade. While many members of Congress supported the scaling back of controls, concerns over national security remained. By 1974, opponents of relaxed controls were expressing grave reservations about the flow of advanced technology to the Eastern Bloc, which they believed threatened to shift the strategic balance against the Free World. As a result of these converns, in the mid-1970s Congress significantly expanded the Department of Defense's role in regulating export controls.

Concerns continued to mount as the bloom of detente faded. The invasion of Afghanistan in 1979 shattered any remaining illusions that the Soviets could be dissuaded from their drive for hegemony. Both the Carter administration and Congress focused a great deal of attention on the renewal of the Export Administration Act in 1979. Subsequently, highly visible hearings in Congress in 1980 revealed disturbing lack of coordination and resources in the enforcement of export controls. With alarm growing on both sides of the aisle in Congress, the stage was set for a dramatic overhaul of the licensing system. The election of Ronald Reagan in November of 1980 ensured that it would happen.

EXPORT CONTROL DURING THE REAGAN ADMINISTRATION

The newly elected president made stemming the flow of advanced technology high priority. Apart from legal Soviet acquisition of Western technology, intelligence information that became available in 1981 clearly demonstrated that the Soviets were conducting a massive program of diversion and espionage.[15] The administration quickly established a program to strengthen technology controls domestically and internationally. Aware that American commercial interests might suffer some dislocation, the administration nevertheless urged their support for expanded controls in the interest of national security. Internationally, the administration initiated diplomatic efforts to sensitize the Allies to this threat to Western security. The president also chose to use America's powerful position in high technology to set an example for other countries.

Revitalizing Domestic Controls

On the domestic front, the existing mechanisms to control technology exports were woefully inadequate. The president requested, and Congress approved, a series of substantial increases in funding and personnel. Government agencies scrambled to redefine their roles and initiate new programs. A few examples will illustrate the extent of this shift in emphasis.

The Department of Commerce retained the leading role in the administration and enforcement of nonarmament export controls. In the period since 1980, the Export Administration staff in Commerce has expanded by approximately 400 percent. Today, the Bureau of Export Administration is headed by an Under Secretary, has 500 people, and a budget for fiscal 1988 of $37.5 million. Within the Bureau, enforcement operations have increased by 300 percent.[16]

Other agencies have also greatly expanded. United States Customs, which shared enforcement responsibilities with Commerce, launched Operation Exodus in 1981 to verify that shipments of controlled commodities leaving the United States were properly licensed. A year later, Customs established the Strategic Investigations Division, complete with a 24-hour command center, which centralized responsibility for export control investigations.[17] Customs claimed, and eventually won, the right to conduct overseas investigations into alleged violations of U.S. export control regulations.

In the Department of Defense, the Defense Technology Security Administration (DTSA) grew from 4 people in 1980 to 150 by 1987. Generously funded, DTSA quickly set up an automated data base that allowed them to play a powerful role in decisions on export control policy.

The Department of State, asserting its prerogative to conduct foreign policy discussions, expanded both the Political–Military and the International Trade Controls sections. Later, the Department of State appointed a technology transfer "czar," with the rank of ambassador, to coordinate multilateral control initiatives. Other agencies within the Executive Branch, including the intelligence community, substantially expanded their activities in response to the president's mandate.

Multilateral Cooperation

On the international front, in 1981 the U.S. government set out to energize the Allies on a bilateral and multilateral basis. Previous experience had made it clear that no embargo could be effective without the support of the Allied nations. The effort to revitalize COCOM began with high-level meetings and dramatic presentations on the extent of the strategic threat. While the Allies recognized that the unlimited flow of dual-use technology represented a threat to Western security, they balked at the scope of the American proposals to restrict trade. Convinced that the danger to Western security warranted extraordinary measures, the U.S. government exerted strong pressure on the Allies and extended its own enforcement activities to unprecedented lengths.[18] This produced an outcry from Western trading partners who were now less inclined to accept the American assertion of jurisdiction over U.S.-origin technology outside the United States. The question of extraterritoriality became a major irritant among COCOM member governments.

Despite the inherent limitations of such an informal organization (COCOM had grown to include 15 countries, each of which had a veto), the United States and its COCOM allies did agree on major changes. Among other accomplishments, COCOM revised the International Control List and set up an ongoing review process; it focused more attention on the transfer of technology as well as commodities; and members upgraded the support facilities in the COCOM secretariat itself.[19]

The Impact on American Business

The decision to insist on rigorous unilateral standards, instead of compromising at the lowest common denominator in COCOM, had a predictable impact on American exporters. The United States had established a stringent set of controls on U.S.-origin technology, including commodities not controlled by COCOM. Moreover, among COCOM members, U.S. penalties for violation of the export control laws continue to be the most severe. The steady increase in license applications further strained the licensing office, resulting in delays of weeks, months, or longer for some licenses, also hurting U.S. exporters. American firms complained about these and other commercial handicaps.

The Department of Defense, however, countered that the Warsaw Pact could have saved up to a billion dollars per year in research and development costs had export controls not prevented their acquiring American technology. They estimated that NATO would have spent an equivalent amount to equal these Soviet advances.[20] In proportion, Defense contended, the economic cost of foregoing sales to the Warsaw Pact was more than justified. Furthermore, the temporary inconveniences in the processing system were being overcome and progress in COCOM was ameliorating the disparities between national regimes. The Department of Defense asserted that businesses should focus on the long-term survival of the free enterprise system rather than on the limited, short-term impact of export controls on their balance sheets.

American companies countered that they suffering serious competitive disadvantages that went far beyond lost sales to embargoed countries. These disadvantages resulted in long-term losses of markets due to the uncertainty and difficulty of dealing with a complex and often overburdened licensing system. They warned that American suppliers were being "designed out" of foreign-made systems. Specifically, foregin customers would select a non-U.S. product—even if technically inferior—that could be easily obtained and reexported, instead of an American product that came with many conditions attached.[21] Lost markets diminished the ability of U.S.

firms to retain their technical edge. These complaints from the business community were not lost on members of Congress when they began to review the Export administration Act.

The Export Administration Amendments Act of 1985

Congress opened discussions on renewal of export controls in 1983, in light of the vigorous, enforcement-oriented policies of the administration. At the center of the ensuing 2-year debate were long-standing divisions over the scope and economic cost of strategic controls. As in previous debates, there were widely divergent views over the best approach to dual-use controls. Many who believed in the inherently aggressive nature of the Soviet leadership fought to control any dual-use items that might reduce the Western lead in any technology with military applications. They cited the use of trucks, made with Western help, to carry troops into Afghanistan as an example of the need for a broad embargo. Others advocated controlling only commodities and technologies that are truly strategic and would significantly enhance the military capabilities of the Warsaw Pact. These "reformers" argued that the economic and political costs of controlling lower level, dual-use technology outweighed the strategic benefits and that it was simply not possible to effectively control an extensive list.[22]

Further complicating the debate was the lack of hard data.[23] How do you measure the costs versus the benefits of specific export controls? How do you determine whether a specific commodity or technology "significantly enhances the military capabilities" of our adversaries? How can we know what is already available to the Warsaw Pact forces? What is the cost of strained relationships with our allies?

All of these questions and many others had been examined by Congress in previous debates, though few of them were answered with finality. Not surprisingly, the Export Administration Amendments Act of 1985 (EAAA) did not represent a consensus but another hard fought compromise. The 1985 Act set new guidelines in a number of important areas. For example, it:

Strengthened the decontrol process for commodities found to be available in face and in quantity to the Warsaw Pact. This was done by creating the Office of Foreign Availability within the Department of Commerce and by giving decontrol authority to the Secretary of Commerce;

Mandated the creation of a new agency in Commerce to be headed by an Under Secretary of Export Administration; this separated export control from trade promotion and gave Commerce the senior government official in strategic trade matters;

Established in section 5(k) that non-COCOM countries with a control system "comparable in practice" to COCOM should be accorded COCOM equivalent status in export licensing matters;

Established tighter deadlines for the processing of license applications, especially for COCOM countries; and

Attempted to clarify jurisdictional boundaries within the Executive Branch, for example, giving U.S. Customs authority to investigate alleged violations of export controls overseas.

The Export Administration Act, as amended in 1985, remains the principal legislation for U.S. policy. Because the 1985 Act represented a compromise rather than a consensus, the debate over the scope and enforcement of controls continued, though at a lower level of intensity. Some of the same issues were raised again in the debate over the Omnibus Trade Bill of 1988.

The Quest for Balance

In the aftermath of the 1985 EAAA, a number of trends began shifting the emphasis from stemming the flow to achieving a balance of strategic and economic security. By the beginning of President Reagan's second term, the United States had made substantial strides in controlling the flow of technology to our adversaries. The sense of crisis had passed, though much remained to be done. In the meantime, mounting evidence indicated that America was paying a high cost for rigorous technology controls.

By the mid-1980s, it became apparent that America no longer dominated technological advances. With the increasingly rapid transfer of technology came a growing interdependence in the development of products and markets. Fewer products were entirely of American manufacture and the sale of U.S. origin products for use as components became an increasingly important market. In some fields, such as telecommunications and computers, a system might consist of major components from half a dozen or more different countries. The "internationalization" of technology made the administration of a broad list of products increasingly complex—and costly to American firms.

Despite progress in COCOM, American firms continued to lose markets to competitors from neutral and COCOM countries that operated under much less stringent controls. The spread of technology enabled many non-COCOM nations, especially the newly industrialized countries (NICs) of the Pacific Rim, to compete aggressively against American firms for international markets. Some foreign firms, frustrated by the complexity of American reexport controls, instituted policies to "de-Americanize;" that is, to eliminate controlled American content from their products.

The danger inherent in these trends was graphically illustrated by the precipitous decline in our balance of trade in high technology. In 1980, the United States ran a $27 billion trade surplus in high technology; by 1986, we had fallen into deficit.[24]

Balancing the National Interest

In early 1987, a highly regarded panel of scientists, businessmen, and former Defense Department officials crystallized these concerns in a study undertaken by the National Academy of Sciences (NAS). Entitled *Balancing the National Interest: U.S. National Security Export Controls and Global Economic Competition,* this study emphasized the importance of economic vitality as a component of national security and drew attention to the high economic cost of overly broad controls. Certain conclusions were particularly striking.

First, the NAS study found that the scope of national security controls undermined the effectiveness of the program. The study also noted that technical development was no longer predominantly driven by "spin-offs" from defense contracting but, on the contrary, products developed by the private sector for commercial use make up an increasing share of new defense technology. Finally, the study noted that excessive controls dampen private sector innovation and ultimately diminish our technological lead over the Soviets.[25]

While the panel found that "A comprehensive cost/benefit analysis of controls is currently infeasible," the panel did publish, in an appendix, a paper that drew some general conclusions based on an examination of statistical data. The paper stated that the "security benefits are not uniformly distributed across all levels of criticality but are concentrated in the region of highly critical technology and/or products." A substantial portion of the controlled commodities, however, consist of comparatively "low technology items," which are most likely to be available from non-U.S. sources; hence, "the more likely it becomes that U.S. export controls will drive foreign customers away from U.S. sources. The result is that the cost borne by U.S. firms due to lost sales associated with export control compliance is greatest for those items with the lowest degree of military criticality."[26]

The NAS panel recommended sharply reducing the scope of export controls. "Pragmatic control lists must be technically sound, narrowly focused and multilaterally coordinated."[27]

Progress and Reform at Commerce

Shortly after the NAS panel released its findings, the Secretary of Commerce initiated a series of reforms designed to lessen the administrative burden on companies, decrease the extraterritorial reach of U.S. regulations, and facilitate legitimate trade with COCOM and the Free World countries. In addition, strenuous efforts to improve and automate the licensing system were accelerated. Average waiting times for most licenses dropped steadily through 1987.

In parallel with these regulatory and processing advances, the Administration redoubled its efforts to improve multilateral enforcement and remove disadvantages for U.S. firms. Finally, the United States announced its intention to further liberalize the range of permissible exports to the People's Republic of China, as warranted by continued improvements in relations.

The Omnibus Trade Bill

In Congress, advocates of reform decided not to wait for the next legislatively mandated renewal of the Export Administration Act in 1989. They attached a series of amendments to the Omnibus Trade Bill, thereby placing export controls in a trade context rather than a national security context. If Congress agrees on a package of reforms acceptable to a broad spectrum of opinion, it may also extend the Export Administration Act beyond the September 1989 renewal date. This would obviate the need to review export controls in the first year of a new administration. Both houses of Congress have passed provisions that would enhance economic vitality. The difference tend to be more in degree than in nature.[28] The Export Administration section of the pending Trade Bill would:

Confirm many regulatory reforms already implemented by Commerce;

Reduce the size of the Controlled Commodity List, though the House and Senate versions differ greatly in degree and approach;

Strengthen the authority of Commerce within the Executive Branch, especially on Foreign Availability findings and interagency dispute resolution;

Liberalize licensing toward the People's Republic of China; specifically, allow exports under Distribution License to China and authorize the Executive Branch to negotiate an expanded Green Line with COCOM.

There are other amendments that would impose mandatory, retroactive sanctions on foreign companies for violations of COCOM regulations, even if no U.S. laws were broken. They stem from the recent Toshiba/Kongsberg incident.

Toshiba/Kongsberg and Its Consequences

News of this diversion of strategic milling technology by firms in two COCOM countries burst on the scene like a bombshell in early 1987, and the reverberations continue to be felt. Toshiba Machine, a subsidiary of the huge Japanese conglomerate, Toshiba Corporation, diverted nine-axis milling machines to the Soviet Union where they were linked to advanced control systems supplied by the Norwegian defense contractor Kongsberg Vaapenfabrik. Individuals in both companies knew the equipment could be used to enhance Soviet naval capabilities.

Congress reacted with outrage to this stunning example of our vulnerability to instances of corporate greed and governmental laxity. Some congressmen questioned the seriousness of Allied commitment to export controls and the effectiveness of COCOM. Others called for highly punitive sanctions on Toshiba and Kongsberg. The most serious of these is the so-called Garn Amendment, which would deny the American market to foreign companies that violate COCOM regulations, even if no American law is broken. This breath- taking extention of extraterritoriality would have extremely negative ramifications. The administration resolutely believes that such sanctions would:

Undermine the entire COCOM organization, which is based on a *voluntary* agreement among 16 member governments;

Bring strong cries from other governments on the extraterritorial application of U.S. laws;

Prevent the United States from gaining better cooperation on multilateral controls from all COCOM members and from forging COCOM-like agreements with other Free World countries;

Sour U.S.–Japanese relations and perhaps undo some of the changes the Japanese have instituted;

Reduce incentive for Japanese companies to invest in the United States;

Cost thousand of jobs in the United States (4,000 for Toshiba America alone);

Cause serious economic damage to American firms with long-standing ties with Toshiba and its subsidiaries; and

Possibly lead to retaliatory measures that would hurt U.S. business even further.

Rather than imposing sanctions, the administration has used this grave breach of Western security to press our COCOM partners for major improvements in their administration and enforcement of export controls. Many of the changes proposed by the United States—which has the severest penalties for violations of export control laws—have been accepted by other member governments. The Japanese, in particular, have passed new legislation and are allocating increased resources to this area. There is some evidence that Japanese companies have also instituted control systems to ensure compliance at all levels.

The United States will continue to seek "harmonization" of export controls among COCOM members to eliminate competitive disadvantages for American firms and to make diversions more difficult and costly. Dr. Paul Freedenberg, the senior policy official for export controls, told Congress in November 1987 that: "Our goal is and remains essentially to have equivalent control regimes across the spectrum of allied cooperation countries. . . . Indeed the enhancement and harmonization of COCOM enforcement efforts has been a top priority of Commerce."[29]

The Direction of United States Government Policy in 1988

In retrospect, 1987 turned out to be a watershed in the history of U.S. strategic controls. The year opened with the publication of the NAS study and the government's announcement of important regulatory changes. Congress decided to address export controls well before the statutory review of the Export Administration Act in 1989 by attaching a series of amendments to the Omnibus Trade Bill. The Toshiba/Kongsberg diversion presented the U.S. government with opportunities to improve multilateral enforcement, which it used well. As relations continued to improve with the People's Republic of China, the U.S. government also declared its intention to further liberalize permissible exports to the People's Republic of China.[30]

Easing the Burden on American Exporters

Improved administration of export controls relieves the business community while enhancing security. The Department of Commerce places high priority on the efficiency of its licensing system. Commerce initiatives include:

Increasingly efficient license processing to greatly ease export licensing for U.S. businesses. Average licensing times have dropped from 46 days in 1984 to 14 days in 1987; those licenses still necessary for COCOM countries (our major trading partners) are routinely processed in 3 to 5 days.

Holders of some 560 distribution licenses may ship a wide range of commodities to over 18,000 consignees around the world without having to apply for individual validated licenses (IVLs).

An automated tracking service (STELA) gives applicants the latest information on the progress of their applications and can even give verbal authorization to ship when no conditions are attached.

The creation of ELAIN, an electronic application submission network that enables subscribers to transmit applications directly to the Office of Export Licensing and receive replies by telephone line. This cuts up to 10 days off the license processing.

Revising the Technical Data Regulations: In response to concerns from the business community, the Commerce Department's Bureau of Export Administration (BXA) has held public hearings on Part 379 of the Export Administration Regulations (EAR) that govern the export of technical data. At a minimum, BXA wants to clarify these regulations. Wherever possible, BXA will also streamline and simplify the regulations.

Commerce initiatives have considerably facilitated West–West trade. By broadening the parameters of general licenses to COCOM countries (G-COM) and Free World destinations (GFW), Commerce effectively delicensed sizable amounts of low-end technology bound for Western customers. Raising the dollar limit of the General License for computers and related equipment from $1,000 to $5,000 for Free World destinations further reduced the need for validated licenses.

Revisions in the Parts and Components regulations eliminated the reexport licensing requirements where U.S. parts and components comprise 25 percent or less of the total value of foreign-made products destined for Free World countries. For embargoed or restricted countries, foreign-made products containing both 10 percent or less and $10,000 or less may be shipped without a reexport license. Almost all limits on the exports of one-for-one replacement parts have also been lifted. Besides facilitating trade, these regulatory changes significantly reduce the extraterritorial reach of our regulations.

The combination of new or expanded general licenses, regulatory changes and improved bilateral cooperation has reduced the number of applications for individual validated licenses from 140,000, 3 years ago, to 100,000 in fiscal 1987. Licensing volumes leveled off in 1988, but overall waiting times for license applications should continue to improve significantly as more companies take advantage of ELAIN and as the Bureau of Export Administration completes its automation program. Additional reductions in the number of licenses should result from the administration's commitment to streamline and reduce U.S. and COCOM control lists.

Although the administration opposes those provisions in the trade bill that would remove entire categories of technology from control, the administration intends to significantly reduce the list. As Paul Freedenberg, then Under Secretary of Commerce for Export Administration, said in February 1988:

> National security depends on a strong industrial base which, in turn, depends on the strength and vigor of our economy. We must stop subjecting to overcontrol and undue control the very same private sector companies upon which we rely to keep us technologically superior to our adversaries. We must limit the role of government to doing *only* that which is *truly* necessary to protect national security. . . . We must ensure that U.S. policy keeps pace with the changes represented by an increasingly interdependent global economy and rapid diffusion of technology.[31]

Reductions in the COCOM list will allow member governments to focus enforcement resources on a narrower range of strategic items. Particular consideration is being given to reduction of the computer equipment category, which "alone represents almost 50 percent of the export license applications submitted by U.S. exporters."

Progress in COCOM

In January 1988, ministerial level representatives of COCOM member governments gathered in Versailles, France, to demonstrate their strong commitment to strengthening the enforcement of multilateral exports controls. Among other things, they agreed to rationalize the International Control List, improve cooperation with Third World countries, harmonize national controls, and facilitate the flow of goods within COCOM countries. They also recognized the need to share more information with the business community regarding the objectives of COCOM. To maintain momentum, member governments will hold high level meetings annually to evaluate progress made in each of these areas.[32]

Cooperation with Third World Countries

A number of commercially powerful and technically sophisticated countries have remained outside of COCOM due to long-standing policies of neutrality or nonalignment. One of the administration's most impressive achievements has been to use the 5(k) provision of the 1985 Export Administration Act to enhance *both* strategic and economic trade security through better cooperation with these non-COCOM, Free World countries. Section 5(k) empowers the Secretary of Commerce to grant COCOM equivalent status to nonparticipating countries provided that their export control systems are "comparable in practice to those maintained by COCOM."

Furthermore, 5(k) benefits can be granted incrementally as the nonparticipating country strengthens its export controls. Sweden was the first country to receive partial 5(k) benefits, while Switzerland was the first country to receive full COCOM equivalence.[33] Subsequently, Finland, Austria, and Singapore have been granted various 5(k) benefits. The net result for the United States is freer trade in key markets coupled with enhanced security for our strategic technology.

Prognosis for 1990 and Beyond

No one can predict with any certainty the future course of export control policy, but it is possible to identify some of the factors that will influence it. The dynamics of strategic trade controls suggest that radical shifts in direction are unlikely. The philosophical orientation of the Bush administration may have the greatest impact in defining the scope of controls, the policy toward China, and the management of the export control bureaucracy. Underlying pressure to reconcile economic and strategic concerns will continue. Continued improvements in license processing and multilateral harmonization of regulations should make export controls a less contentious issue. Strong bipartisan interest will ensure, however, that export control policy remains closely linked to national security issues, even if it enjoys less visibility in the future.

The rapid diffusion of high technology will mean continued emphasis on multilateral enforcement cooperation. The Pacific Rim countries will become increasingly important participants in multilateral discussions due to their growing technical prowess. The European Community's drive for a unified internal market by 1992 will encourage a trend toward increasing liberalization of West–West trade in return for better enforcement within Europe.

The policies of the Bush administration will also be shaped largely by events, especially:

Relations with the Soviet Union;
The trade balance, particularly in the high technology sector;
Relations with the People's Republic of China;
Congressional action on relevant provisions of the Trade Bill;
The institutionalization of export controls.

Relations with the Soviet Union

The cautious "opening" in Soviet society may produce some important changes in that society, but probably not the dramatic economic and political shifts that would promote the rapid growth of Soviet indigenous technology. On the contrary, as the pace and complexity of technological advance increases, it will be harder for them to assimilate and copy Western technology.[34] The Warsaw Pact will have to run faster just to keep from falling further behind. The resulting pressure on the Soviets may push them toward better relations, or it could produce an aggressive backlash. The manner in which their leadership addresses this Soviet dilemma will have immensely important implications for America through the 1990s. This factor will influence the course of strategic trade controls in the next administration. In particular, it will be a factor in determining whether the United States uses export controls as an instrument of foreign policy (i.e., to retard the overall strength of the Soviet Union), or narrows controls to cover only truly strategic commodities and technologies that directly enhance Soviet military capability.

The Balance of Trade in High Technology

The balance of trade, especially in the high technology sector, is bound to influence the search for "balance" between economic and strategic security. If the high technology sector falls into deep deficit, or is perceived to suffer serious competitive disadvantages due to U.S. government policy, the new administration might opt to reduce controls, counting on the drive of the free enterprise system to maintain the overall Western lead in technology. The president could make sizable cuts in the control list by Executive Order. Congress would probably not resist, if our adversaries are not engaged in military adventurism.

Relations with the People's Republic of China

The course of economic and political reform in China promises to be one of the most fascinating and important phenomena of the coming decade. Assuming China's economy continues to develop, it will play an increasingly significant role in world affairs. Given the keen interest the Chinese have manifested in Western technology, controls on strategic trade with China have broad foreign policy implications. Although the president must work with both Congress and our COCOM Allies to broaden the China Green Zone, this is an area in which he could make a considerable difference.

The Trade Bill

The Export Administration provisions of the pending trade bill will obviously have an important impact—if they become law. The absence of new legislation would draw the president into a congressional debate over extending the current Export Administration Act that expired in September 1989. Assuming some new laws are passed, they may set important parameters on everything from reductions in the Commodity Control List to the division of authority within the Executive Branch. If no legislation emerges, the administration's reforms to the negotiations would not be affected. Liberalization of trade with China would be hampered by the lack of a clear mandate, but the administration would not be left entirely without options.

The Institutionalization of Export Controls

The mechanisms for controlling strategic trade are now firmly established within the Executive Branch. Once policies have become institutionalized in this fashion, they tend to develop a certain momentum that carries over from one administration to the next. Funding levels may shift according to priorities, but the consensus for controlling strategic trade is broad enough to sustain institutional momentum in strategic controls for some years to come. The president could, however, define interagency responsibilities differently to focus authority and accountability in one agency. Alternately he might reorder the interagency process to ensure that no single agency can block progress. With proper management and funding, the administrative and enforcement organs should continue to become more efficient and more effective. This would help to reduce the administrative burden on business, increase our strategic security, and make export controls less contentious in Congress.

SUMMARY

Through this overview, I have tried to present certain issues and approaches that are part of the national debate on export control policy. While new issues and approaches may appear, the basic underlying balancing of national security objectives will continue. In short, the issue is how we can fashion solutions that accelerate the pace of technological change while simultaneously protecting the most militarily critical technologies. Ideally, we can make the choices that maximize our ability to promote a strong and dynamic economy that promotes the development of emerging technologies while effectively controlling the most sensitive dual-use technologies.

NOTES

1. *Soviet Military Power,* 1987, an annual publication of the U.S. Department of Defense, describes Soviet capabilities in depth. The following data are selected from a comparison chart found on pages 92–93.

Marine battle tanks:	WP	52,000	NATO	24,250
Artillery:	WP	42,000	NATO	18,350
Total Submarines:	WP	258	NATO	206
Fighter-Bomber:	WP	2,600	NATO	3,450
Fighter-Interceptor:	WP	2,800	NATO	1,170

These figures represent fully deployed strength. The Soviets usually have higher percentages of force in place and would have to cover shorter distances to reinforce the front lines.

2. Foreign policy controls restrict trade to convey disapproval of another government's policies or behavior, whereas strategic trade controls attempt to deny a foreign government technology or products that could be used to threaten the security of the United States. Foreign policy controls may be imposed or lifted in response to specific events, while strategic controls tend to be based on long term national security considerations.
3. Marshall L. Goldman, *Gorbachev's Challenge: Economic Reform in the Age of High Technology* (New York: W.W. Norton & CO., 1987) pp. 119–135.
4. *Ibid.*, p. 127
5. *Soviet Acquisition of Militarily Significant Western Technology: An Update* (Washington, D.C., Department of Defense, 1985), p. 12.
6. Gorbachev, Mikhail, *Perestroika* (New York, Harper & Row, 1987).
7. Linda Melvern, David Hebditch, and Nick Anning, *Techno-Bandits* (Boston: Houghton Mifflin, 1984), p. 42.
8. "America's Domestic and International Role in Protecting the Free World's High Technology," *Business America,* (January 18, 1988), p. 8.
9. *Techno-Bandits,* pp. 42, 258.
10. Harold Paul Luks, "U.S. National Secretary Export Controls: Legislative and Regulatory Proposals," *Balancing the National Interest: Working Papers* (Washington, D.C.: National Academy Press, 1987), pp. 98, 108.
11. *Balancing the National Interest: U.S. National Security Controls and Global Economic Competition* (Washington, D.C.: National Academy Press, 1987), p. 73.
12. The Arms Export Control Act of 1976 imposed controls on the import and export of military weaponry and authorized the Department of Defense to maintain the U.S. Munitions Control List. The Department of State implements the controls through the International Traffic in Arms Regulations, administered by the Office of Munitions Control. See Luks, p. 8.
13. Luks, p. 90.
14. *Ibid.*, pp. 90–91.
15. *Soviet Acquisition of Militarily Significant Western Technology: An Update.* Op. cit. Published by the Department of Defense, this "white paper" updates a report given to the U.S. Congress in May 1982, which was drawn from intelligence gathered in 1981.
16. From $1.7 million and 39 people in fiscal 1980 to $8.3 million and 185 people in 1987. *Business America,* (February 29, 1988), pp. 21–24.
17. *Techno-Bandits,* pp. 88–90.
18. *Ibid.*, pp. 124–130.
19. *Balancing the National Interest,* pp. 135–137.
20. *Ibid.*, p. 110.
21. *Ibid.*, pp. 9–12.
22. Luks, p. 88.
23. *Ibid.*, p. 92.
24. William Finan, Perry Quick, and Karen Sandberg, "The U.S. Trade Position in High Technology: 1980–1986" (Washington, D.C.: A Report Prepared for the Joint Economic Committee of the United States Congress, October, 1986), pp. 2, 57.

25. Luks, *Ibid.*
26. William F. Finan, "Estimate of Direct Economic Costs Associated with U.S. National Security Controls," *Balancing the National Interest, op. cit.*, Appendix D, p. 363.
27. *Balancing the National Interest,* p. 18
28. While the Congress is likely to pass a Trade Bill, the export administration provisions may be jettisoned before passage, if a compromise version cannot be reached. The House and Senate provisions share much common ground, but these provisions have become entangled with proposed sanctions on Toshiba/Kongsberg, which the Administration strongly approves.
29. Statement by Dr. Paul Freedenberg, Under Secretary of Commerce for Export of Administration to the Committee on Foreign Affairs, Subcommittee on International Economic Policy and Trade, U.S. House of Representatives, November 3, 1987.
30. This was temporarily sidetracked by Chinese sales of missiles to Iran, but the fundamental Sino–American relationship remained strong.
31. Dr. Paul Freedenberg, "What Effect Will the U.S. Trade Bill Have on the Department of Commerce?" Remarks before the Pacific Basin Economic Council's 1988 Washington Meeting, February 9, 1988.
32. "Results of the Senior Political Meeting on Strengthening COCOM," U.S. Department of State Press Release, January 29, 1988.
33. As described in the Federal Register notice of August 28, 1987, full 5(k) benefits include listing as an authorized destination on three general licenses (G-COM, GCG, G-CEU), expedited license processing times, and U.S. Permissive Re-export Authorization for China Green Zone items to the People's Republic of China.
34. *Soviet Acquisition of Militarily Significant Western Technology: An Update,* p. 12.

4

Technology Transfer and Economic Growth: A Historical Perspective on Current Developments

RAJ AGGARWAL

In recent years, U.S. and Western European business and industry have been battered by increasingly intense international competition. Western companies in traditional manufacturing industries, such as automobiles, steel, and textiles, seem particularly threatened. Now a new source of competition is emerging—a source with which even the Japanese find difficult to compete successfully in some industries.

This new source of competition is the emergence of multinationals based on the newly industrialized countries (NICs) such as South Korea, Taiwan, Hong Kong, Singapore, India, and Brazil. Companies based in these emerging industrial states are taking over significant shares of North American and global markets for products, such as steel, electronic products, microcomputers and peripherals, and small automobiles, and are beginning to displace U.S. and even Japanese producers of these and other products. If these trends in the global economy continue, learning to compete successfully with the Japanese may be a case of "too little too late" for U.S. and Western European companies. In addition to these new sources of competition, Western companies are also facing major information-based technology driven changes that include the globalization of product and financial markets and increased instability in global financial markets.

A number of authors have argued that the study of economic history can prove useful in understanding contemporary economic phenomena (e.g., Hicks, 1969; Stigler, 1969; McCloskey, 1976; North, 1978). Specifically, North (1978, p. 963) contends that the purpose of economic history is "to analyze the parameters held constant by the economist." Technology transfer often alters the nature of an economy, and the parameters that describe it, by changing the nature and possibilities of production and choice in an economy. Thus, the historical perspective on technology transfer may present fresh insights.

This chapter explores historical evidence that may help us understand the nature and sources of recent technologically driven changes in product and financial markets. It examines the role of technology transfer in the economic development of various European and Asian economic centers. It is contended that this perspective can provide useful insights into the current movement of technology between the United States and Asia and the rise of major economic centers in Asia.

This chapter also explores the two-way relationship between technology and economic growth. On the one hand, an economic center needs a certain level of wealth and economic surplus to invest in education, research, and other inputs that are necessary to develop a new technology, which is then often expected to provide the basis for future economic growth. On the other hand, technology often migrates, leaks, or is transferred among competing economic centers. Many times in the past, the economic center originating a new technology has not been able to exploit it as rapidly as a competing economic center to create the next wave of global economic growth. Thus, recent Japanese economic growth based partially on technology initially developed in the U.S. does not seem unusual in a historical context.

In such a case, what should be the role of the United States in a global economy? How should U.S. companies plan to compete in global markets? In this chapter, relevant historical evidence is reviewed in an attempt to provide some answers to these questions.

This chapter is organized as follows: this section concludes with a very brief overview of the definition of technology and its role in economic growth. The second section reviews historical evidence regarding the role and source of technology underlying the growth of industries and economic centers. The third section presents an overview of the process of technology transfer consistent with the historical evidence presented in the prior section. The last section discusses the possible lessons of historical experience in understanding and coping with the rapidly changing global product and financial markets.

Technology and Economic Growth

The role of innovation and new technology in economic growth has been widely recognized. For example, innovators and innovation are central sources of economic growth in Schumpeter's analysis (Schumpeter, 1934). According to Schumpeter, capitalism is characterized by periodic waves of innovation whereby older, inefficient firms and industries are replaced by new, more efficient firms with newer technologies. More recently, the Nobel prize winning economist Robert Solow has also contended that technology is the main source of economic growth (Solow, 1970). Consequently, an extensive body of literature on technology transfer has accumulated in recent years (e.g., Sagafi-Nejad, 1981).

Technology is usually defined as "know-how" or the sum of knowledge, experience, and skill necessary to establish an enterprise that will manufacture and market a product economically. While this definition may be adequate for many purposes, it should be noted that technology needs to be viewed not only as the specific production process or manufacturing technology, but also various other types of knowledge and expertise necessary for the planning, establishment, and operation of a manufacturing plant and associated enterprises. Transfer of technology should be interpreted as the communication, adaptation, and use of technology from one economic region by a firm into a second region. Thus, technology transfer is not simply the reproduction of an identical enterprise in a second area, but is in fact an adaptation of the original that has been modified to fit the second region's peculiar social, political, technological, climatological, economic, and educational environment (UNIDO, 1973). Thus, technology transfer involves innovation in creation of a viable new enterprise that fills a market need by solving an end-user problem.

As this very brief review indicates, technology transfer is a complex process that involves innovation in manufacturing, marketing, organization, or other aspects of managing an enterprise. It is an important input for economic growth. Technology assessments involve high information costs and the market for technology is, thus, imperfect. Economic modeling of technology transfer must address this market imperfection. As contended in the previous discussion, studies in economic history can provide an excellent perspective to understand the role of technology in economic growth. The next section reviews selected studies in economic history.

A HISTORICAL PERSPECTIVE ON TECHNOLOGICAL LIFE CYCLES

This section presents historical evidence regarding the evolutionary nature of technology, its occasional inflow from less developed countries, and its two-way relationship with economic growth. The role of recipient entrepreneurship in facilitating technology transfer is also examined.

Evolutionary Nature of Technologies

The recent experience of the automobile and steel industries in the United States illustrates the evolutionary nature of technology and international competitiveness. The automobile was developed in Europe and was first successfully mass produced in the United States. U.S. companies grew to dominate the automobile industry during the mid-1900s. Lately, this United States dominance has been successfully challenged by Japan and is now beginning to be challenged by firms from South Korea, Taiwan, and other countries. Consequently, U.S. automobile companies are now taking defensive measures such as engaging in joint ventures and production agreements, not only with Japanese firms, but lately with Korean and Taiwanese firms.

Another example is the steel industry that, in its original form, was developed in West Germany and Great Britain. Steel was initially mass produced in Western Europe, but the United States became the dominant producer in the early 1900s. However, the U.S. steel industry started to lose its dominance to the Japanese in the mid-1930s. Interestingly, the Japanese have now started to lose their dominance in steel to producers from NICs such as Brazil and Korea.

A similar shift is taking place at the lower end of the semiconductor industry. The low-cost location for manufacturing, at least for the commodity-type integrated circuits, such as memory chips, moved first from the United States to Japan and is now moving to Korea and Taiwan. Companies in Korea and Taiwan are already planning to be the lowest cost suppliers of the 256K memory chip. A similar movement can be expected for semiconductor products at successively higher levels of technology.

These very brief industry reviews serve to illustrate a basic phenomenon, that is, the S-shaped life cycle of technologies, and perhaps economies, at work where the basic stages seem to be growth, maturity, and decline. Like high-technology industries today, industries at the beginning of their S-curve are characterized by a rapid rate of change in the underlying technology, a high proportion of sales as expenditures on research, and a high proportion of highly educated personnel. In addition, industry market structures move from almost pure competition among a large number of firms at the beginning to a gradual consolidation of companies (possibly to gain economies of scale) into oligopolistic competition among a few large firms as the technology matures and becomes less uncertain. The pervasiveness of the S-curve in the evolution of a technology is illustrated by its use in a popular computer program (Techover Plus) based on the S-curve that predicts the rate of replacement of an old technology by a new one (Bryan, 1987).

In many cases, however, operations of the S-curve may be difficult to perceive, especially when using aggregate economic data, as declining sales in one industry are often offset by increasing sales in another. In addition, major new developments in technology can lead to the start of another S-curve cycle of economic growth in an industry or region. The confounding effects of these simultaneous S-curve phenomena are illustrated in the following discussion of the recent evolution of manufacturing in the United States.

The common contention that the U. S. economy is becoming a service economy does not seem to be completely true since manufacturing output as a percentage of the U.S. gross national product (GNP) has not changed significantly since the end of World War II. This proportion was 24.5 percent in 1950, 23.3 percent in 1960, 24.1 percent in 1970, 23.8 percent in 1980, 24.1 percent in 1985, and is above 25 percent for 1988 and beyond.

What has declined, however, is the share of overall employment in manufacturing (from 31 percent in 1960 to 22 percent in 1980), as has the share of spending on manufactured goods (from 28 percent in 1960 to 22 percent in 1980).

Thus, while many manufacturing industries, such as textiles and steel, have declined in the United States, overall manufacturing has maintained its share of the U.S. GNP. U.S. manufacturing, in fact, has become more productive. It now accounts for a smaller proportion of employment, and manufactured goods are becoming less expensive relative to other items as their share of spending has decreased. The U.S. economy is becoming a service economy, but only in terms of employment and spending, not in terms of output.

Furthermore, it is possible that with the advent of robotics and the introduction of other computer-based intelligent machines, the efficiency of U.S. manufacturing may be rapidly improving. Thus, it can be argued that at least in certain style- or quality-sensitive and high-technology sectors, U.S. manufacturing may once again be able to compete effectively against production bases in lower labor-cost overseas locations. An example of the beneficial impact of the application of these new technologies in United States manufacturing is the U.S steel industry where the "mini-mills," with new and flexible capital equipment and over 25 percent of the steel market, are doing extremely well especially in relation to the large traditional steel producers with outdated plants.

On an overall basis, manufacturing in the United States may now be at a stage where agriculture was half a century ago. During this period there was a large decline in the number of farm workers accompanied by a large increase in farm output. The manufacturing sector of the U.S. economy not only has not declined in importance in recent years, but it may be at the beginning of a new cycle of growth as it becomes more productive with the adoption of new information-based technologies.

Thus, it seems that technology has been and continues to be an important determinant of economic growth in an economy. In addition, technologies seem to follow an S-curve in their life cycle and the decline of one technology can be offset by the introduction of a new one. Is the source of this new technology always internal or does it come from a more advanced foreign country? Can and does technology flow backward?

Cross-Border Reverse Movements of Technologies

American economic growth since at least the middle of the nineteenth century has been favorably influenced by the American development of the technology of interchangeable parts. This "American system" was well developed by the time of the Crystal Palace Exhibition held in London in 1851. At that time, nothing comparable was being used in Britain, then the most advanced country (Habakkuk, 1962). The development of this technology in America took place in the early parts of the nineteenth century and has been tied to the American development of the milling machine (Smith, 1973). This technology of machine production of interchangeable parts was then transferred in the late nineteenth century to Britain from America—a reverse flow of technology (Floud, 1974).

Similarly, while British textile technology was transferred to the Philadelphia region between 1770 and 1820 (Jeremy, 1973) in spite of significant governmental efforts and regulations to keep it in Britain, the much superior ring spinning technology developed in the United States was transferred to Britain in the late 1800s. Numerous studies (e.g., Feller, 1974) document the subsequent shift of the textile industry to the U.S. south, and thereafter, to foreign locations in less developed countries (LDCs).

As this very brief historical review indicates, technology not only crosses borders but occasionally flows back. What are the implications of the cross-border flows of new technologies for relative international competitiveness? What is the historical evidence regarding an economy's ability to continue to generate and exploit new technologies? The next section takes a longer historical perspective to try to answer these questions.

Technology and Economic Growth

Consider the major periods and centers of growth over the last few centuries. As an example, the science and practice of navigation and shipping was developed in the Arab countries of the Middle East and borrowed by southern Europe. In the Middle Ages (to about the sixteenth century), Italy and other countries of the region used and further developed this technology of navigation to generate a great deal of wealth and economic surplus. Based on this economic surplus, they developed new skills in international trade and banking.

Subsequently, the Dutch took these international trade and banking skills developed in southern Europe and added significant advances in administrative capabilities to make Amsterdam the leading center of trade and commerce in the late seventeenth and eighteenth centuries. Amsterdam was the origin and headquarters of the first limited liability corporation and modern multinational firm, The Dutch East India Company. These multinational organizational skills were subsequently adapted by the British to run their expanding empire. It has been contended that the exploitation of the markets in the British and other European colonies contributed to the economic surplus necessary for the development of the set of technologies that formed the basis for the industrial revolution in the United Kingdom and other European countries (e.g., Braudel, 1982).

The United States used technologies developed in the industrial revolution to generate extraordinary wealth and economic growth in the late nineteenth and early twentieth centuries. In the mid-twentieth century, the wealth generated by these traditional industries provided the economic surplus necessary for the development of the scientists and basic technologies that have led to the information and biotechnology industries. While

Table 4.1 Technology Transfer and Shifts in Economic Growth Centers

Geographic Focus of Development		Geograpic Temporal Focus of Economic Surplus	
Technology/Industry	Region of Initial Development	Region of Economic Surplus	Century
Navigation/shipping	Middle East	Southern Europe	Mid-13th to mid-16th
Trade/banking	Southern development	Mainland N. Europe	Mid-16th to mid-18th
Administrative/governance	Mainland N. Europe	United Kingdom	Mid-18th to late 19th
Industrial revolution	United Kingdom	Eastern United States	Early to late 20th
Informational industries	Eastern United States	Western United States and Pacific Rim	Late 20th to early 21st (?)

The development of a major new technology seems to depend on the economic surplus generated by an earlier major industry. The economic potential of this new technology does not seem to be fully realized by the inventing region/culture, but only by another proximate region/culture. Perhaps, in generating an economic surplus, an economy loses its original ability to generate growth and develops institutions/groups resistant to change.

the two main centers of industrial revolution-based economic growth in the United States were the East Coast and the Midwest, the center of the region that is using the economic surplus from these old technologies to develop new information and biotechnology based industries seems to have shifted to the West Coast of the United States. Table 4.1 summarizes this discussion of the development and cross-border movement of economic surplus and technology over the past few centuries.

As this brief historical discussion indicates, it seems that there has often been a movement in technology from where it was initially developed to create an economic surplus for a neighboring but different location. This second region then used its economic surplus to create the next wave of new technology. This wave of new technology can be exploited by the region that created it, but is often exploited by another region.

Conditions for Technologically Based Growth

It seems that the economic surplus created by a technology not only enables the development of the intellectual environment necessary to generate the next wave of technology, but often can lead to social and institutional developments that tend to protect the economic positions and privileges of various groups in that society and, thereby, prevent local exploitation of the new technology (Olson, 1965).

Olson (1965, 1982) suggests that the decline in the ability to attain rapid economic growth and exploit new technology is related to the lack of desire for further rapid economic growth in a society that is already relatively well-off. Barry (1978) contends that rapid economic growth takes place only "where the controls inherent in a civilization have for some reason broken down." He posits that this happens because of the trade-off between rapid economic growth and the maintenance of civilizing institutions. According to him, with greater levels of wealth, people are decreasingly tolerant of the "uncivilizing" disruptions caused by the needs of economic growth. As an example, while migration has been widely recognized as a source of economic growth (Kelley, 1965; Neal and Uselding, 1972), its disruptive effects have also been noted (e.g., the *Economist,* 1983). Thus, this institutional resistance to change in a stable, well-off society seems to reduce, and perhaps even eliminate, such a society's ability to exploit the new wave of technology it just helped create.

It is clear that recipient entrepreneurship facilitates technology transfer and that they both have positive influences on economic growth (Ozawa, 1986). Historical evidence indicates that economic growth suffers, as it did in the mid-eighteenth century in America and in nineteenth century India, when external (e.g., colonial) forces suppress innovation (Woodman, 1977). Similarly, internal rigidities that may suppress economic growth include commercial laws in fourteenth century Northern Europe and Indian social rigidities prior to the Moslem and British invasions. According to Tuchman (1978, p. 37), writing about commercial laws as such rigidities, "To ensure that no one gained an advantage over anyone else, commercial law prohibited innovation in tools or techniques." Similarly, Nehru (1946) writing about the role of social rigidities notes that "the loss of political freedom leads inevitably to cultural decay. But why should political freedom be lost unless some kind of decay preceded it?" Nehru noted and attributed this decay to "the static nature of Indian society—probably as a result of the growing rigidities of the Indian social systems." Likewise, Olson (1982, p. 152), writing about the Japanese economy of the nineteenth century when established commercial groups in Japan (before the 1850s, before Commander Perry) enjoyed protection by the state, noted that "protected markets enjoying a period of stability will become cartelized." After the treaty of 1866 that humiliated and opened Japan to foreign trade, he notes that the Japanese economy saw a period of explosive growth and "the Japanese were humiliated all the way to the bank." As Hirschmeier (1964) noted, this rapid export-led growth in late nineteenth century Japan unsettled established commercial groups and was mostly created by small new entreprenuers.

What are the implications of this historical evidence for our understanding of technology transfer and for the United States' role in the global economy? The next section examines the nature of technology transfer and the section following that examines recent changes in the global economy and possible strategies for U.S. companies.

Table 4.2 Channels for Transfer of Technology: Selected Examples

Transfers to / From	Governments	Institutions	Business	Individuals
Governments	Exchange of scientists and technical cooperation agreements	Funding of equipment, research, etc.	Financing and other assistance	Sponsored training programs
Institutions	Consulting contracts for study of specific problems	Agreements to cooperate; exchange of faculty and	Supply and sale of process know-how	Training programs for foreign students
Businesses	Turnkey contracts for construction of high technology plants	Supply of research equipment, data, etc.	Joint ventures, licensing agreements, foreign acquisitions, etc.	Jobs and training programs for LDC individuals and expatriate workers
Individuals	Foreign consultants hired for specific problems	Faculty and researchers from foreign countries	Foreign workers, managers and researchers	Cooperative research projects and other professional interaction

THE PROCESS OF TECHNOLOGY TRANSFER

Technology transfer (TT) among nations and regions can and does take place through a number of different channels and mechanisms that may in some cases exist independently of other channels. One useful taxonomy to understand TT is based on the organizational complexity and nature of transferring and recipient entities as illustrated in Table 4.2. The nature and extent of TT and the channels used can be influenced by internal government policies as well as by national political and economic alliances. The absorptive capacity of the recipient may also influence the channels used and the rate of TT. The importance of these channels for TT will also depend on the intrafirm, interfirm, or the international dimension of the TT. While some have emphasized the importance of personal contacts and networks in TT (e.g., Aggarwal and Khera, 1987; Komoda, 1986; Rogers, 1983), the major mechanism for TT has been the international extension of the life cycle of new products by business firms. New products have usually been developed by a firm through extensive investment in research and development, which it then recovers by progressively developing and supplying markets for that product in as many countries as possible.

The Product Life Cycle Theory of Technology Transfer

To understand the product life cycle theory of TT, it is important to examine the underlying assumptions and limitations, especially since these assumptions differ significantly from those of traditional international trade theory. Until 1953, the factor proportions theory (generally known as the Heckscher–Ohlin theory) was used extensively to explain international trade. According to this theory, a country will produce for export products that require the greatest use of its abundant factors and conversely will import those products that require relatively more of its scarce factors of production. While traditional trade theory is based on free availability of information and stable production functions, the product life cycle theory is based on assumptions that the flow of information and skills across regions or national borders is restricted and that products undergo predictable changes in production and marketing characteristics over time.

In addition, the product life cycle theory also assumes that the production process is characterized by economies of scale, that it changes over time, and that market characteristics (consumer tastes) also change over time. The product life cycle theory is an outgrowth of these assumptions.

> That information does not flow freely across national boundaries leads to three important conclusions: (1) innovation of new products and processes is more likely to occur near a market where there is a strong demand for them; (2) a businessman is more likely to supply risk capital for the production of the new product if demand is likely to exist in his home market; and (3) a producer located close to a market has a lower cost in transferring market knowledge into product design changes than one located far from the market (Vernon, 1966).

Although a number of versions of the international product life cycle have been discussed in the literature, the version discussed here assumes three categories of regions or countries: the technologically advanced home country where the product is developed, followed by a group of countries that may be at the same or a somewhat lower technological level, known for convenience here as the more developed countries (MDCs), and finally, a group of countries that are at a lower level of technology and economic development classified here as the LDCs.

In the international product life cycle (PLC) theory of TT, the international involvement of a business is viewed as following sequential stages in the life cycle of the product or process it develops. As indicated earlier, because of the restrictions in the flow of information across regions or national boundaries and the evolution of demand for high-income consumer goods and labor-saving producer goods, innovation of new products is more likely to occur in well-developed, highly industrialized nations. These same innovations are more likely to be used in less developed nations later as they emerge and develop economies and consumer tastes similar to those of the highly developed nations. Although new product innovation can and does take place in all countries, for the sake of convenience, we will hereafter consider only the cases where new product innovation takes place in the United States. However, the analysis applies equally well to cases where new product innovation occurs in countries other than the United States. Similarly, while TT across national boundaries is discussed here, the analysis also applies to TT among geographic regions.

The first phase of product development and domestic sales growth is critically important in the life of the product. It is during this stage that the product undergoes test marketing, product redesign and reengineering, and production scale-up. Only if a product gains acceptance in the domestic market is there any need for discussion of the international TT. Generally, if a product does not gain domestic market acceptance, it will probably not be exported. If, however, the new product is accepted and during this phase domestic sales volume grows, the product reaches phase two. During this phase, domestic sales continue to grow but probably at a decreasing rate, and exports begin to other MDCs and, to a lesser extent, to LDCs. Up to this point, all production is still in the United States. Export of the product may begin for three basic reasons:

1. Similarities between the markets in the MDCs and the United States evidence demand for the product.
2. The price for this product has decreased because of economies of scale that accompany market growth.
3. The income level of the MDC may have increased.

During this phase, technological changes take place in the MDCs that in fact lead to the next phase. Because the expertise of MDC residents increases regarding this product, the probability of their being able to set up a manufacturing operation in their country increases. By this time, the industry will have extensive price competition as other domestic firms develop a similar or substitute product that is also being sold in the United States and in the MDCs. Finally, MDC governments could have increased tariffs or set quotas to encourage the U.S. firm to invest in their country. Because of these and other reasons, the U.S. firm is likely to make the decision to transfer technology and to invest in the MDC in the third phase of the life cycle of the product.

In the third phase of the cycle, when production has begun in a foreign market, U.S. exports to that market cease to grow as rapidly as before, and they may even decline. U.S. exports continue to go to markets where production has not begun. In the fourth phase of the cycle, U.S. exports to nonproducing countries begin to be displaced by exports from other nations. Markets overseas reach sufficient sizes such that MDC manufacturers do not suffer from the high costs associated with small scale production. In fact, the MDC-producing unit may be a subsidiary of a U.S. parent. Armed with lower labor costs, but the same transportation and tariff charges, these firms take away markets in Third World countries that were previously supplied from the United States. In the fifth phase, foreign production in some countries reaches sufficient scale that costs are low enough to overcome the transportation and tariff protection of the U.S. manufacturer. The United States now becomes a net importer of the prod-

Table 4.3 The International Product Life Cycle

Phase 1:	The product is invented or innovated. Domestic sales begin and domestic production rises to near full capacity. Production and sales are still only in one country.
Phase 2:	Domestic sales grow at a declining rate and export sales to MDCs and LDCs begin. There is no overseas production yet.
Phase 3:	Domestic sales begin to decline and production begins in MDCs. U.S. exports are now mainly to LDCs because MDC demand is being supplied from local production.
Phase 4:	Domestic sales continue at a low level with no exports from domestic production. MDC and LDC markets now are supplied by MDC-based production.
Phase 5:	Domestic market begins to face competition from MDC exports as MDC exports to LDCs begin to be displaced by LDC production.
Phase 6:	Domestic and MDC production now displaced by LDC producers, which begin to supply most demand globally.

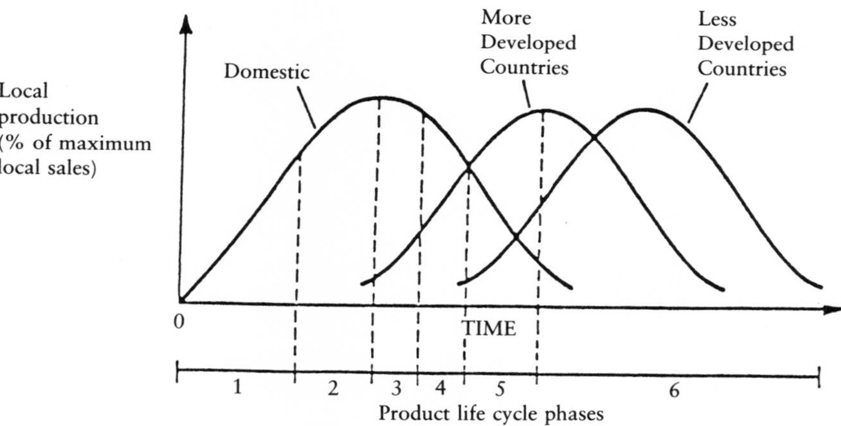

uct, and in the final phase the LDCs become exporters to the MDCs and the United States.

The international product life cycle theory of TT has been applied to a wide range of technologies including the spread of agricultural technology (Hiyami, 1974) and textile technology (Feller, 1974). Table 4.3 depicts the process of how technology, production, and sales of a given product move across the three sets of countries through a cycle of growth and decline in each area.

A major implication of the PLC theory of TT is that investment in research and development can be recovered over a much longer product life. Research and development is a high risk and often expensive activity and successful products, on average, must also pay for expenses incurred in developing unsuccessful ones. This means that an LDC may find it cheaper to purchase new technology rather than develop it locally, since a multinational company can spread the research and development costs across a worldwide market. In addition, by the time a technology is made available to LDCs, the company is likely to have recovered the major portion of the fixed costs and thus may be able to price the technology based on only its much smaller marginal cost. Therefore, it seems that there may be considerable room for negotiation, and both LDCs and business firms are likely to gain from TT. To better understand and negotiate TT, the next section examines the costs and benefits of TT for firms and countries.

Costs and Benefits of Technology Transfer

For the firm transferring the technology, there may accrue a number of advantages or benefits. A major benefit is, of course, the possibility of making an adequate or even above normal rate of return. Another strategic advantage may be the ability to maintain its market share and competitive position vis-à-vis competing firms. A third advantage is that expansion into another country and market not perfectly linked to its existing operations or markets provides for a reduced level of overall risk because of diversification or portfolio effects. A fourth advantage of a firm engaging in TT to LDCs may be the achievement or sustenance of high rates of growth. A fifth advantage is that the firm may be able to tap the capital markets of these countries, thereby obtaining access to a possibly more diversified and lower cost source of funds.

In terms of a popular (Gordon's growth) stock valuation model, the price of a company's stock (P) equals the expected dividend $(D1)$ divided by the difference between the rate of return required by investors (K) and the growth rate of the dividends (g), that is $P = D1/(K-g)$. All of the advantages of TT by firms mentioned above serve to increase P, the price of the firms' shares and, therefore, the wealth of its owners. For example, higher profits mean a greater ability to pay dividends and to grow faster—both factors leading to a higher P. The second advantage of TT is defensive in nature and is designed to prevent a possible decline in $D1$ or g and, thus, P. The third advantage of risk reduction or diversification leads to a lowering of K by investors, again leading to a higher P. The fourth factor increases P by increasing g, and the last factor increases P by decreasing K (because of diversification of sources of funds) or by increasing $D1$ (because of lower cost of funds). Thus, a firm may find it beneficial to engage in TT to LDCs if these advantages or benefits are not completely negated by the disadvantages or costs of such TT.

The disadvantages or costs of TT to LDCs include the possible higher costs of production or of doing business in a foreign, alien country located at a distance from its home base. A second disadvantage is the possible higher business risk faced in a new environment. A third cost is the risk of expropriation, forced sale of equity to local partners at lower than economic value, restrictions on repatriation of income and capital, and other forms of interference by the host government. A fourth disadvantage is the risk of incurring losses because of unexpected exchange rate changes. A fifth cost is the higher cost of expatriate managerial compensation and training local nationals. A sixth set of costs are the transportation costs and border taxes incurred in transferring labor, materials, and capital overseas. A seventh cost or strategic disadvantage is the creation of potential new competition, that is, some recipient LDCs will eventually emerge as global competitors, competing even in the original firm's markets. Other disadvantages include possible negative effects on the firm's relations with its labor union and on its public image in its home country because of the decision to create jobs overseas. Naturally, a firm will try to minimize these disadvantages.

For the recipient LDC, the costs and benefits of TT are not so easy to define. It seems that a useful distinction may be to separate the first order or direct effects of TT on LDCs from the second and third order or indirect effects of TT on LDCs. This distinction does not imply that the indirect effects are less important than the direct ones.

Included in the first order or direct advantages is that the capital involved in such TT may help meet the gap between the net actual local savings rate and investment rate needed for the planned or desired rate of economic growth. Thus, the capital related to TT may be an important supplement to local capital in generating economic growth. A second but related advantage to the LDC is that TT adds to national income, encourages development of ancillary industries, and creates jobs in the LDC. A third related advantage is that it generates tax revenues for government expenditure. TT may also accelerate economic growth and the development of the country's export potential because of the likely adoption, by diffusion, of more sophisticated technology by local entrepreneurs.

Among the costs of disadvantages to the LDC are the direct or first order costs including the outflow of dividends, profits, management and royalty fees, interest on loans, and other remittances by the firm including the possible use of high transfer prices. An indirect or second order cost arises when too much or uncontrolled TT crushes local "infant" industries, creating an undesirable dependence on foreign firms that may not be safe for the LDC in the long run or for its national defense capability. Such costs are, of course, hard to measure. A second indirect and hard-to-measure effect of TT on the LDC economy is that the foreign firm(s) will generally have preferential access to scarce local capital, slowing the growth of other local industry. This is likely to be the case since the foreign firm is often larger and is viewed by lenders as less risky than comparable domestic firms. Similarly, a third related disadvantage that may be suffered by domestic firms would be their inability to compete with the foreign firm for other scarce resources such as trained manpower and raw materials.

Thus, markets for technology are usually imperfect and are generally characterized by many externalities. It seems that technology transfer best takes place through the international extension of the product life cycle where the market for technology is internalized by a firm and there is considerable flexibility in negotiating arrangements that are beneficial for all of the parties involved. TT seems to be increasing in importance in recent years, especially with the emergence of new global competitors. The next section considers recent changes in the global economy in light of the historical evidence and the process of technology transfer presented above.

GLOBAL ECONOMIC CHANGES AND U.S. CORPORATE STRATEGIES

Driven by significant advances in technology, telecommunications, and transportation, the global economy is currently in a period of rapid change characterized by:

Shifting technological, strategic, and commercial advantages;
Increasing international integration; and
The emergence of new economic power centers.

In recent years, many government and corporate managers have often been "blindsided" by these developments that begin and develop outside their normal sphere of attention.

The term *economic revolution* has been used to convey the simultaneous occurrence of two types of change: a fundamental change in society's productivity and a consequent change in its economic organization (North, 1978). According to North (1978), the first economic revolution was the development of agriculture in the eighth millennium BC while the industrial revolution of the eighteenth and nineteenth centuries was the second economic revolution.

It is contended here that we are probably at the beginning of the third economic revolution based on the widespread application of the new information-based technologies of the microprocessor, telecommunications, and genetic manipulation (biotechnology). These new technologies designed to supplement human intellectual and genetic abilities are based on the creation, manipulation, and transmission of electronic and genetic information. These technologies are likely to transform the global economy even more fundamentally than the industrial revolution, when human and animal power was supplemented by mechanical power (Simon, 1987). The pace of technology transfer is likely to increase as the costs of information processing and transmission continue to decline.

Role of the Nation–State

One structural change being brought about by this third economic revolution is that the importance of the nation–state as an economic unit may be starting to decline. The economies of most nations and regions have become more open to international influences, and their relative economic importance is shifting. Newly industralized countries, especially those located in the Orient, are making their presence felt in global markets. International financial markets are now playing a more important role than previously was the case.

Thus, the international dimension of business has become particularly important in recent years because of the increasing globalization of product and financial markets that has been associated with recent rapid advances in the technology of information processing and its transmission. As an example, it is estimated that more than a quarter of all global output now moves across borders; the Eurocurrency market is larger than any domestic money supply (including the U.S. M2), and the weekly volume of trading in foreign exchange markets exceeds annual trading on the world's equity markets.

Cross-border investments continue to increase as does the role of multinational companies that finance, produce, and distribute simultaneously in a number of countries. There have also been extraordinary increases in the international dimension of business through increased cross-border trade, financing, licensing, franchising, and management contracts. This growth in global business organizations and activity has taken place in spite of the various costs of operating overseas. For example, these costs include the costs of overcoming linguistic, cultural, political, institutional, and other barriers to the operation of cross-border businesses. As a matter of fact, astute managers realize that they usually find extraordinary profit opportunities if they can overcome these and other barriers to the free cross-border movement of capital, labor, technology, and other factors of production.

Because of the increased openness of most economies, there are very few companies that can afford or claim to be purely domestic. Today, almost every business is affected by events in the international economy. Either a business imports or exports directly, or it competes in its sales or raw material markets with foreign firms or firms that export or import or are multinational in nature. Even if a firm faces purely domestic product markets, it certainly faces financial markets that are influenced by global forces.

Multipolar Global Structure

This rise in the importance of international business activity has been accompanied by other changes in the business environment. For example, the U.S. economy is not as dominant as it used to be. In the past quarter century, the economies of Japan, Western Europe, Eastern Europe, and the NICs of Asia have all grown to rival and overtake various sectors of the U.S. economy. Just as the change in trade flows from the Mediterranean sea to the Atlantic foretold the relative decline of Europe compared with North America, the recent displacement of trade across the Atlantic by trade across the Pacific may foretell the relative economic rise of the nations of the Pacific rim. It seems that the economic center of gravity is continuing its move westward toward the Orient.

Consequently, we may be returning to a multipolar world where there are a number of economic and military centers that are important instead of global dominance by one or two superpowers. However, as a result of the nondominant global position of the U.S. economy, there may be continuing difficulty in providing leadership to maintain a free and open trading system or to contain instability in international financial markets.

Displacement of Bureaucratic Systems by Markets

In addition, recent years have seen a marked rise in the acceptance of market mechanisms and individual initiative as important determinants of economic growth. Socialism and state ownership and control of economic enterprises are on the decline globally. More and more countries realize the benefits of private ownership as exemplified by statements such as "A leased garden is likely to turn into a desert while an owned desert is likely to turn into a garden" or "A sick cow is more likely to get better when it is owned by a private farmer." These changes in attitude mean that the role of markets is becoming more important in more countries.

Thus, the world economy is in a period of rapid change. New market forces are emerging as the economic center of gravity continues to move westward toward the Orient. The information revolution is likely to equal or exceed the industrial revolution in its impact on the global economy. What are some useful responses to these changing markets and technologies?

Public Policy and Corporate Responses

To develop some answers to this question, it is useful to keep in mind that the changes in relative standing of the various economies and the globalization of product and financial markets are being driven by fundamental forces such as technology and telecommunications. Therefore, it may not be easy or wise to attempt to reverse or oppose these changes. Opposition is likely to be expensive, and it will probably only buy time.

Furthermore, the relative importance of various industries and countries is changing more rapidly than in earlier times. Companies in the United States and Western Europe must face up to the fact that Japanese low-cost production is being replaced by even lower cost producers from the "new Japans": Hong Kong, Korea, Singapore, and Taiwan. Industries at successively higher levels of technology are facing this threat. Consequently, companies in these industries must engage in a never-ending process of moving to higher value-added operations, using even higher levels of technology. How can this be accomplished successfully when it is usually impossible to know the exact nature of industries with emerging technologies?

Bureaucratic systems were developed in an age when change was much slower. These systems are not very good at responding to rapidly changing markets and technologies. In addition, a large, modern economy or even a large company may be too complex a system to manage or even understand. Therefore, tight government control or management of an economy or similar bureaucratic control of a large corporation may be an exercise in frustration.

Almost every country in the world seems to be discovering these limitations of bureaucratic systems, as evidenced by the global rise of entrepreneurial activity and the movement toward the privatization of government-owned and government-run companies. Government companies are being sold in countries ranging from the United Kingdom and France to Turkey and Thailand. Even the People's Republic of China and other centrally planned economies are beginning to transform their economic systems to take greater advantage of systems that reward individual initiative, which is the essence of free enterprise.

To stay competitive in rapidly evolving global markets, the United States must depend on a system that can respond quickly and efficiently to change. A number of fields, from quantum mechanics to sociobiology, are coming to similar conclusions regarding the nature of optimal growth strategies in an uncertain environment. It seems that the most effective long-run strategy for large, complex systems to adjust to rapid environmental changes is a process of trial and error undertaken in the form of numerous random changes among the individual units.

For example, it has been contended that one reason for the rise of Europe after the Renaissance, compared with the relative decline of other empires of the sixteenth- century (Ottoman, Ming, etc.), was that, unlike the other empires of that era, sixteenth century Europe lacked a central unified culture that succeeded in suppressing initiative or experimentation (Kennedy, 1987).

It seems that the economic system best able to keep an economy growing and competitive in an increasingly dynamic global economy is a market-force-driven free enterprise system with appropriate, but minimal, government regulation. This is especially true for the United States, whose role in the global economy seems to be that of developing and exploiting ever newer technologies.

Consequently, if the United States is to stay competitive in the global economy, the United States must continue to encourage innovation in our companies and economy. We should continue to emphasize corporate and social systems that encourage and reward entrepreneurship (Gilder, 1984). Our tax and investment banking systems should ensure a continuing supply of venture capital and the ability to retain the rewards of taking the risks inherent in new ventures.

Similarly, companies should also develop systems to encourage and reward entrepreneurship (Pinchot, 1984). Worker input should be valued, and employees should feel they have a stake in the success of the company. Traditional approaches to merit pay systems should be supplemented by an emphasis on profit sharing and decentralized decision making to encourage individual initiative and risk taking, even in large corporations (Weitzman, 1984).

In addition, to avoid the problems that prevented other cultures and economies from adjusting to change, the United States needs to shift the focus of public policy toward the generation of a bigger economic pie and away from the recent obsession with its distribution. It seems that public policy in the United States needs to recognize and encourage this shift in emphasis to prevent a further relative decline. It has been contended that, in general, great power decline can be traced to an overextension of obligations and power (Kennedy, 1987). Although in the past, overextension by a state has generally meant taking on extensive military obligations, the same effects may result if the overextension is in the form of excessive domestic social obligations that drain the resources of such a state. Thus, it seems important that the United States cut government spending and reduce the growing budget deficit, as funding the deficit leaves less capital with an attendant higher cost for business and industry. As a matter of fact, the United States must continue to encourage and reward a higher savings rate to fund higher levels of research and development and new capital spending.

CONCLUSIONS

This chapter has reviewed historical evidence regarding the economic role and the cross-border movement of technology. It also developed a paradigm of technology transfer that is consistent with historical evidence. It seems that technology and its movement has often played a significant role in generating economic growth. Its movement across economic centers is best understood using the life cycle paradigm.

New technology generally seems to be generated in a continuing process of Schumpeterian change and is best exploited by societies open to economic change. Often, a wealthy society seems to lose this openness to change and, in such cases, technology it has developed is often transferred to and exploited by another upcoming economy that is less resistant to change. Thus, the recent economic rise of the Pacific Rim nations such as Japan, based on technology initially developed in the United States, does not seem at all unusual in a historical context.

Last, this chapter analyzed recent changes in the global economy to examine the insights provided by historical perspective. The global economy is facing a new period of rapid change, driven at one end by the newly emerging information-processing and biological technologies and at the other by the successive emergence of countries at ever lower levels of economic development as global competitors. With the rapid rise of the Asian Pacific region, the global economic center of gravity continues its westward move toward the Orient. In response, developed countries must continue to encourage higher levels of savings and investment in new capital equipment and the development of new technology.

In view of the rapid pace of economic change, all countries must continue to develop corporate and public policies that focus on encouraging and rewarding individual initiative in responding to market signals. Government and corporate managers increasingly operate in product and financial markets that are global in nature and that are characterized by shifting competitive and technological advantages. History seems to indicate that to ignore these significant changes in the global economy is to invite disaster.

REFERENCES

Aggarwal, R. and Khera, I. P. (1987). "Exporting Labor: The impact of expatriate workers on the home country," *International Migration,* 25 (4, December): 415–425.

Barry, B. (1978) *Sociologists, Economists, and Democracy,* Chicago: University of Chicago Press.

Braudel, Fernand. (1982). *The Wheels of Commerce,* New York: Harper & Row.

Bryan, M. (1987). "Package predicts technological obsolescence," *PC Week* (December 15): 78.

Economist, The. (1983). "Ergophobia," *The Economist,* August 12:29.

Feller, Irwin. (1974). "The diffusion and location of technological change in the American cotton–textile industry, 1890–1970," *Technology and Culture,* 15 (October): 569–593.

Floud, R. C. (1974). "The adolescence of American engineering competition, 1860–1900," *Economic History Review,* second series 27 (February):57–71.

Gilder, G. (1984). *The Spirit of Enterprise,* New York: Simon and Schuster.

Habakkuk, H. J. (1962). *American and British Technology in the Nineteenth Century,* Cambridge, England: University Press.

Hiyami, Yujiro. (1974). "Conditions for the diffusion of agricultural technology: An Asian perspective," *Journal of Economic History,* 34 (March): 131–148.

Hicks, J. R. (1969). *A Theory of Economic History,* Oxford: Clarendon Press.

Hirschmeier, Johannes. (1964). *The Origins of Entreprenuership in Meiji Japan,* Cambridge, Mass.: Harvard University Press.

Jeremy, David. (1973). "British textile technology and transmission to the United States: The Philadelphia region experience, 1770–1820," *Business History Review,* 47 (Spring):24–52.

Kelley, A. C. (1965). "International migration and economic growth: Australia, 1865–1934." *Jornal of Economic History,* 25 (September): 333–354.

Kennedy, Paul. (1987). *The Rise and Fall of the Great Powers,* (New York: Random House.

Komoda, F. (1986). "Japanese studies on technology transfer to developing countries: A survey," *Developing Economies,* 24 (4, December):405–420.

McCloskey, Donald N. (1976). "Does the past have useful economics?" *Journal of Economic Literature,* 14 (2, June):434–461.

Neal, L., and Uselding, P. (1972). "Immigration, a neglected source of American economic growth: 1790–1912," *Oxford Economic Papers N. S.,* 24 (1 March):68–88.

Nehru, Jawaharlal. (1946). *The Discovery of India,* New York: Anchor Books.

North, Douglas C. (1978). "Structure and performance: The task of economic history," *Journal of Economic Literature,* 16 (September): 963–978.

Olson, M. (1982). *The Rise and Decline of Nations,* New Haven, Conn.: University Press.

Olson, M. (1965). *The Logic of Collective Action,* Cambridge, Mass.: Harvard University Press.

Ozawa, Terutomo. (1986). "Entrepreneurship and technology in economic development," *Asian Development Review,* 4 (1):91–102.

Pinchot, G. (1984). *Intrapreneuring,* New York: Harper & Row.

Rogers, M. (1983). *Diffusion of Innovations,* New York: Free Press.

Sagafi-Nejad, Tagi. (1981). *A Bibliography on Technology Transfer,* New York: Praeger.

Schumpeter, J. (1934). *The Theory of Economic Development,* London: Oxford University Press.

Simon, Herbert A. (1987)., "The steam engine and the computer: What makes technology revolutionary," *EDUCOM Bulletin,* (Spring):2–5.

Smith, Merritt Roe. (1973). "John Hall, Sineon North and the Milling Machine: The nature of innovation among antebellum arms makers," *Technology and Culture,* 14 (October):573–591.

Solow, R. M. (1970). *Growth Theory: An Exposition,* Oxford: Clarendon Press.

Stigler, G. J. (1969). "Does economics have a useful past?" *History of Political Economy,* 1 (2, Fall):217–230.

Tuchman, Barbara. (1978). *A Distant Mirror,* New York: Ballantine Books.

UNIDO. (1973). *Guidelines for the Acquisition of Foreign Technology by Developing Countries,* New York: United Nations Industrial Development Organization.

Vernon, Raymond. (1966). "International investment and international trade in the product cycle," *Quarterly Journal of Economics,* 80 (May):190–207.

Weitzman, Martin. (1984). *The Share Economy,* Cambridge, Mass.: Harvard University Press.

Woodman, Harold D. (1977). "Imperialism and economic development: England, the U.S. and India in the nineteenth century," *Research in Economic History,* 2:141–172.

II
SOME ELEMENTS OF TECHNOLOGY TRANSFER

The first section of this book presented a broad picture of the general macro nature of technology transfer and its relation to major historical trends (Chapter 5), to current international business practices (Chapter 2), and to political concepts and practice (Chapters 3 and 4). The purpose of the next section of this book is to relate technology transfer (often considered a specific or segmented topic) to a more general framework of economic, managerial, and political behavior. In so doing it is possible to understand the problems posed by the successes and the failures of technology transfer, in general, and the cases of given industries or countries, in particular. The four chapters in Part I provide a multidisciplinary view of the roots of technology transfer, while maintaining sufficient specificity required for in-depth understanding of the different fields reviewed and analyzed in Part II.

At the risk of oversimplification, a major dialectic emerges. The technological development in the decades since the 1950s has created a strong impetus for integration and globalization. In some ways, as both Simon and Aggarwal argue, technology is one of the main reasons for the integrating force in world business. Technology development also enhances economic growth, which itself contributed to an increase in world trade, yet another force for globalization. The need to acquire technology has also contributed to greater similarity in science and following that, a greater cultural similarity that adds another dimension to the force of integration.

These same factors, however, also created opposing forces. Globalization reduces the control of national governments, and many of them (including the U.S. government) set out to correct what was in their opinion a problem. The net result was a contradiction in the attitude of individuals, institutions, and even business firms, between what is regarded as nationalism and what may be called internationalism. Often, individuals and corporations alike behave inconsistently; they professed to prefer nationalism in some cases and internationalism in others. But then human behavior is often unpredictable or inconsistent, and in trying to understand the complexity of international technology transfer it is useful to recognize this point.

Therefore, the four chapters in Part I should not be treated as representing different complete approaches, but rather different facets of the same phenomenon. The question is not whether the global approach (based on economic considerations such as the maximization of economic welfare) is superior or "more correct" than the nationalistic approach based on political considerations. Both approaches exist, often they co-exist and appear to be compatible. The observed outcome results from the dialectics of the economic thesis and the political and behavioral antithesis.

Given this background, the question is, then: How the recognition of the complexity of what drives technology transfer is expressed in specific policies and in specific cases? In Part III we examine the expressions of technology transfer in relation to the functional fields of managemment and economics such as international trade, international management, and development policy, production, and marketing. But before we embark on that, it is useful to discuss the vehicles of technology transfer, in general, and international technology transfer, in particular.

Three general vehicles are presented and discussed in Part II: individual, spatial, and organizational. In general, and again at a risk of projecting our interpretation based on the three chapters taken together (Chapters 6, 7, and 8) the first vehicle is consistent with the global approach, the second is closer to the nationalistic approach, and the third provides a compromise by using the organization (the firm) as a bridge between the two.

Aharoni discusses education as a primary vehicle for technology transfer, international or domestic. The only responsibility of the state is to provide education, or to allow its residents to seek education where it is available. The rest will take care of itself. Rogers and Valente provide a design for a locational vehicle for technology transfer. Its spatial characteristics make it ideal for maintaining local, national control on the production and the transfer of technology. Pucik focuses on the corporation as the vehicle for the production, the development, and the transfer of technology. The ambivalent nature of the corporation on the economic/political scale, and the mix of financial, behavioral, and national goals of many corporations put the corporation as a vehicle for technology transfer in between the two major approaches descirbed earlier. Indeed, focusing on the corporation as a vehicle for technology transfer as we do for the rest of this book, and focusing on technology transfer as an integral part of international business serves to highlight the complexity of this issue, as well as its importance.

5 Education and Technology Transfer: Recipient Point of View

YAIR AHARONI

TECHNOLOGY AS A STRATEGIC VARIABLE

Technology can be defined as knowledge about products, processes, or managerial actions that have applications in a business setting. Therefore, technology is knowledge related to the techniques and methods of the production of goods and services. To some, technology has a second meaning, namely, the goods themselves as well as the tools of production or the production systems that are the embodiment of technological knowledge. This distinction is crucial in judging what is or is not successful technology transfer. Knowledge can be created through research and development or accumulated through experience.

Technology is a firm's most important source of competitive advantage. A firm achieves a high level of competitive advantage if the technology it possesses is difficult for other firms to copy or simulate. The more unique the knowledge, the more difficult it is for competitors to copy the technology and to offer exactly the same product. By the same token, these are also the cases in which the transfer of technology—even willingly within the firm itself—is becoming, almost by definition, more difficult.

Because of the implications for long-term growth, technology is also of utmost importance to the nation–state. (For some attempts at quantification see Solow, 1957; Denison, 1962, 1980, and 1982.) The receipt of up-to-date technology gives firms a better chance to compete in the global marketplace. There has been a gradual shift from science as a solely intellectual endeavor, occupied with the creation of a body of knowledge, to science as a reason for change in economic and political power. The recognition that global industry and commerce are being reshaped by technological change has made both governments and businesses very concerned about the level of technological sophistication of their nations. We are witnessing a new era with the development of entirely new materials as well as existing materials acquiring vastly enhanced new properties to add flexibility, or improve strength or reduce costs. Accelerating advances in microelectronics, biotechnology, and biogenetics in photonics and ceramics as well as the spin-off into information sciences have altered the patterns of world trade. A country's comparative advantages increasingly lies in its ability to use effectively new technology, which is generally a function of the capacity of its population to absorb new technologies and incorporate them in production processes.

In the 1980s, labor rate differences or proximity to raw materials sources have become much less important considerations in determining the location of manufacturing and service facilities relative to the availability of engineers or market considerations. As one example, robotics and automation reduced the labor cost in car assembly from 30 percent in the 1950s to around 7 percent in the 1980s. The increasing speed and pervasiveness of technical change also reduced the gap between basic and applied research. While basic research is still concerned with fundamental issues, it is often of a nature that creates clear, long-term benefits for exploitation.

Furthermore, as more and more industries are becoming globalized, products and services, components, subsystems, and parts are intermingled in a way that makes it difficult to determine the national origin of a certain final product. A significant percentage of world trade today is intra-trade within subsidiaries of multinational enterprises (MNEs). Indeed, by the late 1980s, almost half of the total exports of U.S. MNEs came from their production facilities outside the United States. In 1985, U.S.-owned corporations sold the Japanese almost $54 billion of products they produced in Japan—a sum greater than the American trade deficit with Japan that year (while the Japanese sold the United States $15 billion worth of goods they made in the United States in that year). More than a third of Taiwan's trade surplus with the United States is due to American corporations manufacturing or purchasing products in Taiwan and selling them in the United States.

While many researchers are looking for similarities among firms emphasizing market efficiency, a growing number of scholars recognize the crucial role of firm-specific advantages. One essential element of a firm's success in a competitive world is to attempt to create and sustain, at least in the mind of the consumer, an image of difference between itself and others, or singular attributes that allow it to charge higher prices and command higher margins. These unique characteristics are based on particular knowledge in production, marketing, or organization.

Multinational enterprises expand their operations largely because they possess firm-specific, intangible assets that they internalize (Caves, 1982; Dunning, 1981). These internalized advantages are outright control of technological assets in the form of patents or other industrial property rights or of accumulated expertise in management, organization, and know-how. Once it is recognized that such advantages reduce the risk of loss for a firm and give it a competitive edge, explicit efforts are made to gain these advantages or at least to participate in a system enjoying them. In other words, the more technology becomes a key element in competition, the more it is viewed as a key resource that must be strategically managed.

To be sure, much of the so-called unique knowledge is based on a combination of standard knowledge, but when this combination is immersed into a firm's basic culture, it becomes unique. To accomplish this, it is necessary to indoctrinate the entire organization to achieve certain results and effect certain tasks, an ability that is generally the result of a long process.

Certainly, not every technology (or knowledge) is unique. Much of the know-how of the world is very standard. The more standardized the knowledge, the easier it is to transfer it through standard operating procedures, through teaching, or through learning by observing others. The more unique the knowledge, the more difficult it is to transfer and the less willing top management is to risk loss of competitive advantage through its transfer outside the organization (and in the East–West context, the more reluctant a government is to allow the transfer).

Generally available technology can be easily transferred. Firm-specific technology is created, and usually transferred, only within an organization. It is transferred less by licensing than by a long process of meetings, training, even indoctrination, and by following strict procedures and creating shared values.

Many of the firms that have accumulated know-how in some critical technology area are unique and irreplaceable except at great expense, and over a long time. Furthermore, the ability of the country to maintain a technological lead is a function of accumulated knowledge, resulting from large public investment in education and in research and development (R&D). Technological capabilities are also crucial for defense and security reasons. Therefore, it is highly unlikely that governments will leave issues of technology to the market alone. This is true for donor countries, anxious to maintain their hard-earned technological advantage in critical areas and to avoid jeopardizing their comparative advantage, and/or security, as well as for the recipient country, attempting to ensure that only appropriate technology will be purchased. As for the recipient countries, profound disparties exist among them in terms of their capacity to absorb technology.

The purchase of already developed technology is usually possible at bargain prices, since the large investment in developing the technology has already been made. Most new technologies require a very large investment in R&D and, therefore, a large scale of production and sales to reduce the average unit cost of the development. Therefore, MNEs are willing to transfer technology to their subsidiaries. Some firms are willing to trade know-how with other firms through markets. The more unique the technology, the less it is traded on the open market.

Technology, or society's pool of knowledge regarding the industrial art, is not equally distributed in the world. Technology transfer from the developed to the developing countries has been advocated as the single most important step to accelerate Third World development (Emmanuel, 1983; Samli, 1985). It has also been seen as a major reason for *dependencia*. The MNE has been a very important transfer agent, and many in developing countries see MNEs as promoting the perpetuation of dependence of the Third World on the industrialized countries.

It is well to remember that not all technology transfers are commercially oriented: transfer may be the result of technical exchange programs, or simply movement of people. Indeed, the developing countries today have more options in selecting the donor of the technology, the technology itself, and the channels of transfer than ever before.

However important technology is today, there is every reason to believe that its importance will grow rapidly. With that growth, there is bound to be a further increase in the transfer of technology, mainly to the developing countries. Samli (1985) even claims that technology transfer is a viable alternative to war and poverty.

Problems of technology transfer have been discussed in the literature from different points of view. One is the point of view of the macroeconomists interested in development: for them, the major problem is that of appropriate technology, how to receive it cheaply and not as part of a "bundle." Another is the transfer within the firm from R&D to production facilities. A third is that of the managers of multinationals: how do these managers choose the technology they import or export, and how do they decide the channels through which technology will be transferred? This chapter takes the point of view of the technology transfer recipient, discussing the relations of transfer and indigenous capabilities. It explores the major characteristics of technology transfer, the constraints to effective transfer and the issues to be dealt with by an effective technology transfer policy.

TECHNOLOGY AS A FACTOR OF PRODUCTION

Technology may be related to the product, specifying its characteristics and uses; to the process by which a specific product is produced, or to management—the knowledge used in operating a business (Baranson, 1970). As technology is based on knowledge, it is a public good once it has been created, but its creation entails costs, usually borne by a specific firm. Obviously, the innovative firm would not like its hard-earned technological gain to be withered away just because the cost of diffusing a technology is much smaller than that of creating it.

The recognition that technology is a separate (and important) factor of production, the possession of which enables firms to create sustainable competitive advantages, came about only in the early 1960s. In a world of homogeneous products and a high degree of competition, firms are forced to choose that technology that would minimize manufacturing costs and optimize the use of the factors of production, usually assumed to be labor and capital. As a result, each firm will use the same technology. For example, firms in countries with an abundant and cheap labor supply will use similar labor-intensive technologies. This simple model was unable to explain the decisions actually made by managers of real-life firms. Clearly, firms in the same country were using different technologies to manufacture ostensibly identical products. Contrary to expectations, developing countries' firms used capital intensive technologies and expanding manufacturing sectors were not creating more job opportunities. Moreover, Leontief (1954) clearly demonstrated that the United States exported labor intensive products.

In search for explanations for the Leontief paradox, several studies (Hufbauer, 1966; Gruber et al, 1967; Horst, 1972; Caves, 1974) focused on the technology intensity of U.S. exports. These studies concluded that U.S. exports, and United States' direct foreign investments, rather than being labor intensive, have been technology intensive. Technology intensity has been operationalized as the ratio of the R&D expenditures to sales, or as the number of scientists and engineers employed relative to the total number of employees.

Once technology is recognized as an important and separate factor of production, several questions arise. First, how can technology be created and what are the major incentives that may be used to enhance the rate of new technology creation? Second, once the technology has been created, how does management choose to use the technology? Third, how is the technology transferred from the R&D laboratory to actual production and sales? Fourth, how can it be diffused to other firms or transferred across national boundaries?

No attempt is made in this chapter to summarize the many works on these issues, only to highlight some major conclusions. A distinction is generally drawn between scientific invention, aimed at understanding, and technological innovation, aimed at use. The amount invested in a search for new technology depends on the anticipated profitability of the investment, but also on supply factors such as the number of scientists and engineers. To some extent, the quantity of resources devoted by other industries can also affect the rate of technological innovation in an industry by a spillover process (Mansfield, 1968). The process by which the use of innovations spread (diffusion) was found to have been accelerated in recent times both within a country and in the international arena (Nabseth and Ray, 1974). Yet, a considerable time may lapse before a new technology is used. In addition, only a few companies are able to make a successful transition to a new technology (Foster, 1986).

When technology is transferred across national boundaries, the problem is often perceived as one of choosing the "appropriate" technology, usually understood to mean more labor intensive technology in the case of a developing country with an abundant labor supply and a relative scarcity of capital. More precisely, appropriate technology is product, process, or marginal knowledge optimally adapted to local conditions. This choice, again, is often perceived as the responsibility of the technology giver. Yeoman, in a seminal study of the choice of technology problem in 1968 (summarized in Stobaugh and Wells, 1984, pp. 21–46), argued that the degree to which U.S. multinationals adapt their technology to foreign cost conditions is a function of the ratio of manufacturing costs to the total cost and the degree of price elasticity of demand to the firm's products. The higher any one of these two variables, the greater the adaptation. Other studies stressed certain institutional factors. Wells (1973), for example, argued that labor laws and customs may severely limit the discretion of management to lay off workers, making capital intensive technology more flexible. Michel Amsalem (1983) argued that the choice of technology was limited by ignorance of the full range of techniques available elsewhere. Amsalem thus stressed the importance of the search process.

Having chosen a technology, managers face another set of choices: that of the appropriate channel through which the technology would be transferred. Essentially, there are three mutually exclusive forms of commercial international proprietary technology transfer: one is arm's length licensing: sale of the know-how to a third, unrelated party; the second is use of the technology in a joint venture, partially owned by the provider of the technology; and the third is the transfer of the technology to a wholly owned subsidiary of the multinational enterprise, internalizing the transfer process within the organization. Therefore, one way of looking at technology transfer is to inquire when it will be more efficient through the market and when efficiency will be enhanced by internalizing the transfer within a firm. Another is to inquire how technology transfer can build indigenous capabilities in science and technology. To deal with these questions, a typology of transfers is needed.

A TYPOLOGY OF TRANSFERS

Technology can be bought, borrowed, stolen, or developed indigenously. Technology transfer is a poorly defined catch-all phrase for all activities and mechanisms causing the movement of technology from the laboratory to the marketplace or from one individual or organization-unit to another.

The major elements that define any transfer matrix may include (Frame, 1983; Robock, 1980):

The Phases of Transfer

The technology process starts with the generation of new knowledge and then moves to its diffusion. That diffusion starts within the firm and then moves to transfers between places, institutions, and nations.

The Type of Technological Knowledge Transferred and the Characteristics of the Transfer Item

The transfer may be that of the *result* of knowledge (machine or any other technological artifact itself, turnkey operation, or subcontracting operations in the developing country that assembles components). In all these cases, the transfer does not give the recipient an ability to reproduce the knowledge, only to consume or use it.

The other extreme is an active transfer. It allows the recipient to reproduce the knowledge and change it, adapting it to different conditions. An active transfer can allow a firm to achieve sustainable competitive advantage and a developing country to enter into self-sustained growth. For obvious reasons, an MNE will not willingly transfer such knowledge outside its own system, although by training local persons, it can aid in achieving such a goal.

In between these two, there is a transfer of design elements: blueprints, formulas, patents, documents, and technical data. The recipient firm can produce the machines or the products, but remains dependent on the foreign supplier for any changes in design. Thus, in 1929, Ford Motor Company engineers transferred to the Soviet Union the know-how for producing Model A cars. The Soviet Union continued producing the same car without changing it long after Ford stopped production.

The Technology Donor

The donor could be a commercial firm, a university, or a government body.

The Channels of Transfer

As already mentioned, there are a myriad of possibilities: turnkey projects, foreign direct investments, license agreements, joint ventures, patents, licensing, training, commercial visits, commercial literature, sales of products in which the technology is embodied with or without maintenance, and after-sale service or on-the-job training.

Different channels mean different amounts of skills and actual knowledge transferred. Transfer may be an explicit objective of an international transaction, as in the case of patent licensing by one firm to another or other licensing agreements, joint ventures, technology sharing, and training programs. Transfer may also come as a by-product, as when a firm receives the technology embodied in a machine it acquired. Technology may also be transferred without being received or received without being transferred. An example of the first case is a turnkey project where the donor builds an entire factory but no one in the recipient country knows how to replicate it. An illustration of the second is when engineers in the recipient country create a new product through reverse engineering.

The choice of an appropriate channel is a joint function of the goals of the technology donor and the absorption capacity of the recipient. Thus, if absorptive activity is low, a turnkey project may be more appropriate than licensing.

The Cost of Transfer

Much of the discussion on technology transfer seems to be based on the implicit assumption that the transaction costs of the transfer are zero or negligible. It is not always recognized that technology transfer, both through market mechanisms and within a multination enterprise, involves heavy costs. An effort to understand the nature of these costs and then to minimize them may be a much more beneficial avenue for reducing the technology gap than restricting foreign direct investment.

For the most part, technology transfer literature discusses the transfer of commercial technology. However, most available technology in the world can be acquired free of charge by reading scientific articles, by participating in international conferences, and by reverse engineering. To use the wealth of available information, one has to possess a minimum knowledge of the field. To put it in the extreme, an illiterate person cannot read any of the published articles, even though the articles are easier to access by the creation of computerized systems. For transferred technology to be absorbed, the receiver must have certain basic knowledge.

Even if technology is transferred by selling products, there is still a need for knowledge on the receiving end. The receiver of the technology should be able to search for the technologies to be transferred, to choose the product, to scan intelligently for the most appropriate source of technology, to upgrade it, and to have after-sale service to maintain the usefulness of the products. Therefore, each firm absorbing technology must have a core of technical personnel with certain minimum educational and training-acquired capabilities that will make the transfer possible and effective.

In most cases, the costs of licensing fees are miniscule compared with the total costs of overcoming technological barriers and achieving technology transfer. Governments may argue that they pay hefty prices for patents or know-how. Much heavier costs, however, are those usually not recorded as part of the cost of transfer. Sending engineers with little previous experience for training abroad may be recorded as costs, but the costs of a long period of underutilization of equipment while the engineers are trying to figure out what to do next is rarely so regarded. Other invisible costs include supplying defective parts, charging excessive prices because of import substitution protection, failing to honor delivery commitments, or delays in construction and in commencing production.

To be in the technology business, a developing country must be prepared to leap into the dark, taking great gambles. The greatest gamble is whether it will be able to develop the human capital that would be able to use the sophisticated machines, produce the sophisticated products, and, even better, adapt them for local use.

There are significant differences in the capacity of different societies to generate technical innovations suitable to their economic needs (Rosenberg, 1982, p. 8) and effectively to receive technology. A society may not possess the capability to improve the transferred technology, but may still be able to use a certain technology or even to alter it to local conditions. Without minimal indigenous capabilities—fostered by a broad system of education—technology transfer will not strengthen learning by doing or by using. Transfer without fostering domestic capabilities is possible, sometimes necessary, but is less beneficial to economic growth.

TECHNOLOGY TRADE

No comprehensive data are available that identify all international technology flows: Much of this flow is in the form of R&D intensive goods exports, in which the technology is embodied. Thus, the available statistical measurements on international trade in technology are sketchy. It is even harder to estimate the degree of technology transfer embodied in products or achieved by free flow of information. Certainly, however, this trade has been growing very fast. As one example, for the five leading developed market economies (United States, United Kingdom, France, Federal Republic of Germany, and Japan), the total value of receipts for licensing and technical services, to the extent they are recorded, grew from $1.9 billion in 1965 to $16 billion by the mid-1980s (UNCTC, 1987, p. 7, table 1). These figures are only the tip of the iceberg as they do not include the value of more implicit forms of technology transfers, such as direct foreign investments, franchising agreements, or international subcontracting or turnkey contracts. Nor do these figures estimate the value of information transmitted across countries as a side effect of other sales, that is, know-how received from machinery equipment manufacturers or simply by reading journals.

While it is not easy to define the international market for technological information, such a market clearly exists and is growing in size. Part of this market consists of free exchange of information such as among scientists at conventions. Another part of the market can be measured by the size of the royalties and management fees paid and received as well as by the registered foreign patents. Technology can also be transferred by immigration of engineers and skilled workers or by exports of the goods and services that embody the technology.

Some international trade is even more invisible, as in the case of reverse engineering or training of foreign students (for the limitations of different measurements, see Robock, 1980, pp. 14–16). Furthermore, there is no statistical means to estimate how much technology transfer develops local capabilities. It may well be that the transfer of proven technologies by MNEs to highly protected markets discourages local learning.

From the point of view of the innovative firm, it is best to maintain the technology within the firm and protect it against becoming universal to achieve an extremely important firm-specific advantage. There are many cases, therefore, in which the interests of the host government and those of the innovative firm diverge. When the innovative firm owns a subsidiary in the host country, it may have a strong incentive to transfer the proprietary technology. When this is the case, the firm would want to minimize the cost of technology transfer. An effective transmission of technology may be hindered by all sorts of costs, some of which may be reduced by governmental action.

Less developed countries (LDCs) complain bitterly that MNEs exploit them. Some of the most bitter complaints are in the area of technology transfer. Consequently, there have been many attempts to develop rules of conduct in this area—by large MNEs, by the international Chamber of Commerce, and by governmental bodies. The OECD Guidelines for Multinational Enterprises, promulgated in 1976 and revised in 1979, enumerated several areas of responsibility in the realm of technology transfer. The attempt by the United Nations Conference on Trade and Development (UNCTAD) to develop a code of conduct for technology transfer originally focused entirely on the responsibilities of the MNEs. Throughout the negotiations of the code, it has been clear that the North and the South approach this issue from entirely different conceptual platforms, and "each side appears somewhat blind to the claims of others" (Frame, 1983, p. 172).

TECHNOLOGY TRANSFER AS A LEARNING PROCESS

Technology transfer can sometimes take place between an inventor and a commercial firm, or between the central laboratory and other divisions of the same firm, or between two firms in the same country. In other cases, the receiver is situated in one country and the technology is transferred across international borders but within the same MNE. The transfer of existing technologies may be made through a market transaction between two firms from different countries, leading to an assimilation of these transferred technologies by indigenous agents in the host economy. Ideally, technology transfer should result in the ability of local scientists and engineers to acquire enough knowledge of the technology to be able to use it without continuous aid. Hopefully, the indigenous engineers may be able to improve the designs and the production system. The word *transfer* may imply that an owner of technology takes active steps to convey technology to the receiver by teaching.

A great deal has been written and researched from the point of view of the managers of the sending organization, such as on the strategies used by the givers of the technology, the transfer agents and their role, and the cultural barriers to international technology transfer, as well as the institutional arrangements and the different methods of transfer. There also has been a body of literature dealing with national security issues and other problems a supplier may have regarding a transfer, such as the allegations of job exportation, creation of competition, or inability to maintain control. Much less attention has been paid to the barriers to technology absorption by the receiver.

Most proposals for modifying transfers are designed to improve the negotiating capabilities of the developing countries' representatives. A more important goal is that of improving the ability of the firm in developing countries to achieve technological adaptation. Technology transfer is easiest when the absorption capacity needed is that of the use of the product. Certainly, the skills needed to assemble electronic components can be learned quickly, while the design of new electronic devices takes much greater technological capability.

For the receiver, technology transfer is a learning experience. The firm receiving the technology must learn how to use it effectively. Paradoxically, very little knowledge has been transferred from the realm of organizational behavior theory to that of technology transfer literature.

Learning allows a reduction in costs, since the time required by an individual to perform a task declines as experience increases. This so-called learning curve was later found to exist not only in individual learning but also in small group performance (Leavitt, 1951; Guetzkow and Simon, 1954; Baloff, 1967), in organizations (first documented by Wright, 1936), and in industry (Sheshinski, 1967). The Boston Consulting Group has made a series of strategic recommendations based on what they believe to have been the predominance of experience curves in business firms.

Economists attempted to reconcile the learning-by-doing phenomenon with standard production theory (Hirshleifer, 1962; Oi, 1967) and analyzed the implications for both competitive (Arrow, 1962; Rosen, 1972) and noncompetitive (Spence, 1981, 1984; Fundenberg and Tirole, 1983; Smiley and Ravid, 1983) equilibrium.

Learning theory clearly shows the importance of experience, an almost insurmountable barrier to entry for most developing countries. As one example, when India started its production of heavy electrical equipment in 1956, it competed against firms established many years before: Siemens in 1847, ASEA in 1883, Brown Bovery in 1891, General Electric in 1892. The relative newcomer was Hitachi, established in 1910 (Ramamurti, 1987). Only enormous aid from the Indian government and its import substitution policies allowed the firm (BHEL) to overcome the initial period of learning.

The problem of intraorganizational transfer from newly found knowledge in a research laboratory to a business product has been studied by several researchers. A common characteristic of these works is the emphasis on the importance of communality of goals and close communication between the giving and receiving units in the transfer of the new knowledge. Some degree of cultural proximity between the giver and the receiver should exist, which will facilitate communication between them. Furthermore, the receiving organization should possess technical expertise that complements that of the giver. It is often noted that the reward system of the donor organization and that of the recipient do not necessarily motivate transfer and that successful technology transfer is not rewarded (Ounjian and Carne, 1987).

Another stream of papers, starting with Eckaus's (1955) seminal work, investigated potential problems in transferring production techniques developed in one country to another economy with different factor proportions. Several studies concluded that a wide range of technological choices and of capital and labor intensities permit increases in productivity (Mason, 1973; Forsyth and Solomon, 1977; Rhee and Westpahl, 1977). It was also recognized that the transfer of technology entails costs to the donor (Teece, 1977) and the recipient (Dahlman and Westphal, 1982).

Two more variables may complicate the technology transfer process. First, the receiving organization does not necessarily know how and where it should look to find the most suitable technology to be acquired and transferred. In fact, if the receiving organization really knew what it was buying, it would not have to buy it. Second, the organization holding the technology is not motivated to share its unique technology with another organization. True, a new development of technology or innovation is very costly. The innovative firm is interested in spreading these high costs over a large number of products to be sold. Under certain circumstances, it may also have the incentive for the technology itself to be transferred, such as in the form of licensing as the marginal cost of additional sale is very low compared with the original and sunk costs of creating the technology. The likely price to the buyer would be relatively low, in particular when the technology can be acquired from several sources. However, the technology transferred would usually be restricted. Moreover, only firms that show an ability to create technology on their own are able to acquire the technology with fewer restrictions. Most important, to be effective the technology transfer must be absorbed by the recipient organization. For that, there must be an ample supply of technical, professional, and managerial cadres that can receive the technology as well as a well-developed scientific infrastructure.

Any technology transfer process involves a donor and a recipient. The donor transfers an item of technology through a certain channel (licensing, turnkey operations, joint venture, patent rights, in-house transfers to foreign subsidiaries, purchase of technology or of technology embodied in a product, etc.). To achieve an efficient transfer, one needs to look at the supplier's needs, knowledge, and skills as well as the absorptive capacity of the receiver. Technology transfer has many technical dimensions, but it is first and foremost a human communication issue. One obstacle to a better transfer is that persons in different countries, organizations, or departments have their own way of doing things. Making sure that the giver and the receiver are willing and able to work together in an effective manner is a major issue and a precondition of any effective transfer.

TECHNOLOGY GAP

For a technology transfer to occur, there must be a technology gap among firms or among the countries. Theoretically, free trade in technology should close the gap and equally endow all countries. The scientific and technical resources needed to develop new theories are heavily concentrated, however, as are the engineering resources required to develop new products or processes and to carry out essential modifications in the new product after its embryonic commercial introduction. OECD (1984) figures show that 88 percent of the R&D expenditures by business in the market economies of OECD were spend by five countries: United States, United Kingdom, Japan, West Germany, and France. The United States originated about 80 percent of the major innovations in the world during the period 1953–1958, but only 57 percent for the period 1965–1973 (National Science Board, 1975). Clearly, knowledge and know-how are unequally distributed. Only very few countries today can discuss the possibility of having an active technology policy in the sense of the creation of new products or the development of indigenous capacities for innovation in areas on the frontiers of knowledge. Even Europe suffers a trade deficit in information technology. According to UNESCO (1987) estimates, the number of R&D scientists and engineers per million population in 1980 was 2,986 for the developed countries and only 127 for the developing countries. In Africa, this number was 49—much higher than the 27 per million in 1970, but still miniscule compared with 5,172 in the Soviet Union.

When technology is salient, enterprises may be assumed to operate in oligopolistic markets. Furthermore, institutional arrangements vary among countries. The market structure, the external environment, and the firm's position in the market are important variables in explaining the degree of a technology gap.

In the 1950s, it was believed that development would be achieved by capital infusions that would break the so-called vicious cycle of poverty. However, the mere funneling of capital was found to be inadequate. While Europe was able to reconstruct itself once it received Marshall Aid funds, most developing countries were unable to use the capital inflows in an effective manner. Clearly, technical knowledge was a crucial variable on the road to economic growth. This recognition is the first among many that lead to the assertion that absorptive capacity is a crucial variable.

For some time, fueled by the many obvious examples of misapplied technology through the developing world, the major focus for discussion was whether or not the technology was appropriate to the economic conditions of the host country. Others, Emmanuel (1983) in particular, argued that appropriate technology is often an underdeveloped one that would perpetuate the problems of underdevelopment rather than eliminate them. One reason for this contrasting point of view is that countries differ in their ability to absorb technology. This ability depends on several factors, including the political environment and the economic incentive structure.

The most important of these factors seems to be the educational level of the population. Educational programs geared to vocational training in useful skills is the first requirement for any ability to absorb technology.

The organized pursuit of knowledge is an international activity, and its transfer is generally free. Scientists and engineers travel, visit plants in other countries, read journals, participate in conferences and in international fairs, and often correspond with colleagues in other countries. All these modes are important means of international technology transfer. Technical assistance of the sort provided by the United Nations or by the United States through the Agency for International Development (AID) is another source. Postdoctoral work, and even studies toward a degree in a foreign university or on-the-job training in a foreign firm all allow persons to transfer knowledge. The transfer of processes from one place to another has often been achieved by the migration of skilled persons.

As already noted, almost all new knowledge through scientific R&D is undertaken in highly industrialized countries where 98 percent of all R&D expenditures are spent. Yet, this phenomenon is changeable: The United States was dependent on British technology in the seventeenth century and Japan become a technological power only recently. Transfer of knowledge through individuals is as important today as it was when steam engine technology was transferred from England to the United States.

Unfortunately, in some countries, science is an intellectual item enjoyed only be the elite. Competent scientists can certainly use the results of discoveries made elsewhere, all of which are not subjected to intellectual property rights protection. However, scientists are often uninterested in engineering applications, and the dominant culture among institutions of higher learning encourages participation in the world product of knowledge more than relevant research for domestic use or the preparation of vocationally competent individuals. Thus, in most Latin American countries, vocational training is neglected and universities concentrated on the humanities and professions such as law.

At least as important as vocational training is the availability of the entrepreneurial class, able to give dynamic leadership for industrial growth. In many developing countries, the relatively most modern sector of the economy is the defense sector. Defense-related R&D is very often of a high priority. On the one hand, this means that the military becomes an important training ground for vocational training as well as a source of entrepreneurs and an effective builder of large infrastructure projects. This has been true for the Roman legions, the U.S. corps of engineers, and many developing countries. The army has often been the largest vocational school in the country, training many mechanics, nurses, and so on. Unfortunately, defense-related R&D seldom spills over to civilian products, in which trade competitiveness is an overriding criterion of success. Because licensed technology is often restricted, particularly in terms of access to world markets, developing countries are much better off if their relatively small number of entrepreneurs and engineers concentrate their skills and efforts on achieving excellence in those areas in which a firm may be able to compete in the global marketplace.

Vernon (1982) hypothesized that information flows may be an important substitute to trade. He based this expectation on the declining relative cost of transmitting information relative to transportation, the expected continued increase in the speed and efficiency of transmitting information across international borders, and the rapidly increasing protectionist trends. Clearly, there has also been an increase in the number of prospective sources of new technology—at least for receivers capable of searching out and using the information. Again, most technology can be acquired free of charge, if one has the capability of searching for and using the available information. Indeed, many of the real life problems of technology transfer are encountered because the receiving organization is not able or ready or willing to absorb the technology either because of lack of knowledge or wrong incentives.

THE BASIC STRATEGIC CHOICES

It is sometimes claimed that the developing countries are relegated to the position of low labor cost assemblers of products to be designed by MNEs in developed countries and marketed in the industrialized part of the world. This is one reason for the claim of *dependencia.* Yet, if countries build their capabilities in science and engineering, they will be able to change this role. MNEs can become change agents, introducing advanced technologies, and therefore changes in value systems and social norms. Governments may seek to tie technology transfer to building capabilities for adaptation. A corollary of the above is that countries at an incipient level of development have limited possibilities in absorbing technologies, in particular in an unbundled form, because they have very limited cadres of educated technicians and engineers. For such a country, the only short-run, viable alternative is to accept technology transfer via direct foreign investment, often managed by expatriates, or by turnkey projects selling to MNEs.

Depending on the availability of skilled personnel, some countries may find that foreign direct investments are the only realistic alternative for economic growth in the short run and that technology transfer is possible mainly in terms of learning how to assemble components. Others may find that the local firms are able to carry out successful production under licensing, and only a few would be able to adapt and create new products, as Brazil did in the case of its Bandeirante aeroplane. The more emphasis placed on building domestic capabilities instead of technology transfer, the greater the local learning will be. Government policies may encourage MNEs to take the role of coaching local entrepreneurs.

In the long run, a country can aim for a major strategic change by increasing its educational capabilities. The investment in education is intended to develop a cadre of people capable of understanding technology.

These persons achieve the capacity of effective global scanning and of absorbing and disseminating technologies that originated elsewhere.

Only when educational levels have been raised, and a larger number of engineers are available, can one hope to achieve not only the import of technology, but also its assimilation and adaption. With a higher number of engineers, the country may also be able to create unique technologies. This may be one lesson to be drawn from the undisputed success of the Japanese. The Japanese industry was absorbed with catching up to its United States counterparts. To achieve its goal, it concentrated on technology acquisition, quality improvement, and productivity gains. Later, the Japanese moved to the creation and mastery of advanced technologies in the process of achieving larger market shares.

The Japanese experience underlines the importance of increasing local capabilities by developing the physical and human technological infrastructure. The same has been true for South Korea. The secondary school enrollment for that country grew from 27 percent in 1960 to 95 percent in 1986. This allowed the country to increase the number of its engineers. In another example, in 1955–1956, India had 65 degree granting institutions that produced an annual output of 4,000 degree holders. By 1978, the number was increased to 13,000, compared with more than 70,000 engineering graduates in Japan and about 24,500 in much smaller-sized South Korea (but also compared with only 91 in Morocco).

Only after increased investment in education creates human capital can the government use its purchasing policies (and that of the state-owned enterprises) to encourage the development of a technology-based industry. The major role that state-owned enterprises can play may be seen in the cases of Brazil and India (Ramamurti, 1987). Other countries have subsidized financing for technological activities of the private firms.

In conclusion, one way a firm may want to compete is by receiving technology that would allow it to achieve lower costs. These lower costs are due in part to economies of scale, but also to an experience effect whereby the costs of the product declines by a certain percentage each time the firm's experience in producing it doubles. The cost reduction with cumulative production has been observed and carefully measured in a wide range of products. To some extent, this experience effect is a result of standardization.

Another way for a firm to compete is to develop a firm-specific capability, based on the adaptation of its product to market needs. This type of competitive advantage requires much greater availability of technical persons that can redesign a product and managers that can manage this process. A few of the more advanced developing countries were able to achieve this kind of expertise. Japan is perhaps the most well publicized case, but Brazil's Embraer and Petrobras, India's Hindustan Machine Tool Company, and Korea's personal computer industry are only a few of many other examples of success with this type of strategy. In all these cases, the success was due, at least partially, to the government's technology policy, including specific efforts to develop more and better educational institutions.

The decade of 1990 is certainly going to be a decade of knowledge-intensive production. Countries will be much better off if they can develop world class global companies, whose competitive advantage will be based on unique knowledge. For that, there will be a need for greater investment in education and on-the-job training.

A firm gains a crucial competitive edge through technological advantage only if it can exploit this advantage. This means that skilled engineers and experienced managerial personnel must be available and that this personnel must have the capacity to earn economic rent from proprietary technology and know-how. Technology that is widely disseminated and available does not differentiate one firm from another. Therefore, a firm that is able to search, select, negotiate, acquire, and assimilate successfully the most relevant technology for its purposes, and also to adapt, improve, or modify the technology or develop a new production system that will create differentiated products, will enjoy a sustainable competitive advantage. A firm that cannot achieve such modifications, but possesses the technological ability to assimilate a known technology, may be able to compete on the basis of lower prices, but not on the basis of differentiated products or a leading edge technology. A firm that does not possess even this minimum technical capability depends on foreign manpower, often supplied by an MNE. The MNE, for its own reasons, would often attempt not to transfer the leading edge technologies for the critical skills required for the product to be differentiated. In most cases, if the receiving firm does not possess the necessary skills, it can compete only by purchasing a turnkey plant of known technology or by becoming a subcontractor to an MNE.

This chapter does not discuss problems related to the use of MNEs as change agents. One should remember that cultural and language barriers may be important as well as salary differences: the expatriates' level of compensation in MNEs is often a source of envy.

CONSIDERATIONS IN THE DESIGN OF TECHNOLOGY POLICY

From the point of view of a host government, it is much more sensible to allocate resources to the development of search and use capabilities of individuals and indigenous firms than to evaluate the technologies and try to reach an agreement on a code of conduct of the grantors of technology. To participate in the fruits of modern technology, a country is often portrayed as having to spend large sums for licensing fees. In fact, as shown earlier, licensing costs are miniscule compared with the total costs of absorbing technology and, therefore, the large amount of attention to the problem is ill directed. Furthermore, relevant technology can be received free of charge or as a side-effect of turnkey project or purchase of machines.

How can an efficient technology strategy be achieved? First and foremost, by strengthening and enhancing technological and vocational education in the country. Without engineering and technicians, a country cannot receive technology or assess the appropriateness of such a technology. The more people who understand the new technologies and know-how to evaluate them, the better off the country is. Ideas, concepts, and innovations come from people, and it takes a long time to train these people.

Society's investment in education enhances technological change because it creates the basic knowledge for the harnessing of a new technology and because it facilitates technology diffusion. The major failure of the market is not in transferring inappropriate technology, but in not being able to transfer a technology because the recipients are not sufficiently educated.

The ability to create, maintain, and nurture a modern industrial system depends on the existence of a cadre of scientists, engineers, and technicians and on high literacy rates of the total population. Educational levels lead to technological capabilities and these capabilities are the creators of new income and higher standards of living. These capabilities are absolutely necessary for technology transfer to lead to increased capacity, not merely to the purchase of goods.

For technology to be developed and diffused, there is also a need for a learning environment and for certain infrastructures that do not offer proprietary advantages to firms and, therefore, may not be developed by each individual firm. This includes measurement methods and processes as well as standards. Standards provide information, compatibility, variety reduction, and quality. Thus, the transfer of complex technological information requires a comprehensive terminology. Standards can define the interface between several pieces of equipment that work together. Standards can also be used to reduce or limit the variety of product types or sizes, allowing greater economies of scale and substitution of products in different countries.

Second, a special effort should be made to establish and operate better global scanning and search procedures for technology waiting to be acquired. Existing technology is usually purchased at bargain prices and this technology can be used to manufacture products with which the country can be competitive in world markets.

Third, the process of transfer is made much easier if there is a congruence of goals between the receiving and supplying organizations. In this sense, achieving the transfer within multinational enterprises is more efficient because the MNE possesses a high degree of transaction economies. If one is interested in differentiation, however, one needs a more complex method of transfer based on adaptation and redesign. Here, much can be learned from the Japanese experience.

One major difference between Japanese and U.S. firms is that the latter's design and development groups are much less closely linked to manufacturing. In Japan, the manufacturing divisions are in effect internal clients of the central corporate lab. In addition, people are constantly moving from the labs to manufacturing and back. Perhaps for this reason, people in manufacturing divisions are a more important reference group for the research engineers in Japan than in the United States (Westney and Sakakibara, 1986, p. 224).

The responses of firms to changing external circumstances are sometimes viewed as totally determined by market structure. In fact, organizations learn, adapt, and search for solutions consistent with their governing values and beliefs to achieve new equilibria. When individuals and organizations learn effectively, a transfer is made more effectively.

CONCLUSIONS

There are many problems throughout the long process from the initial idea stage to the development to the manufacture and marketing of a new product; very few firms have been able to transfer technology efficiently, even within the firm itself, across these stages. In fact, the more we know about technology transfer, the clearer it becomes that the strategies needed to facilitate the process must be holistic, based on an analysis of the entire transfer process and the environment in which it is embedded.

The major thrust of this chapter lies in the discussion of the conditions necessary on the receiving side for a technology transfer to be successfully implemented. It is argued that technology cannot be transferred from one unit to another or from one country to another unless the receiver is able and willing to learn the new technology and apply it. The absorptive capacity of the receiver of technology is a necessary ingredient in the transfer process and this cannot be taken for granted. Unless the recipient has a substantial scientific and technological capability, the diffusion of the technology will be very small and its transfer will become rather impossible. Moreover, specific policy measures can be used to enhance this capacity. One such policy is an increased investment in the betterment of human capital through formal education as well as on-the-job training.

The motto on the seal of the University of Chicago reads *Cresat scientia, Vita excolatur* (Let knowledge grow that life may be enriched). Yet for knowledge to enrich life, it has to reach the people who need it in a form that they can put it to use. As Glaser and Marx (1966, p. 6) succinctly argued:

> All over the world people struggle with problems and seek solutions. Often those who struggle are unaware that others face similar problems, and in some instances, are solving them. It is destructive and wasteful that people should be frustrated and often defeated by difficulties for which somebody else has found a remedy. . . . The gap between what we know and what we put to effective use bedevils many fields of human activity.

Many in the developing countries would argue that technology is a public good, and that the cost of technology transfer is unnecessarily inflated. As they see it, an already developed technology is part of human knowledge that should be diffused free of charge. Firms in developed countries emphasize the private property nature of technology (Chamber of Commerce, 1977); they argue that technology would flow to the developing countries only if these countries would attract such flows (National Research Council, 1986). Furthermore, they argue that technology is expensive and funds must be earned from existing technology to allow the development of new ones. Multinational enterprise managers are frequently confused by what they see as contradictory demands for easier transfer of technology to developing countries, but also for the strengthening of local capabilities, local R&D and more adept technologies. Many also feel that it is a mistake to export technologies since one loses one's competitive advantage in the process. The spearhead of the assault on the MNEs on these counts has been the trade unions in the United States, concerned about job losses in the domestic market, which they see as stemming from technology transfer.

It is also pointed out that the transaction costs are high: negotiations on the conditions of the transfer may be lengthy, costly, and tedious. It is argued that much of these transaction costs can be saved if the transfer is done within a multinational system by creating an enclave, often divorced from its surroundings, of a subsidiary of the MNE or by the sale of products that embody proprietary technology.

The best technology policy depends on the availability of personnel for the assimilation, modification, and adaptation of imported technological knowledge. A wholly owned subsidiary of an MNE may be the best choice for technology transfer if local technical manpower is very limited and largely unavailable for civilian use. An active technology policy may allow not only a selection of the direction of the foreign investments, but also creation of new products or adaptations of existing ones. To achieve such a goal, greater investment must be made in education and in scientific and technological infrastructures. In addition, there should be greater willingness to take the risks inherent in new product development. In the 1990s, the issues to be discussed should be less those of technology transfer and technology replication than those of new production systems and new technologies and the means by which firms in developing countries can create and sustain firm-specific advantages by modifying, adapting, and improving imported technologies, and by taking advantage of the wealth of noncommercial transactions—from journal papers to machinery producer's literature—to create an indigenous technology base.

Researchers will gain from a transfer of knowledge among the different disciplines producing the scattered literature on learning, change, transfer, diffusion, and innovation. If accord can be reached on common definitions, both the variables making transfer more efficient and the policy implications can be agreed on. The common problem dealt with by many researchers is that of transferring knowledge from one organization to another to change the practices procedures employed by the receiving organization. The common theme in many studies of different intellectual origin is that of the application of available knowledge by a new user. This new user must be willing to learn and ways must be designed to make the learning effective. Therefore, the process of technology transfer, or knowledge adoption or utilization or diffusion involves many political, organizational, attitudinal, social, and economic components. The capacity of the receiver to learn the uses of the technology (and to choose the technology to be adopted) is a crucial variable.

REFERENCES

Amsalem, Michel. (1983). *Technology Choice in Developing Countries*, Cambridge, Mass.: MIT Press.

Arrow, Kenneth J. (1962). "The economic implications of learning by doing," *Review of Economic Studies*, 29:155–173.

Baloff, Nicholas. (1967). "Estimating the parameters of the startup model—An empirical approach," *Journal of Industrial Engineering*, 18:248–253.

Baloff, Nicholas. (1970). "Startup management," *IEEE Transactions*, EM-17: 132–141.

Baranson, Jack. (1970). "Technology, United States investment, and European economic growth," in C. Kindleberger, (ed.), *The International Corporation*, Cambridge: MIT Press.

Caves, Richard E. (1982). *Multinational Enterprise and Economic Analysis*, New York: Cambridge University Press.

Caves, Richard E. (1974). "Effect of international technology transfer on the U.S. economy," *The Effects of International Technology Transfer on U.S. Economy*, Washington, DC: Government Printing Office.

Chamber of Commerce of the United States. (1977). Report of the Task Force on Technology Transfers, "Technology transfers and the developing countries: Guidelines and principles for consideration in development of national policies governing transfers of technology between industrial and developing countries," Washington: Chamber of Commerce, April.

Dahlman, C., and Westphal, G. (1982). "Technological effort in industrial development: An interpretative survey of recent research," in F. Stewart and J. James (eds.), *The Economies of New Technology in Developed Countries*, London and Colo.: Frances Printer and Westview.

Denison, Edward F. (1962). *The Source of Economic Growth in the United States*, New York: Committee for Economic Development.

Denison, Edward F. (1980). *Accounting for Slower Economic Growth in the United States in the 1970s*, Washington, D.C.: The Brooking Institution.

Denison, Edward F. (1982). *Accounting for Slower Economic Growth: An Update*, paper presented to the Conference on International Comparisons of Productivity and Causes of the Slowdown, American Enterprise Institute for Public Policy Research: Washington, D.C.

Dunning, John H. (1981). *International Production and the Multinational Enterprise*, London: Allen and Unwin.

Dunning, John H. (1983). "Market power of the firm and international transfer of technology: A historical excursion," *International Journal of Industrial Organization,* 1:333–351.

Eckaus, R. S. (1955). "The factor proportions problem in underdeveloped areas," *American Economic Review,* 45:539–565.

Emmanuel, Arghiri. (1982). *Appropriate or Underdeveloped Technology?* New York: Wiley.

Forsyth, D. J. C., and Solomon, R. F. (1977). "Choice of technology and nationality of ownership in manufacturing in a developing country," *Oxford Economic Papers,* 29(2):258–282.

Foster, Richard N. (1986). "Timing technological transitions," in Mel Horwitch (ed.), *Technology in the Modern Corporation: A Strategic Perspective,* New York: Pergamon Press, pp. 35–49.

Frame, J. Davidson. (1983). *International Business and Global Technology,* Lexington, Mass: Lexington Books.

Fudenberg, Drew, and Tirole, Jean. (1983). "Learning-by-doing and market performance," *Bell Journal of Economics,* 14: 522–530.

Glaser, E. M., and Marx, J. B. (1966). "Putting research to work," *Rehabilitation Record,* 7(6):6–10.

Gruber, William, Mehta, Dileep, and Vernon, Raymond. (1967). "The R and D factor in international trade and international investment of U.S. industries," *Journal of Political Economy,* 75: 20–37.

Guetzkow, Harold, and Simon, Herbert A. (1954). "The impact of certain communication nets upon organization and performance in task-oriented groups," *Management Science,* 1: 233–250.

Hirshleifer, Jack. (1962). "The firm's cost function: A successful reconstruction?" *Journal of Business,* 35:235–255.

Hollander, Samuel. (1965). *The Sources of Increased Efficiency,* Cambridge, Mass.: MIT Press.

Horst, Thomas. (1972). "Firm and industry determinants of the decision to invest abroad: An empirical study," *Review of Economics and Statistics,* 54:258–266.

Hufbauer, Gary. (1966). *Synthetic Materials and the Theory of International Trade,* Cambridge, Mass.: Harvard University Press.

Leavitt, Harold J. (1951). "Some effects of certain communication patterns on group performance," *Journal of Abnormal and Social Psychology,* 46:38–50.

Leontief, Wassily, W. (1954). "Domestic production and foreign trade: The American capital position reexamined," *Economia International,* 7:3–32.

Link, Albert N., and Tassey, Gregory. (1987). *Strategies for Technology-based Competition,* Lexington, Mass.: Lexington Books.

Mansfield, Edwin. (1968). *The Economics of Technological Change,* New York: Norton.

Mansfield, Edwin, et. al. (1982). *Technology Transfer, Productivity, and Economic Policy,* New York: Norton.

Mason, R. H. (1973). "Some observations on the choice of technology by multinational firms in developing countries," *Review of Economics and Statistics,* 55(3).

National Research Council. Report of the Council. (1986). *U.S. Science and Technology for Development: A Contribution to the 1970 U.N. Conference*, Background on suggested U.S. initiatives for the U.N. Conference on Science and Technology for Development, Vienna 1979, Washington, D.C.

National Science Board. (1975). *National Indicators: The 1974 Report*, Washington, D.C.

National Science Board. (1986). *National Indicators: The 1985 Report*, Washington, D.C.

Nasbeth, L., and Ray G. (eds). (1974). *The Diffusion of New Industrial Processes: An International Study*. New York: Cambridge University Press.

Oi, Walter Y. (1967). "The neoclassical foundations of progress functions," *Economic Journal*, 77:579–594.

Organization for Economic Cooperation and Development (OECD). (1984). *OECD Science and Technology Indicators: Resources Devoted to R&D*; Paris; Organization for Economic Cooperation and Development.

Ounjian, Moira L., and Carne, E. Bryan. (1987). "A study of the factors Which affect technology transfer in a multilocational, multibusiness unit corporate," *1EEE Transactions of Engineering Management*, VEM-34, pp. 194–201.

Ramamurti, Ravi. (1987). *State-owned Enterprises in High Technology Industries: Studies in Brazil and India*, Praeger: New York.

Rhee, Y. W., and Westphal, L. E. (1977). "A microeconomic investigation of choice of technology," *Journal of Development Economics,* 4: 205–238.

Robock, Stefan H. (1980). *The International Technology Transfer Process,* Washington, D.C.: National Academy of Sciences.

Rosen, Sherwin. (1972). "Learning by experience as joint production," *Quarterly Journal of Economics,* 86:366–382.

Rosenberg, N. (1982). *Inside the Black Box: Technology and Economics,* New York: Cambridge University Press.

Samli, Coskun A. (ed.). (1985). *Technology Transfer: Geographic, Economic, Cultural, and Technical Dimensions,* Westport, Conn.: Quorum Books.

Sheshinski, Eytan. (1967). "Tests of the learning by doing hypothesis," *Review of Economic and Statistics,* 49:568–578.

Smiley, Robert H., and Ravid, S. Abraham. (1983). "The importance of being first: Learning price and strategy," *Quarterly Journal of Economics,* 98:353–362.

Solow, Robert. (1957). "Technical change and the aggregate production function," *Review of Economics and Statistics,* 39:312.

Spence, A. Michael. (1981). "The learning curve and competition," *Bell Journal of Economics,* 12:49–70.

Spence, A. Michael. (1984). "Cost reduction, competition, and industry performance," *Econometrics,* 52:101–121.

Stobaugh, Robert, and Wells, Louis T., Jr. (eds.). (1984). *Technology Transfer Crossing Borders: The Choice, Transfer, and Management of International Technology Flows,* Boston, Mass.: Harvard Business School Press.

United Nations Centre on Transnational Corporations (UNCTC). (1987). *Transnational Corporations and Technology Transfer Effects and Policy Lines,* New York: United Nations.

United Nations Educational, Scientific, and Cultural Organization (UNESCO). (1987). *Statistical Yearbook,* New York: United Nations.

Vernon, Raymond. (1982). "Emerging technologies: Consequences for economic growth, structural change, and employment," in Herbert Giersch (ed.), Rubinger, Germany: Institute fur Weltwirtschaft an der universtat Kiel.

Wells, Louis T., Jr. (1973). "Economic man and engineering man: Choice of technology in a low-wage country," *Public Policy,* 21 Summer.

Westney, Eleanor, and Sakakibara, Kiyonori. (1986). "The role of Japan-based R&D in global technology strategy," in Mel Horwitch (ed.), *Technology in the Modern Corporation: A Strategic Perspective,* New York: Pergamon Press.

Wright, T. P. (1936). "Factors abbeting the cost of airplanes," *Journal of the Aeronautical Sciences,* 3:1221–1228.

6
Technology Transfer in High-Technology Industries

EVERETT M. ROGERS AND THOMAS W. VALENTE

The purpose of this chapter is to describe the unique nature of the technology transfer process in high-technology industries. We draw on a variety of recent research efforts in the United States and Asia that deal with technology transfer in high-technology microelectronics. Our general theme is that technology transfer in high-technology industries is different from technology transfer in the manufacturing, service, or other industries.

Technology transfer is a complex process, yet one that is very important in modern society. Its importance is illustrated by the 1987 Toshiba crisis where the shipment of a high-technology lathe, representing cutting-edge technology, from a Japanese to a Soviet company, created an international scandal that harmed Toshiba's international reputation and cost it millions of dollars. In this instance, the U.S. government was seeking to *prevent* technology transfer to the Soviet Union. More often, governments, individuals, and organizations try to facilitate the technology transfer process, frequently without success.

A *technopolis* is a geographically concentrated high-technology complex that is often characterized by collaborative research and development (R&D) activities between private industry, a research university or institute, and government agencies; and by the presence of venture capital and entrepreneurial spin-off firms. The technopolis phenomenon first occurred in the United States: Silicon Valley in Northern California near San Jose, and "Route 128" in the area around Boston.

The term *technopolis* was coined by the Japanese. In 1980, the Japanese Ministry of International Trade and Industry (MITI) made public its "Technopolis Concept," a plan for a number of high-technology centers patterned after Silicon Valley and Japan's Tsukuba Science City. In 1987, a conference on the technopolis was held in Austin, Texas, and a book of the proceedings is now available (Smilor et al. 1988). In this chapter, we demonstrate why technology transfer is relatively rapid in the technopolis like Silicon Valley.

A new emphasis of the 1980s in the United States has been the collaborative R&D center, funded by a consortium of private companies and usually located on the campus of a research university. The first such collaborative R&D center in the United States was the Microelectronics and Computer Technology Corporation (MCC), created in 1982 as a counter to the Japanese Fifth-Generation Computer Project. A few years later, in 1984, a federal law was passed by the U.S. Congress providing freedom from antitrust regulation for the member companies who collaborate in an R&D consortium. Since then, over 80 collaborative R&D consortia have been established in the United States, mainly in high-technology industries and especially in microelectronics. Later, we explore the special aspects of technology transfer involving R&D consortia.

THE NATURE OF TECHNOLOGY TRANSFER

Technology Transfer

Technology transfer is the process by which technological innovations are exchanged between individuals and organizations who are involved in R&D on one hand, and in putting technological innovations into use on the other hand (Larsen et al., 1986, p. 2). Traditionally, technology transfer was conceptualized as the transfer of hardware objects. Today, we realize that technology transfer often involves information (e.g., a computer software program or a new idea) that may be completely devoid of any hardware aspects. In fact, technology essentially consists of information (Eveland, 1986). We define *technology* as a design for instrumental action that reduces the uncertainty in the cause–effect relationships involved in achieving a desired outcome. Technology is a tool for accomplishing some function; the tool may be a mental model or a machine.

"Since technology is essentially information, 'transfer' is essentially *communication* of that information . . . and the *use* of that information in the recipient system" (Eveland, 1986). In this sense, technology transfer amounts to communicating information about tools to achieve a desired goal. Technology transfer may also consist of persuading an organization or industry to use one kind of tool rather than another (Schon, 1971).

An *innovation* is an idea perceived as new (Rogers, 1983). Essentially an innovation is a new technology or a recombination of closely related technologies. The technology transfer process consists of the exchange or movement of technological innovations.

Technology transfer is usually a two-way process. For example, a study of university–industry technology transfer in microelectronics in the Phoenix area found that technology moved both from Arizona State University to private microelectronics firms, and from these companies to researchers at the university (Larsen et al., 1986, p. 6). So, we define technology transfer as a type of information exchange.

Instead of thinking of technology transfer as an act or an event, we should consider technology transfer as a continuing *process*. For example, a private firm may develop a close relationship with a set of university researchers that is maintained over a period of several years and that fosters the exchange of technology. Technology transfer is a process because it happens over time. Some scholars have described stages or steps that occur in this process, and we shall use a conventional set of such stages (basic research, applied research, development, commercialization, and marketing) later in this chapter.

Technology transfer obviously requires the existence of a technology to transfer. In high microelectronics, from where do technological innovations come? One main source is *research universities,* defined as institutions of higher education whose main function is to conduct research and to train graduate students in how to conduct research (Rozenzweig, 1982). It is no accident that each of the main high-technology centers in the United States is located proximate to one or more research universities: Stanford University and Silicon Valley; Massachusetts Institute of Technology and Route 128; The University of North Carolina, North Carolina State University, Duke University, and Research Triangle, for example. In the United States, the key role of the research university in technology transfer in high-technology microelectronics has been understood only during the 1980s, with the result that many state governments now invest increased funds in research universities as a means of state economic development, which they hope will lead to the creation of jobs and taxable incomes through the spin-off of new high-technology companies (Fig. 6.1). Outside the United States, technological innovations in microelectronics are less likely to come from research universities (in many nations, universities do not conduct research or teach graduate students how to conduct research), and more likely to come from government research institutes and private firms.

High-technology industries are characterized by a rapid rate of change in the underlying technology. High-technology industries include telecommunications, pharmaceuticals, chemicals, aerospace, biotechnology, and microelectronics. Microelectronics and biotechnology are the highest of high technology, because the basic technology in these two industries is chang-

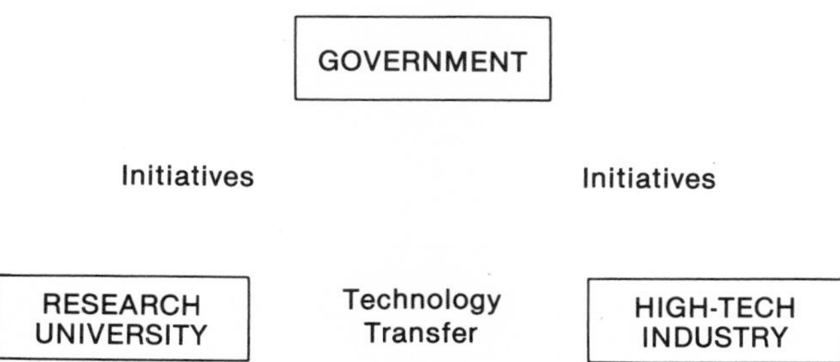

Figure 6.1 Role of government, research universities, and private industry in high-technology microelectronics.

ing most rapidly. This rapid rate of change means that a large number of technological innovations are generated each year. Each such innovation provides an opportunity for a new business venture, as an innovation is usually the entry ticket for a start-up firm into an industry.

The high rate of innovation explains why venture capitalists (the special financial institutions who invest in high-technology start-ups in exchange for an ownership share in the new firm) are especially interested in the microelectronics industry. This chapter centers on microelectronics because of its high rate of innovation, and because technology transfer is so important to the microelectronics industry.

TECHNOLOGY TRANSFER IN SILICON VALLEY

The technology transfer process has been pervasive in Silicon Valley, which represents a model being copied internationally. As mentioned previously, the conventional model of new product development consists of five stages: (1) basic research, (2) applied research, (3) development, (4) commercialization, and (5) marketing (Table 6.1). Basic research was mainly conducted in universities, and applied research was mostly undertaken by private corporations. In the 1970s, universities accounted for 60 percent of basic research conducted in the United States and industry accounted for 40 percent; today, these percentages are reversed (Larsen et al., 1986, p. 6). Corporations conduct applied and developmental research to create products. Corporations then commercialize their products and take the product to market.

Table 6.1 The Model of the Conventional Stages in the Technology Transfer (or new Product Development) Process

Stages	Who Carries it Out?	Definition
1. Basic research	Universities and government research labs	Original investigations conducted to advance scientific knowledge that do not have the specific objective of applying this knowledge to practical problems
2. Applied research	Private companies	Scientific investigations that are intended to solve practical problems
3. Development	Private companies	The process of putting a new idea into a form expected to meet the needs of potential users
4. Commercialization	Private companies	The process through which a technological innovation is converted into a commercial product to be sold by a company
5. Marketing	Private companies	The process by which a product is packaged, distributed, and sold by a company to its customers

A central feature of this new product development process is that separate individuals and departments are responsible for each stage, often with little communication between units. Consequently, a new product may be modified incorrectly and changes in the innovation's original design may cause problems at other stages of the process. These problems are particularly serious at the R&D/marketing interface in high-technology microelectronics companies, where a certain amount of disagreement and conflict often occur (Rogers, 1988).

The conventional staged model of new product development does not represent the reality of technology transfer in Silicon Valley. Market forces, the rapid rate of change in the underlying technology, and the spontaneous ways in which Silicon Valley grew, showed that the conventional conception of stages in technology transfer was inadequate. A more efficient and less formal system of technology transfer developed in Silicon Valley. The Silicon Valley model rests on a system of informal personal networks among technical people.

Personal Networks

Personal networks are composed of the people that an individual talks to about a particular topic. A personal network may include people that one meets through random contacts at work, school, and elsewhere. Personal networks, by serving as communication channels, affected technology transfer in Silicon Valley, which led to informal collaboration that resulted in (1) innovation and (2) the creation of spin-off companies. Thus, technology transfer á la Silicon Valley is informal, entrepreneurial, and rapid.

The Wagonwheel Bar in Mountain View, California is a famous Silicon Valley institution because so many noteworthy events have occurred there: Endless technology transfers, a start-up's business plan that was sketched out on a cocktail napkin, and meetings of entrepreneurs and venture capitalists. The Wagonwheel is located near Fairchild Semiconductor and from the early 1960s was a favorite after-work watering place for engineers. Innumerable deals were cut here, hirings, firings, and endless amounts of technical talk. A German electronics executive told one of the authors about his experience in the Wagonwheel Bar. The executive flew to Silicon Valley to help his company's engineers with a complicated problem they had encountered. Still stumped for a solution at the end of the day, he and his technical people retired to the Wagonwheel. One of his engineers invited an acquaintance to come over from an adjoining table to discuss their problem. The acquaintance yelled across the bar for three others to join them. Two hours later, the problem was solved, and the German executive flew home to Stuttgart the next morning. That's how technology transfer works in the Silicon Valley.

Personal networks in the Silicon Valley enable entrepreneurial individuals to create spin-off companies around a technological innovation. Only in a high-technology industry characterized by a rapidly expanding market and a high degree of agglomeration could technology transfer take place so effectively. In the high-technology microelectronics industry, a new product is often a modification of an existing product that may fill only a small market niche. In Silicon Valley, an R&D specialist must also be aware of a new product's potential market. The usual distinction between R&D and marketing often does not exist in Silicon Valley, especially in small start-up firms where everyone is *both* an R&D worker and a marketer (and perhaps a half-dozen other specialized jobs as well).

Engineers and other technical specialists in the microelectronics industry of Silicon Valley are more dedicated to the electronics industry than they are to the particular firm that employs them, evidenced by the high rate of job mobility, about 30 percent annually. Engineers readily change companies or start new firms where they expect to find more exciting or rewarding work.

The majority of the companies in Silicon Valley are very small; 70 percent of the 2,000 high-technology microelectronics manufacturing firms have fewer than 10 workers, and only 2 percent of the companies have more than 1,000 employees (Rogers and Larsen, 1984). Many of these new, small companies market a specific product with a narrow range of applications. The product is often developed for use by a few companies for a very specific application. Perhaps the product is a component, sold by the supplier to a major company. Employees of small start-up companies must rely on personal contracts with individuals in other companies to obtain technological information.

A typical Silicon Valley spin-off company illustrates how innovation and technology transfer occur. A start-up firm begins with (1) an inspiration, the creation of a new product or service that serves an unmet need; the entrepreneur then (2) forms a new business around this vision, and (3) forms a management team of several individuals, who (4) focus on new product development, and (5) on formation of a new business plan for the new company, which is then (6) used to attract venture capital.

For example, Apple Computer, Inc. was created when two young employees (Steve Wozniak and Steve Jobs) of established Silicon Valley firms (Hewlett-Packard and Atari, respectively) recognized the need for an already assembled microcomputer that users could program themselves. They created a marketable microcomputer in Jobs' parents' garage in Sunnyvale, and formed a team whose first task was to write a business plan and to secure venture capital for the new company.

This typical scenario includes two key components: (1) recognition of a market niche for the innovative product (neither Wozniak's nor Jobs' supervisor felt that the microcomputer represented a large enough market niche for Hewlett-Packard or Atari), and (2) the two entrepreneurs found business partners and secured capital through acquaintances in Silicon Valley. Thus, technology transfer from established companies to the start-up company is highly reliant on the entrepreneur's personal networks. Apple

Computer, Inc. represents a good example of the typical sequence of events in a start-up company.

Personal networks also provide role models for budding entrepreneurs. If an individual's co-workers create successful start-up companies, the individual may envision himself in such a role. A young engineer working side-by-side with someone who later becomes successful in such an entrepreneurial venture is likely to perceive such achievements as attainable. Through this comparative process, entrepreneurial fever rises in Silicon Valley.

The entrepreneurial spirit is contagious. It comes from being around people who start companies and bring new products to market, and retire as millionaires by age 40 (there are presently 15,000 self-made millionaires in Silicon Valley). Silicon Valley also contains numerous examples of people who started a company that then failed. These individuals then were considered even more valuable because of their increased experience in business matters. They may be rehired by their original employer at a higher salary. Since there is no great penalty for failure, perceived risk is lessened.

Research Universities

One crucial ingredient of technology transfer in Silicon Valley was Stanford University. Research universities are essential for technology transfer in the U.S. high-technology industry. There are 50 to 75 such research universities in the United States (Rozenzweig, 1982). Dave Packard and Bill Hewlett were students at Stanford University in the late 1930s: With a loan of $538 from their professor, Fred Terman, these two electrical engineers were able to launch Hewlett-Packard (H-P) in a garage in 1938. Today, H-P has 80,000 employees and is a major computer company.

What role do research universities play in technology transfer? Obviously, universities are important sources of research-based knowledge. They also provide a basis for personal contacts. Hewlett and Packard met as bench-warmers for the Stanford football team. University professors are important gatekeepers in placing their students in the high-technology marketplace. High-technology firms are especially eager to hire graduate students as R&D workers. Also professors may play a key role in redefining new product trends. Dr. Terman advised Hewlett and Packard on their first product, a variable oscillator based on Hewlett's Master's thesis.

The university/private industry interface is important since the university is an agglomerating agent. *Agglomeration* is the degree to which some quality is concentrated spatially in one area. The agglomeration of a technopolis occurs because the first new high-technology firms often spin-off from a research university, and, later on, newer firms spin-off from the previous spin-offs. Thus, a technopolis begins to sprout around the research university.

Agglomeration has several advantages for high-technology microelectronics because it (1) facilitates collaboration, (2) encourages the sharing of intellectual resources, and (3) provides the needed infrastructure for new high-technology companies to arise. Agglomeration occurs because the written word is seldom sufficient for the effective transfer of research-based knowledge into practice. The transfer of research-based knowledge may require a linking agent who acts as an interpersonal bridge. A *linking agent* is an individual who helps others engaged in problem-solving by connecting them to appropriate resources.

Critics of university/industry collaboration in microelectronics state that recent industry-funded research is concentrated on applications, and thus may take universities away from conducting basic research. Too much attention and funding is devoted to engineering research, critics say, and not enough to the arts and humanities. Some scholars also point out that industry-funded research sometimes cannot be published, or else publication must be delayed, yet a university's major function is to disseminate information.

Government Agencies

Government military spending played an important role in the growth of the Silicon Valley's microelectronics industry. The U.S. Department of Defense (and NASA) purchased semiconductors in the early 1960s; at that time, 80 percent of semiconductor sales were to the military. This funding helped the microelectronics industry grow when there was no immediate domestic consumer market. Today, military sales for the U.S. semiconductor industry are only 8 percent of total sales (although the dollar amount of such sales is much higher than in the 1960s).

Thus, in addition to the university/industry interface, high-technology transfer includes government agencies. Local, state, and federal government agencies today are involved in high-technology transfer since they define it as important for economic development and growth. Government initiatives may be involved in increasing industry university linkages, as the following section of this chapter shows.

Although government in the United States generally facilitates technology transfer, the federal government can also impede technology transfer. FBI and U.S. Customs agents try to prevent the sale and shipment of advanced technologies to the Soviet Union or to third party vendors who might transfer advanced technologies to the Soviet Union. Direct sales of advanced technologies to the U.S.S.R. by U.S. manufacturing firms are expressly prohibited under U.S. law.

Numerous microelectronics companies complain about these technology transfer restrictions. A main complaint is that efforts to impede the transfer of advanced technology are fruitless, and hurt business. A highly secret chip design may become common knowledge in the international semiconductor community within months of its first sale. U.S. firms may lose a certain competitive advantage due to delays caused by the inspections imposed to enforce the "technology slippage" laws.

Competing microelectronics firms also seek to impede technology transfer. The main basis of competition as technological innovation means that to develop new products a microelectronics company must protect its R&D activities from competitors. Intelligence and counterintelligence activities are pursued by every major electronics company in Silicon Valley. In this case, the agglomeration of the microelectronics industry is a disadvantage, as it makes it especially difficult to prevent technology transfer.

To obtain knowledge about a competitor's chip design, a company may conduct "reverse engineering," the disassembly of a competitor's semiconductor chip to determine how it was designed and produced. To prevent reverse engineering, a competitor may do "potting," the addition of superfluous details to a computer chip to disguise its true nature. Activities like potting can only partially slow down technology transfer.

One company may hire a key R&D worker from a competitor. After 6 months or so, the original employer may rehire their R&D worker (thus acquiring everything that he has learned at the competition). High-technology companies also employ "moles," individuals who work for another company to obtain technical information for their original employer. Moles may draw two salaries, one from the original company they worked for, and one from the company on which they are spying.

These elaborate attempts at impeding, or accelerating, technology transfer are all affected by the highly informal nature of personal networks à la Silicon Valley. A 10-minute conversation at the Wagonwheel Bar with a well-placed employee of a competing company can overcome months of reverse engineering or of potting. Technology transfer is very difficult to prevent, on the occasions when we try to do so.

TECHNOLOGY TRANSFER IN JAPAN

An extreme example of government initiatives increasing university-private industry agglomeration is Tsukuba Science City in Japan. In 1963, the Japanese Cabinet designated Tsukuba, an agricultural town about 35 miles north of Tokyo, as the site for Tsukuba Science City. Over the next 17 years, 43 research institutes and Tsukuba University constructed their facilities in the area (Bloom and Asano, 1981), and today Tsukuba includes 6,500 government R&D workers (plus 500 R&D employees of private firms), representing one-third of the nation's research personnel and 50 percent of Japan's national R&D budget.

Tsukuba Science City represents an investment of over $5 billion in public funds.[1] The city was constructed to help relieve congestion in Tokyo and to create a site for construction of modern research facilities. A large number of government research institutions in Tokyo were in desperate need of modern facilities if Japan were to continue its rapid rate of economic development (Bloom and Asano, 1981). Tsukuba University was completely remodeled in an attempt to make it more democratic and allow undergraduate and graduate students the chance to get involved in research. The university, by deviating from traditional Japanese university policies, hopes to foster the innovative abilities many observers have felt were lacking in Japan (Anderson, 1984, p. 365).

Tsukuba Science City is an attempt to plan a "Silicon Valley," to create high-technology agglomeration using Tsukuba University and the government research institutes as the core of an emerging technopolis. Tsukuba has attracted a number of large, government-funded research projects and will be the focal point of technological development in Japan for decades to come (Bloom and Asano, 1981).

Unfortunately, the planned nature of the city has made it rather unlivable by the standards of most Japanese. Tsukuba Science City has one of the highest suicide rates in Japan, and the "Tsukuba Syndrome" of skin rash, diarrhea, and other minor health problems are common among Tsukuba residents. Although Tsukuba has been successful at attracting some high-technology firms, there have been very few spin-off companies a la Silicon Valley.

One Japanese response to America's lead in microelectronics was the creation of the Fifth-Generation Computer Project in 1981. The objective of the collaborative R&D project was to create a new breed of computers that are much more humanlike in their functioning, by utilizing recent research in artificial intelligence and in expert systems. The Fifth-Generation Computer Project is carried out by an R&D consortium, funded at $400 million over 10 years, whose members include government agencies and the leading computer companies. Each member of the consortium contributes funds and its brightest computer engineers under 35 years of age. One goal of the project is to foster a new generation of young computer engineers in Japan.

The Fifth-Generation Computer Project is a government-initiated collaborative R&D project that brings otherwise competing firms together into a form of limited cooperation. The ability of MITI to persuade arch-rival firms to join collaborative ventures has been nicknamed "Japan Inc." Initially, U.S. electronics companies complained that Japan Inc. gave their Japanese counterparts an unfair advantage, a so-called sloping playing field. Soon, however, U.S. microelectronics companies responded by forming their own collaborative R&D consortia (as we detail in a later section).

Japanese Personal Networks

In Japan, a company's employees spend a great deal of personal time together. After work, groups of work associates go to restaurants and bars to drink, eat, and talk about company business. Much sharing of information occurs via *intra*organizational communication. Conversely, Silicon

Valley employees visit certain bars to discuss technical matters with each other, leading to a high level of *inter*organizational communication. So American employees in Silicon Valley companies display a high degree of loyalty to their *industry,* whereas Japanese employees have a higher degree to their *company.* The closeness of employees in a Japanese microelectronics company, partly due to lifetime employment and company housing, helps bridge the R&D/marketing interface involved in technology transfer.

Initiation Versus Implementation

One of the most important decisions in any high-technology company, especially a semiconductor firm, is the decision to begin producing a new product. A new semiconductor chip ordinarily requires that a company obtain capital for new plant and equipment, additional or different personnel, assign new tasks for marketing and other units in the firm, and requires major changes for suppliers and buyers. In short, the production of a new semiconductor chip is a major decision, usually made only a few times each year by large microelectronics firms.

In the early 1980s, we asked the director of engineering at Toshiba Semiconductor Division to recall the nature of his company's last decision to make a new product. This director stated that this particular decision process began with a lengthy meeting of some 30 Toshiba officials. The meeting's outcome was to decide to begin the new product process with a *ringesii,* a document stating the main conclusion of the meeting, in this case: "Toshiba Semiconductor shall produce a new semiconductor chip, the TS-40004." A junior official was then placed in charge of getting the signature (actually a personal stamp called an "*inkan*") of each official who would be involved in carrying out the decision. Getting all of the necessary stamps on the *ringesii* required several months, as each special provision added by an official to the *ringesii* meant that all of the previous signatories had to re-stamp the *ringesii.*

Finally, all 30 or so of the required signatures were obtained: R&D, marketing, manufacturing, capital (supplied by a large Japanese bank in the same business group as Toshiba), and certain buyers (such as an automobile company belonging to Toshiba's business group) that agreed to purchase the new chip. This lengthy process insured a high degree of consensus, thorough planning, and much anticipation of possible problems that might arise in implementing the decision to make the new semiconductor.

In a Silicon Valley semiconductor company (the U.S. counterpart of Toshiba Semiconductor), this initiation phase of the new product decision process would be made in an hour-long meeting, and then its implementation would begin in the afternoon. When we pointed out this cultural difference to the Toshiba director, he said: "In Japan, we take months to plan a major decision, and then implement it in an hour after lunch."

Undoubtedly there is a trade-off between the time and effort spent on

(1) *initiation,* the information gathering, conceptualizing, and planning for an innovation leading up to a decision, versus (2) *implementation,* the events, actions, and decisions involved in putting an innovation–decision into use (Rogers, 1983, p. 363). It may be noteworthy that the R&D/marketing interface is much less conflictual in Japanese high-technology microelectronics firms than it is in the United States. One reason may be the greater attention to planning and to the anticipation of future problems.

COLLABORATIVE R&D IN THE UNITED STATES

In the late 1970s and early 1980s, the U.S. microelectronics industry was characterized by dog-eat-dog competition (Rogers and Larsen, 1984). This belief in free market forces as a means to make decisions affecting the industry (Adam Smith's "invisible hand") changed during the 1980s in the face of foreign competition, mainly from Japan. Within a few years, a major value shift occurred from pure competition to some limited forms of collaboration, especially in R&D activities, in the U.S. microelectronics industry.

Rise of the Microelectronics and Computer Technology Corporation

The main symbol of this value change is the Microelectronics and Computer Technology Corporation (MCC), an R&D consortium located in Austin, Texas. The chief event leading to formation of the MCC in 1982 was the 1981 announcement of the Japanese Fifth-Generation Computer Projects, formed by MITI, Nippon Telephone and Telegraph, and the seven largest Japanese electronics companies. Previously, in the 1970s, MITI and five large electronics companies had formed the VLSI (Very Large Scale Integration) Project, which resulted in over a hundred patented innovations and which contributed to worldwide Japanese dominance in semiconductor memory chips. The basic strategy in both the VLSI Project and the Fifth-Generation Computer Project was for otherwise-competing electronics companies to cooperate with MITI and other government units in the founding and conduct of an R&D consortium.

The MCC was formed to beat the Japanese electronics industry at its own game (Gibson and Rogers, 1988). The MCC was founded by William C. Norris, Chairman of Control Data Corporation, a mainframe computer company headquartered in Minneapolis. Norris invited the top executives of 15 large U.S. computer and semiconductor companies to a February 1982 meeting in Orlando, Florida, at which it was decided to form the MCC. Ten companies originally became shareholders in the MCC, a number that grew to 20 by 1988. Each shareholder company annually contributes several million dollars to the MCC (the U.S. Department of Defense also has made large research grants to the MCC, but is not a member), and thus has a say in the research directions that are pursued by the R&D consortium.

Shortly after the MCC was launched in 1982, Admiral Bobby Ray Inman, the former Deputy Director of the Central Intelligence Agency, was appointed Chairman of the Board, President, and Chief Executive Officer of the MCC. Inman and the MCC agreed that he needed such absolute authority to handle the disputes that would likely arise among the MCC shareholder companies.

William G. Ouchi (1984, pp. 10–13) argues that an interdependent, collaborative form of industrial organization, called the "M-Form" organization by Ouchi ("M" for Minneapolis, the place in the United States where such an M-Form spirit is especially strong), must be adopted by U.S. companies if they are to compete effectively with their Japanese counterparts. Obviously, the MCC represents just such an M-Form organization.

At the time of its founding, the legality of the MCC regarding antitrust regulations was not clear, and this uncertainty served as a barrier to the participation of major U.S. electronics firms, who feared government regulation. On December 27, 1982, the U.S. Department of Justice gave a "yellow light" to the MCC, stating that it would not be prosecuted for antitrust violation at that time. Later, as a result of lobbying by the MCC and its shareholder companies, the National Cooperative Research Act was passed by the U.S. Congress in October 1984. This new law clarified antitrust regulations, so as to permit R&D consortia like the MCC. By 1988, more than 80 R&D consortia had been organized in the United States.

Technology Transfer and R&D Consortia

R&D consortia pose complicated problems for technology transfer from the consortium to its shareholder companies. The collaborative R&D center is usually located on the campus of a major research university; the MCC is headquartered on a 20-acre tract in the Balcones Research Park of the University of Texas at Austin. In fact, the offer of this land, plus a $22.5 million building for the MCC headquarters, was an important part of the $62.5 million Texas incentive that attracted the MCC to Austin, rather than to one of 56 other competing cities. But obviously a university location means that an R&D consortium cannot always be geographically close to most of its shareholder companies.

Each company contributes a substantial portion of its corporate R&D funds toward the annual budget of the consortium to which it belongs. In return, it expects to receive at least an equal value in the form of useful technology resulting from the R&D investment. The nature of the research carried out by an R&D consortium like the MCC must represent consensual decisions by the shareholder companies. Therefore, the research topics deal with general problems of wide interest that it is hoped will lead to technological innovations potentially applicable to each of the consortium's member companies.

In addition to contributing funds to the R&D consortium, each shareholder is expected to assign a number of its own research employees to work at the consortium. In the case of the MCC, some 100 or so of the 500 R&D employees in 1988 were seconded to Austin by the 20-member corporations. Such company researchers-on-loan are expected to play an important role in technology transfer, both while on their 1- or 2-year assignments at the MCC, and after returning to their employer's R&D laboratory.

Technology transfer is also orchestrated at two higher levels in the case of the MCC. Admiral Inman realized from the beginning that if effective technology transfer did not occur, the MCC would be doomed, so he planned for it very thoroughly. The second level of MCC technology transfer includes managers at member companies who are usually in charge of a particular technology project at their company. They make frequent trips to the MCC, typically monthly, to plan the consortium's research activities, monitor research progress, and then participate in the decision as to when a technological innovation is ready for official release by the MCC and subsequent transfer to the shareholder companies for implementation.

Finally, technology transfer from the MCC also occurs at what the microelectronics industry calls the "tall timber" level: That of a shareholder company's vice-president who is designated by his or her company as their representative to the MCC policy-making council. At this level, a decision might be made for the MCC to launch a new research program. For example, in 1987, the MCC decided to begin a research program on superconductivity.

The MCC is too young for it to have produced very many technological innovations, so its track record of technology transfer is yet to be written. It seems that software technology (for example, a computer software program) is more difficult to transfer than hardware technology. Future research is necessary to understand better the technology transfer process from R&D consortia (1) to their shareholder companies and (2) to others (for example, the MCC will sell the rights to a technological innovation to any buyer 3 years after the innovation's release by the MCC).

To date, only two entrepreneurial spin-offs by departing employees from the MCC have occurred, so little of the Silicon Valley form of entrepreneurial technology transfer has occurred to date. Because the MCC's shareholders have 3-year development rights to the technological innovations flowing from the consortium, potential spin-offs may be more likely to emanate from the distant corporate headquarters of the shareholders, rather than in Austin (Farley and Glickman, 1986). However, the Austin area has a considerable number of high-technology spin-offs from local microelectronics companies (Tracor Inc. is the "mother-hen" in many such cases), and so the MCC may transfer its technology via the entrepreneurial route in future years (Smilor et al., 1988).

One can imagine the special complexities of technology transfer in the case of a collaborative R&D consortium. Each shareholder company in the consortium is competing with the other shareholders in every sense except their collaboration in conducting joint R&D. Consequently, there are competitive pressures on each consortium member company to utilize the technological innovations flowing from the consortium's R&D activities. Whether such competitive forces on the shareholder companies of an R&D consortium result in more (or less) rapid technology transfer than in the case of R&D in the company remains to be seen.

Social Impacts of the MCC

One of the unanticipated impacts of the MCC's 1983 decision to locate in Austin was an increasing agglomeration of high-technology microelectronics in this university city and state capital. Before the MCC, Austin was already becoming a technopolis: Local high-technology employment was about 30,000 (compared with 250,000 in Silicon Valley). The main high-technology companies were Tracor Inc., founded in 1955 as a spin-off from the University of Texas, and local production facilities of Texas Instruments, IBM, Control Data Corporation, Motorola, Data General, Advanced Micro Devices, Rolm, Tandem, and Schlumberger. Following the 1983 MCC decision, which greatly symbolized Austin's role as a high-technology center in the United States, Lockheed's Software R&D operations moved from Northern California, Motorola made a major expansion in Austin, and 3M moved its R&D division from Minneapolis.

In the last three cases, Lockheed, Motorola, and 3M are MCC shareholder companies who wished to move their R&D activities as close as possible to the MCC to facilitate technology transfer from the MCC. Hence, the contribution of the MCC to high-technology agglomeration in Austin was much more than just adding several hundred R&D employees of the MCC. Within the first 2 years after the MCC came to Austin, about 6,000 high-technology workers had been added to the city's workforce, most of whom were employeed by 3M, Lockheed, and Motorola, and many of whom were R&D workers. In microelectronics companies, R&D workers are much more likely to spin-off new start-ups than are production engineers (who were most numerous in pre-MCC Austin).

The high-technology agglomeration in Austin in the mid-1980s set off a spectacular housing and business boom. In 1983, the average price of a house in Austin was $88,464; 2 years later, this figure was $107,000, an increase of 21 percent. From 1983 to 1985, 12 large office buildings were constructed in downtown Austin, more than doubling the amount of office space, resulting in an office vacancy rate of 40 percent (the highest in the nation). While this construction was underway, Austin's skyline was so changed that local wags claimed that the building crane had become the new state bird of Texas. The housing and building boom (in which land values increased about 50 percent in 2 years) was followed, after 1986, by a bust in which housing prices settled back toward their pre-MCC levels.

Although the MCC's spin-off track record in Austin is limited to date,

Austin managed to land another, larger collaborative R&D center in early 1988. Sematech (Semiconductor Manufacturing and Technology Institute) is a consortium of 13 shareholder companies that recently decided to locate its headquarters in Austin. The consortium has a budget of $250 million (with $100 million promised from the federal government). It is expected to employ 800 people and create an estimated 2,100 jobs.

Evidently, the presence of the MCC in Austin helped persuade Sematech to locate nearby, as seven of the members of Sematech were already members of MCC. In fact, MCC sources tipped off Texas leaders in May 1987 that Sematech was coming, thus giving state government leaders a headstart on planning their campaign. The Austin high-technology agglomeration has centered around R&D consortia, instead of just microelectronics companies, and so may evolve differently.

LESSONS LEARNED

Technology transfer in high-technnology microelectronics essentially consists of the communication of information or knowledge in an industry characterized by a rapid rate of change in the underlying technology. In the microelectronics industry, this process has been rapid due to the personal networks typified by the Silicon Valley technopolis. Research universities generally facilitate this process by agglomerating researchers and linking agents with similar technical and entrepreneurial interests.

To compete with the United States, Japanese bureaucrats found it necessary to facilitate technology transfer by forming collaborative R&D projects (such as the Fifth-Generation Computer Project). The U.S. government responded in kind by passing legislation permitting R&D consortia, and private firms formed over 80 such R&D consortia (the MCC is the first and most prominent example).

What lessons have we learned about technology transfer from the major events and investigations in microelectronics during the 1980s?

1. *Governments play a key role in high-technology transfer by (1) direct purchases, (2) planning collaborative R&D activities, and (3) making research grants.* In its early years (the 1960s), the semiconductor industry relied heavily on military purchases. The North Carolina and Texas state governments spent considerable sums of money to attract high-technology investments. The Japanese government has created technopolii to spur collaborative R&D and to create the conditions for agglomeration.

2. *The research university or (in many nations) government-sponsored research institutes are "centers of excellence," and an important source of technological innovations.* In the microelectronics industry, being on the cutting edge with new technological products is essential for effective competition, and for survival. Centers of excellence are also important sources of personal networks and of new employees for a high-technology firm. High quality research personnel are a high-technology company's most

valuable resource. The research personnel must be able to move from the laboratory to private firms to develop the marketplace expertise required to launch a start-up firm (Miller and Cote, 1985).

3. *Difficulties are encountered in attempts to impede technology transfer under certain conditions.* U.S. government efforts to stop the export of technology to the Soviet Union have not been very effective. Major microelectronics firms are engaged in a constant intelligence war with one another, trying to discover each other's technological innovations.

4. *Collaborative R&D may be essential for survival in the highly competitive microelectronics industry.* The collaborative relationship in its numerous forms has become a dominant type of interorganizational relationship in the 1980s. Collaboration, where neither partner has ownership over the other and cannot give orders to the other, is replacing pure competition in the microelectronics industry (and in similar industries). Japan set off the wave of cooperation among U.S. industries, but now U.S. firms cooperate extensively with each other in R&D and even, in some cases, with Japanese and other internationally based firms.

5. *Everyone is trying to be dealt into the high-technology microelectronics game.* Every state in the United States is trying to establish one or more high-technology centers or technopolii. Many industrial nations in the world are competing to become leaders in microelectronics. Unfortunately, this "tragedy of the commons"[2] may result in an overemphasis on high-technological economic development. Not every state can have a "Silicon Valley," and not every nation can be the leader in worldwide microelectronics competition. Experience has shown that many of these efforts to attract high-technology industries are misguided and have led to failure (Miller and Cote, 1985).

How many "Silicon Valleys" can survive and grow in the decades ahead? How many collaborative R&D centers can the U.S. microelectronics industry support? How long can the current wave of cooperation continue before technological innovation is stymied and markets are sated? The answers to these and other questions will be found in a continuing watch over technology transfer here and abroad.

NOTES

1. Much of this $5 billion was financed by the sale of very high-priced office buildings and land in Tokyo, where the various institutes had been.
2. The "tragedy of the commons" is a situation in which individuals sharing a common resource each decide to use an additional increment of the resource, leading the system to break down. Unfortunately, when each member of a system slightly increases their use of a resource, the system is often overwhelmed as the resources are overconsumed. The classic example is the case of the medieval commons pasture in which each shepherd using the common grazing area increased his herd by one sheep, resulting in overgrazing and eventual destruction of the commons. Notice that each shepherd is rationally pursuing his individual goal, but thus the system is ruined.

REFERENCES

Anderson, A. M. (1984). *Science and Technology in Japan,* Harlow, U.K.: Longman.

Bloom, J. L., & Asano, S. (1981). "Tsukuba Science City: Japan tries planned innovation," *Science,* 212: 1239–1247.

Eveland, J. D. (1986). "Diffusion, technology transfer, and implementation: Thinking and talking about change," *Knowledge: Creation, Diffusion, Utilization,* 8(2): 303–324.

Farley, J., and Glickman, J. (1986). "R&D as an economic development strategy: The Microelectronics and Computer Technology Corporation comes to Austin, Texas," *Journal of the American Planning Association,* 52: 407–418.

Gibson, D. V., and Rogers, E. M. (1988). The MCC comes to Texas, in F. Williams (ed.), *Measuring the Information Society: The Texas Studies.* Newbury Park, Calif.: Sage.

Larsen, J. K., Wigand, R. T., and Rogers, E. M. (1986). *Industry–university technology transfer in microelectronics,* Los Altos, Calif.: Cognos Associates, Report to the National Science Foundation.

Miller, R., and Cote, M. (1985). "Growing the next Silicon Valley," *Harvard Business Review,* 63(4): 114–123.

Ouchi, W. G. (1984). *The M-Form society: How American teamwork can recapture the competitive edge,* Reading, Mass.: Addison-Wesley.

Rogers, E. M. (1983). *Diffusion of Innovations,* New York: Free Press.

Rogers, E. M. (1988). *The R&D/marketing Interface in the Technological Innovation Process.* Paper presented at the Symposium on Managing the R&D/Marketing Interface in the Telecommunications Industry, University of Southern California.

Rogers, E. M., and Larsen, J. K. (1984). *Silicon Valley Fever: Growth of High-technology Culture,* New York: Basic Books.

Rozenzweig, R. M. (1982). *The Research Universities and their Patrons,* Berkeley: University of California Press.

Schon, D. A. (1971). *Beyond the Stable State,* New York: Norton.

Smilor, R. W., Kozmetsky, G., and Gibson, D. V. (eds.). (1988). *Technopolis: Technology and Economic Development in the Modern City State,* Boston: Ballinger.

7

Technology Transfer in Strategic Alliances: Competitive Collaboration and Organizational Learning

VLADIMIR PUCIK

TECHNOLOGY TRANSFERS AND COMPETITIVE COLLABORATION

In the late 1980s, one of the striking patterns in global competition was the rapidly growing number of interfirm cross-border coalitions. While such ventures are intrinsically difficult to manage (Killing, 1983), many experts argue that as business risks soar and competition grows more severe, alliances among firms from different countries are becoming one of the key strategic responses to the emerging patterns of competition: companies are expected to rely on international alliances with increasing frequency (Perlmutter and Heenan, 1986; Harrigan, 1984; Ohmae, 1985).

Many of the new alliances, whether equity joint ventures or nonequity deals, involve some aspect of technology transfer. In contrast to traditional joint ventures or licensing arrangements—in which technology was often transferred from a large multinational to a small local partner who played only a marginal role in the execution of the global strategy pursued by the multinational firm—the new type of alliances often involves an intensive technological cooperation beyond the scope of the local market.

Strategic alliances involving transfer of technology can take many forms: technical exchange and cross-licensing, coproduction and marketing agreements, joint product development programs, or stand-alone joint-venture firms with equity distributed among the partners (Root, 1988). Although the specific deals vary in motivation, scope, and duration, they all involve leveraging the current competitive advantage of the collaborating firms. Some partnerships combine the superior design technology of one of the partners with the efficient manufacturing of the other partner to outsourcing of product development using local engineering capacity. Partners join to diversify the risks inherent in developing new technologies, or to take advantage of the complementary nature of each partner's development skills.

The new partnerships can also provide essential economies of scale in research and development (R&D) to withstand a dominant competitor that neither partner could challenge individually (Contractor and Lorange, 1988; Hergert and Morris, 1988; Porter and Fuller, 1986).

An equally important element in the formation of new alliances is the increasing speed of technological change, which makes it imperative to reap the benefits from new technology in a relatively short time, before it becomes obsolete (Mowery, 1988). Alliances and partnerships can serve as important conduits for diffusion of the new technology that balances the need to control its dispersion with the needs of rapid commercialization. A transnational transfer of technology from the firm that developed the new technology to other international users in return for licensing fees, products, or equity is a major component in such collaborative ventures.

Yet another motivation for joining forces, especially in ventures involving Western multinationals and companies located in newly industrialized countries (NICs), is the desire of multinational corporations (MNCs) to exploit existing technological advantages to penetrate previously closed markets and/or to source low-cost products to its other markets. The principal benefit perceived by NIC firms is access to technology that is otherwise not available in the open market or too expensive to acquire on a stand-alone basis. In this sense, technology transfer is the main point of leverage as well as the objective of the whole venture.

Paradoxically, all of these strategic alliances built around technology transfer are growing in number at the same time as it is increasingly recognized that the past record of such alliances is spotty at best (Pucik, 1988; Reich and Mankin, 1986). In particular, when we consider the history of alliances between Western firms and companies in Japan in the last three decades, there seems to be plenty of evidence that, in the long run, the competitive advantage of many Western firms was more often eroded than strengthened by such alliances (Abegglen and Stalk, 1985; Wright, 1979).

As other Pacific Rim nations gain in economic stature, similar questions are now being raised about the long-term consequences of technology transfer to, for example, Korean and Taiwanese manufacturers. Who will gain and who will lose from such partnerships? The traditional classification of alliances, focusing mainly on their legal forms, does not say much about what is probably the most important variable affecting the long-term outcome of such new alliances, namely, their competitive context. A coalition between partners with complementary strategic interests may evolve in a fashion dramatically different from an alliance between existing or potential competitors. To analyze the impact of competitive conditions on technology transfer strategies, a fresh analytical framework may be necessary.

Of foremost importance is the strategic intent behind the formation of the new partnerships. The underlying assumption in much of the previous research on technology transfer was the desirability of a win/win outcome shared by partners in the alliance. However, such an assumption may not realistically reflect the current competitive environment. In contrast to traditional single-market joint ventures between Western multinationals and much smaller firms in developing countries, the new technological alliances are often formed by partners of comparable strength whose activities are often global and who are or may become direct competitors (Contractor and Lorange, 1988). However, the rapid increase in international collaboration among potential competitors does not necessarily lead to the heralded dawn of a new cooperative era in the global economy (Perlmutter and Heenan, 1986; Ohmae, 1985).

The change from competitive rivalry to collaboration is often merely a tactical adjustment aimed at specific market conditions. Many of these new partnerships should be viewed as hidden substitutes for market competition, not its dissipation. The objective is similar: attaining a position of global leadership through internalization of key value-added competencies. The possibility of a potential competitive relationship between partners distinguishes strategic alliances that involve *competitive collaboration* from more traditional complementary ventures (Hamel and Prahalad, 1988).

The strategic and managerial implications of the two types of alliances are fundamentally different. In a truly cooperative relationship, the underlying assumption is the feasibility (and desirability) of long-term win/win outcomes. In the partnerships that involve competitive collaboration, the strategic intent of ultimate dominance makes the long-term win/win outcome highly unlikely. This does not mean that all partnerships that involve transfer of technology are always competitive in nature. However, many of them are, especially in a long-term dynamic context. An expectation of quasi-permanent technological leadership is unrealistic. The relative endowment of resources, skills, and competencies, and the sources of bargaining power can change over time, especially if one of the partners in the technology exchange is determined to come out on top.

COMPETITIVE COLLABORATION AND INVISIBLE ASSETS

Many firms involved in technology transfers are struggling with a fundamental paradox: market forces push them into new alliances, while their capability to manage such relationships may not be well developed. Two key factors hinder an effective monitoring and control of technology transfers: a lack of attention to the strategic intent of partners in the technology transfer, and a false assumption about the nature of competencies involved in the transaction.

A misreading of the partner's strategic intent may lead to an underestimation of their ability and/or desire to move up on the learning curve (Hamel and Prahalad, 1988). This may not only negatively influence the choice of a partner, but also obscure the need for monitoring the partner's behavior and the urgency of developing alternative sources of leverage. Competitive collaboration cannot be managed, unless the existing and future competitive aspects of the relationship between the partners are taken into consideration. Aligning the technology transfer strategies with the dynamic patterns of competitive behavior is the first precondition of their successful execution.

The logic of strategic intent provides for the structure of the partnership. The nature of the exchange relationship influences the process. The exchanges between partners can be distinguished as those leveraging *resources* and those leveraging *competencies*. The typical licensing deals, technical agreements, joint development programs (pooling of resources), and coproduction or codistribution (resource economies of scale) are examples of alliances that focus primarily on resource leverage. Many traditional technology transfer deals were conceived and executed as some form of resource exchange (e.g., technical know-how in return for licensing fees and royalties).

In contrast, competencies are fundamentally information-based invisible assets (Itami, 1987) that cannot be readily purchased and their market value is difficult to ascertain. Examples are knowledge of the market, manufacturing process capability, or speed of new product development. Invisible assets are embodied in people within the organization. These assets represent a tacit knowledge that is difficult to understand and that can only be appropriated over time, if at all (Teece, 1986). Accumulation of invisible assets through operational experience is seen as the foundation for a sustainable competitive advantage (Itami, 1987), as the traditional sources of leverage (e.g., economies of scale, low factor cost, specific technology) are not sustainable in the new global business environment.

Invisible assets are closely linked to information, its stock as well as its flow. To increase invisible assets or competencies is to increase the amount of information available in the firm as well as its capacity to handle the information. Invisible assets can be accumulated through an explicit action, such as training, or implicitly as a by-product of daily operations (Itami, 1987). Using the transfer of technology as a point of leverage, competencies in different parts of a value chain can be combined to achieve a distinct competitive edge in the market, or at least to protect the existing market position against an aggressive rival.

Technology transfer that leverage competencies usually take the form of an other equipment manufacturer (OEM) supply agreement (superior manufacturing process) or a joint venture aimed at a specific market (superior market access); but, in principle, most cases of technology transfer involve the contribution and leverage of both resources and competencies. However, the bargaining process and the agreements regarding the transfer primarily address the issue of equitable resource exchange. The resources initially contributed into the operation usually have a specific market value, be it patents, equipment, land, labor, or money. Both the contribution and withdrawal of resources are explicit, and thus relatively simple to evaluate, monitor, and control

Usually, in the process of technology transfer, the firm transferring the technology expects compensation from the receiving firm in the form of licensing fees, royalties, and/or equity in the venture. The emphasis is placed on estimating the value of inputs into the alliance. The difficulties come with appraising and monitoring the value of outputs, such as competencies acquired through the technology transfer process. As benefits from the accumulation of new competencies are impossible to ascertain ahead of time, technology transfer agreements seldom provide for the sharing of such benefits. Instead, the emphasis is on reducing the potential competitive threat by legal restrictions and "noncompete" clauses aimed at limiting the strategic options available to the recipient of the transferred technology.

The key premise of successful technology transfer in the context of competitive collaboration is the assurance of a long-term competitive balance. Therefore, an outflow of technology must be complemented by an inflow of some other competencies. The accumulation of invisible assets must be mutual, otherwise the technology transfer is nothing more than a disguised divestiture of valuable corporate assets, often not even properly compensated. It is also important that the "transferor" can benefit from any technological improvement made by the "transferee." Where permitted by law, access to any improvement in technology can be stipulated in the contract. Even in such instances, however, the monitoring and enforcement of the agreement may be difficult (Mowery, 1988), as many of the technological improvements are very subtle and incremental in nature.

As the focus of competitive advantage is moving from resources to competencies (Itami, 1987; Prahalad and Doz, 1987), the attention to accumulation of competencies involved in technology transfers is imperative in all competitive configurations. In partnerships where the strategic intent of the partners is basically complementary, an insufficient accumulation of invisible assets may eventually erode the gains derived from the venture for both partners. The beneficiaries may be the other competitors, but the balance of the relationship between partners would not necessarily change. However, in the context of a competitive collaboration where competencies provide the critical leverage, the lack of attention to the accumulation of invisible assets will likely result in a loss of control over the direction of the alliance. It is for this reason that management processes that support accumulation and control of invisible assets are of such critical importance.

ORGANIZATIONAL LEARNING AND COMPETITIVE ADVANTAGE

When a firm is engaged in a technology transfer process in the context of competitive collaboration, its competitive advantage cannot be easily protected. As pointed out earlier, the distribution of benefits related to visible assets, such as new products or profits, is relatively easy to monitor and protect through administrative protocols and rules regarding the implementation of the technology transfer agreements. However, the asymmetric appropriation of invisible assets—which may lead to the acquisition of technological know-how outside of the partnership framework, or even to a competitive strategy targeted at the partner—cannot be easily detected.

The asymmetry results from the internal dynamics of the technology transfers. Benefits are appropriated unevenly due to differences in the *organizational learning capacity* of the partners. The firms that master new competencies faster than their partners will derive greater benefit from the technology exchange. Over time, asymmetrical learning may tip the competitive balance in the alliance. Yet, in the absence of a hostile strategic move, the losing firm is often unaware of its deteriorating bargaining position until it is too late to stop the slippage.

A good illustration of shifts in relative power in a competitive partnership is the reversal in the relationship between Japanese and Western firms in many industries over the last several decades. The asymmetrical distribution of benefits from technology transfers was the fundamental cause of such a reversal. Japanese firms first used access to technology through licensing or joint ventures to master new competencies. When no additional learning gains were to be made through continuation of the alliance, they moved quickly to apply the newly acquired knowledge to obtain sole control of the market in Japan. In the final step, they proceeded to penetrate markets previously dominated by the Western partners with their own superior products (Reich and Mankin, 1987).

Throughout the postwar period, Japanese companies purchased thousands of product and process technologies from the Western firms for what turned out to be rather modest fees. One factor responsible for the low payments was the well-coordinated bargaining within the framework of Japanese industrial policy (Johnson, 1982). The control over technology transfers exercised by the Japanese government until the mid-1970s made it difficult for Western partners to achieve bargaining power parity. A second factor, probably as important as the Japanese industrial policy, was the lack of appreciation among the Western firms of the benefits associated with a carefully planned accumulation of invisible assets.

Western licensors requested and received compensation for resources invested in the development of transferred technologies, but were not compensated for their weakened strategic position due to the change in the relative distribution of invisible assets, nor did they develop alternative strategies to protect their competitive edge. The list of companies that gave up more than they gained in licensing deals or in joint ventures with Japanese partners is long and is not limited to a single country or industry. This would clearly indicate a systematic problem rather than an error in judgment on the part of a particularly inept group of executives.

In case after case, the Western firms did not invest in learning the competencies necessary to succeed in the Japanese market. While some argue that in "technology-for-market-access" ventures the local partner is in a weaker bargaining position (Porter and Fuller, 1986), the gap in organizational learning skills can make the difference. Much of the imbalance in the appropriation of benefits from technology transfers was caused by the superior learning capabilities of the Japanese.

Many Japanese firms developed a systematic approach to organizational learning (Cole, 1985; Nonaka and Johansson, 1985). This approach involved more than an explicit rejection of the parochial "not-invented-here" syndrome. Japanese firms implemented control systems that encouraged the accumulation of invisible assets through an extensive horizontal and vertical information flow that supported a rapid diffusion of the know-how from technology transfer into the entire organization. A strategic planning process centered on the value of invisible assets, together with corresponding control systems and policies guiding the management of human resources at all levels and functions, constituted a vital part of such a learning infrastructure (Pucik, 1983).

In contrast, the accumulation of invisible assets was not a high priority for many Western firms. This did not happen by chance. The financial measurements and accounting systems of Western corporations are focused on visible assets. The logic behind traditional Western accounting standards favors measurements developed for the benefit of the external financial community (Johnson and Kaplan, 1987). However, these measures seldom provide management with sufficient information about the value and significance of invisible assets and organizational competencies. Invisible assets, such as experience regarding the utilization of the transferred technology, were not viewed as having "value." What could not be measured was consequently left unmanaged.

In alliances that may involve competitive collaboration, a firm's capacity to learn is the key to protecting its long-term competitive advantage. Because information on the accumulation of invisible assets by partners involved in a technology transfer is seldom available, or is at best imperfect, the focus of management's attention has to shift from monitoring the financial outcomes of technology transfer to the control of the exchange process. Managing organizational learning must be assigned the necessary priority at all levels of any organization engaged in technology transfers.

BARRIERS TO ORGANIZATIONAL LEARNING

Organizational learning is not a random process, but a carefully planned and executed set of policies and practices designed to enlarge the knowledge base of the organization. Preventing an asymmetry (or creating an asymmetry in one's favor) in organizational learning is a strategic requirement for firms engaged in competitive collaboration, when technology is transferred between competitors. Win/win outcomes so fashionable in academic literature are not likely to occur with one of the partners placed at a bargaining disadvantage. Not providing a coherent strategy for the control of invisible assets in a partnership is a sure formula for failure.

A systematic effort to reduce the organizational obstacles to learning

Table 7.1 Barriers to Organizational Learning in Strategic Alliances

Functional Areas	Principal Barriers
Strategic Planning	Short-term and static planning horizon No appreciation of incremental learning Strategic intent not comunicated Low priority of learning activities Fragmentation of the learning process
Human Resource Planning	Lack of involvement of the human resource function Insufficient lead-time for staffing decisions Resource-poor human resource strategy Surrendering control over the human resource function Staffing dependence on the partner
Management Development	Low quality of staff assigned to the alliance Lack of cross-cultural competence Unidirectional personnel transfer Career structure not conducive to learning Poor climate for transfer of knowledge
Control Systems	Responsibility for learning not clear Short-term performance measures Limited incentives for learning Tolerance of learning barriers Rewards not tied to global strategy

should shape the design of the strategic planning mechanism, organizational control systems, and human resource management policies. However, this strategic priority often remains unattended, buried under the pressure of daily operational concerns that leave in place a number of barriers to organizational learning. A number of such obstacles identified from research on Western joint ventures in Japan (Pucik, 1988) are listed in Table 7.1.

The obstacles to organizational learning, reviewed in greater detail below, are not limited to a specific organizational climate that can easily be changed. Rather, they result from a complex set of misplaced strategic priorities, unfocused organizational control systems, and inconsistent human resource management policies that, while often rational in the short term, may ultimately lead to a loss of control over the technological domain of the firm, if not to the loss of the entire business. Understanding the obstacles to learning is the first step in the process of restoring competitive balance in the technology transfer process.

BARRIERS TO LEARNING IN THE STRATEGIC PLANNING PROCESS

Short-term and Static Planning Horizon

Planning for technology transfer ventures is often driven by short-term objectives, such as improving current profit margins by cutting production costs through an OEM arrangement, or increasing returns on R&D investment, without consideration of long-term effects on the sustainability of the firm's competitive advantage. General Electric's (GE) recent withdrawal from the consumer electronics field was forced by a series of "correct" short-term decisions during the previous two decades that led to a transfer of critical product and process competencies from GE to its Japanese competitors. The logic behind many short-term decisions is based on an erroneous assumption that the existing balance of competencies in the alliance will not change with time and that the recipient of the technology will not learn faster than its investor.

No Appreciation of Incremental Learning

Frequently, the technology to be transferred is considered fixed and static, not likely to be substantially improved on by the technology recipient. Sharing such technology is viewed as profitable or at least costless and as posing no danger to the competitive position of the technology-originating firm. This strategy has a particular appeal in industries with short technology-development cycles, but it may lead to a dependency on "big bang" breakthroughs, in contrast to incremental innovation through operational experience. A number of technologies were transferred from Western firms to the Japanese, but monitoring the experience of Japanese users was thought to be of little value. By the time it became apparent that incremental innovation allowed the Japanese to catch up or even move ahead, the precious technological lead had already been eroded.

Strategic Context Not Communication Throughout the Firm

Many cooperative agreements that involve technology transfer take place in a highly complex competitive environment. Western top management often emphasizes the cooperative nature of the technology transfer, partly to set the right tone for the partnership, and partly to break down any resistance from those opposed to the cooperative strategy. While a cease-fire in an isolated battlefield does not necessarily mean a permanent cessation of hostilities, what is often not made clear are the boundaries of cooperation. During the implementation of the technology transfers agreement, a competitor with a well-developed capacity to absorb information can often gain valuable insights through inadvertent leaks by uninformed employees.

Low Priority Given to Learning Activities

Invisible assets are not free assets. Their procurement requires a commitment of resources, both financial and human. However, the traditional focus of business plans is on the utilization of and the return on tangible assets. The projected outcomes from technology transfer are scrutinized in terms of returns on equity invested, savings from pooled R&D, cost reductions from outsourcing components and products, and/or increases in sales from added distribution channels. In contrast, as discussed before, the commonly used financial planning systems cannot assign a financial value to the intangible outcomes. Learning activities that cannot be evaluated in financial terms are generally not funded.

Fragmentation of the Learning Process

In diversified and complex multinational firms, the stakes in technology transfer activities may differ by business unit and function. Each subunit has only a partial view of the exchange of competencies involved in the partnership. The perceptions of the potential value of the relationship may, therefore, differ as does the commitment to support competencies needed to defend the long-term competitive advantage. In decentralized firms with independent business units (e.g., strategic business units, SBUs), organization-wide learning activities have low priority in comparison to a business unit's immediate needs. The desirability of cooperation may easily be perceived differently among various parts of the organization depending on their level of involvement in the technology transfer strategy and their responsibility for its execution.

BARRIERS TO LEARNING IN HUMAN RESOURCE PLANNING

Lack of Involvement of Human Resource Function

The objective of the human resource function's participation in the planning of an alliance should be to gain understanding about the possible learning strategies and their long-term impact on the balance of power in the collaborative relationship. In the process of negotiating the technology transfer agreement, however, little effort is made to evaluate the learning capacity of the organization and to take the necessary steps to upgrade the learning skills and climate appropriate to the new competitive situation. Often, the human resource function does not play any role in the negotiation process or becomes involved only at a very late stage. The analysis of philosophies regarding the management of human resources and its implications for organizational learning are seldom a factor in the decision-making process.

Insufficient Lead Time for Staffing Decisions

When technology transfer leads to the creation of a new organization (e.g., a joint venture), decisions regarding the key staff to be dispatched to the partnership should be made well in advance of the commencement of the operations. All relevant future players can thus be involved in the negotiation process. Institutional memory about commitments and trade-offs breaks down when negotiators are replaced by implementators without continuity. Insufficient lead time also forces shortcuts in training for the managers assigned to the partnership. In general, everyone agrees with the idea of training, but many firms are reluctant to invest in the preparation of managers for the new venture until the outcome of the negotiations is clear; yet after the deal is signed, there is no time to train. As a result, what is won laboriously at the front end through long, arduous bargaining is often lost through the inability to control the implementation of the agreement.

Resource-poor Human Resource Strategy

As the transfer of technology is often driven by cost considerations, many Western firms are likely to economize on staff assigned to monitor the agreement. In particular, this tendency is quite visible when technology transfers involve the creation of a separate operating unit, such as a joint venture operation on foreign soil, where the costs of supporting expatriates seems prohibitive. Yet, while the expense of staffing a position in a foreign venture may indeed be substantial, economizing may preclude two substantial benefits derived from expatriate posts: improved control over the management process in the venture and ability to transfer skills from the venture to the home organization (Kobrin, 1988). Organizational learning often requires at least some slack resources. When an overextended expatriate management team just keeps on dousing fires, the last thing on an expatriate manager's mind is the transfer of know-how back to the parent company. Even if the venture is in the home country, short-term "excursions" to the joint venture will not do; long-term participation is essential. As GM learned at New United Motors Industries (NUMI), a videotape of innovative work practices is a far less efficient learning tool than a hands-on experience.

Surrendering Control of the Human Resource Function

The human resource function is seen as a cost burden, not as a powerful tool of control over the strategic direction of the collaborative venture. In particular, when the technology transfer involves an operation inside one partner's territory, responsibility for the human resource function is often delegated to that partner. In fact, the partner's familiarity with local labor market conditions is often a deciding factor in making a choice between a technology transfer arrangement and an investment in a wholly owned subsidiary. However, what is gained in lower cost of entry can be easily lost later on. The boundary between the partner's organization and the partnership operation becomes fuzzy and impossible to monitor. Valuable competence may leak without notice and without reciprocity.

Staffing Dependence on the Partner

When staffing is considered a cost rather than an investment, it is very tempting to go along with the partner's offer to assume the responsibility for staffing the new venture. Naturally, there is always great concern over the composition of the top management team. However, very little learning ever occurs in the board room; learning takes place in the laboratories, on the production floor, and in interactions with the customers. When personnel control is abdicated in favor of the partner, the logic of the learning process is obscured. The partner who controls positions critical to the accumulation of invisible assets also gains substantial leverage over the future strategy of the alliance. The supervision of human resource deployment enables the partner to control the patterns of organizational learning, and thus the distribution of benefits from the partnership. A learning asymmetry is likely to occur.

BARRIERS TO LEARNING IN MANAGEMENT DEVELOPMENT

Low Quality of Staff Assigned to Manage the Technology Transfer

When technology transfer between Western and Japanese firms was implemented through a joint venture, it was often the case that after an initial period of high visibility for the new alliance, management positions in the partnership became a dumping ground for sidetracked executives. The emphasis is on "making the deal," not on its implementation. The dispatched managers do not have the necessary learning skills; they are expected to "watch the books" only. Even if they gain new knowledge, they may lack the credibility to transfer effectively the know-how to the parent firm, especially if this involves challenging existing "sacred cows." The partners in the alliance are generally well aware of the low credibility level of these managers and do not hesitate to freeze them out of important decisions.

Lack of Cross-cultural Competence

Many managers and staff involved in collaborative ventures do not have sufficient intercultural skills (language competence, familiarity with partner's culture, etc.). Expatriates are dispatched to unfamiliar countries, such as Japan, with no or limited training at best, with the assumption that knowledge of the business should compensate for the lack of cultural understanding. While perfect language fluency may not be essential, the ability to understand the basic flow of a business conversation and to interact informally with the customers and employees should be the minimum prerequisite for an international assignment. This is important for an expatriate's effectiveness even in a wholly owned foreign affiliate (Tung, 1984). The price to pay for the lack of cross-cultural skills in a competitive collaboration may be high: both an inability to learn and inability to control.

Unidirectional Personnel Transfer

One of the most effective means of learning is through temporary personnel exchange between the partners. This exchange is often asymmetrical, however, especially when the partnership takes the form of a joint venture. While the flow of personnel from the Western joint ventures in Japan often includes staff temporarily seconded from the Japanese parent, training assignments in the opposite direction are infrequent (Pucik, 1988). Even when transfer of personnel into the joint venture occurs on a regular basis, it is seldom for the purpose of skills acquisition. Rather, staff is transferred either to control or manage the joint venture or to serve as a conduit for transferring know-how into the venture. It is often felt that there is no need to seek (and thus expend resources on) knowledge already possessed in the joint venture. Yet, by gaining independent know-how, a firm can avoid becoming hostage to the uncertain future of the partnership.

Career Structure not Conducive to Learning

Personnel exchange can have a positive impact on the amount of accrued knowledge only if administered in a consistent and planned fashion over time. The amount of time spent learning and transferring know-how is the critical constraint. An effective transfer of know-how requires a long-term commitment of qualified personnel, which clashes with expectations of fast mobility among the most promising executives. While many managers, on a personal basis, may benefit even from a relatively short exposure to the collaborative venture, a single short-term assignment—especially when it comes relatively late in an executive's career—will not do much for the accumulation of invisible assets in the rest of the organization. Also, unless the firm posts returnees from the partnership ventures into positions where the acquired know-how can be effectively used and disseminated, learning will not occur.

Poor Climate for Transfer of Knowledge

A large number of critical invisible assets are embedded in the staff involved in the technology transfer. To what degree these assets are shared with the rest of the firm depends largely on its receptivity to new ideas. When learning from the outside, in particular from abroad, is seen as an admission of weakness, the receptivity will be poor (Westney, 1988). The ossification of the learning infrastructure reflects the low priority given to the accumulation of invisible assets in the execution of a company's strategy. Low receptivity to inputs from the technology partnership will naturally encourage a passive attitude toward the transfer of knowledge among the partnership staff. This tendency is further reinforced if the employees in the venture are socialized to develop a distinct identity, as is often the case in Western joint ventures with Japanese firms, including those located outside of Japan.

BARRIERS TO LEARNING IN CONTROL SYSTEMS

Responsibility for Learning not Clear

Who gains and who loses from technology transfer often depends on the vantage point. As pointed out earlier, a win/win partnership strategy on a corporate level often entails a win/lose scenario at the business unit or business function level. For example, a shift from captive manufacturing to an OEM partnership with a Japanese supplier may contribute to immediate cost reduction and thus enhance the product's position in the market while at the same time the production competence of the Western firm is being eroded. Under such conditions, incentives and responsibility for the acquisition of the knowledge necessary to leverage any emerging competitive imbalance may become unfocused. When competencies are lost, operation managers blame faulty strategy while the corporate staff cites incompetent implementation.

Performance Measures Focused on Short-term Goals

Organizational learning is fundamentally a long-term activity, stretching far beyond a typical 1-year performance evaluation time-frame. Also, the costs associated with learning are immediate, whereas the benefits (most of them difficult to quantify under standard accounting procedures) are accrued over time. Thus, support for organizational learning may have a negative impact on the short-term measurements used to evaluate a manager's performance. The expectation of short tenure in a given job is another critical constraint. The pressure to get immediate results forces managers to economize on expenditures with long-term payoffs, no matter how attractive such payoffs may be. However, the issue is not sacrificing profits for abstract learning, but forfeiting a long-term superior performance to inflate short-term results.

Limited Incentives for Learning

With little or no reward given for contributions to the accumulation of invisible assets, learning becomes a "hobby," not a prerequisite of the job. In many leading Japanese firms, the cross-fertilization of skills across functional areas is actively encouraged. This includes not only individual learning, but the creation of new organizational competencies through cross-functional team interactions. In contrast, due to the organizational emphasis on specialized careers, the skill base of typical Western managers is rather narrow, as is their exposure to parts of their organization outside their professional domain. In a joint venture, asymmetry in the distribution of learning skills will result in an erosion of competitive advantage and the loss of leverage.

Tolerance of Learning Barriers

The reward systems in many multinational firms encourage the hoarding of critical information, not sharing it. Information is treated as a source of power, not as a resource. Smart managers assigned to an overseas venture, who otherwise may expect few opportunities for upward mobility, can make themselves indispensable by blocking the flow of essential information concerning the implementation of the technology transfer agreement. Such a behavior is not only tolerated, but these "cross-cultural experts" are often rewarded in terms of superior compensation and considerable operational autonomy. Any increase in information concerning the activities of the partnership outside of their own domain is seen by these managers as a threat to their power. In a venture that involves competitive collaboration, the other parent and some of the company's own managers may share an interest in limiting the transparency of the technology transfer process.

Managerial Rewards not Tied to Global Strategy

The performance of executives assigned to manage a strategic alliance is often appraised solely on the basis of results in a limited business area or market. There is also often no incentive for the "core" partnership staff to worry about the competitive conditions facing other businesses of the distant parent. These managers have nothing to gain from allocating scarce resources to organizational learning benefiting an organization in which they have no tangible interest. This tendency is especially pronounced if these managers are actually dispatched from the "competing" parent. In such a case, their attitude toward transfer of competencies can easily turn from conservative to downright hostile.

TECHNOLOGY TRANSFER AND ORGANIZATIONAL LEARNING

The challenge of competitive collaboration creates a new agenda and new priorities for companies involved in technology transfers. This challenge cannot be met by avoiding strategic alliances. The economic forces in the environment will continue to push firms into more complex sets of global relationships. Those who learn from these relationships will survive; the others will perish. The organization's ability to learn (or the lack of it) will influence the shape of the global markets for many years to come.

An organization has many tools to manage the process of learning (Hedberg, 1981), but, in principle, the learning ability of an organization depends on its ability to accumulate invisible assets. Organizational learning results from a combination of hard and soft organizational practices anchored in specific management practices. As invisible assets are embodied in people, policies regarding the allocation and utilization of human resources are especially critical to organizational learning. The objective is to complement line management in providing a supporting climate and appropriate control systems to guide the process of learning.

Experience shows that the competitive balance in strategic alliances cannot be controlled through structural solutions. The successes and failures of the alliances are often embedded in the same organizational context (Mowery, 1988; Killing, 1983). Symmetry in the appropriation of benefits from a partnership also cannot be protected through legal clauses. The complexities of international commercial laws and regulations and rapid technological change make legal protection impractical. In fact, the reliance on legal means to safeguard the company interests can be counterproductive as it encourages "we-are-safe" attitudes and thus decreases the stimuli to learn.

The strategic agenda for managers involved in technology transfers in the context of competitive collaboration must be centered around the protection and enhancement of core competencies involved in the exchange. In the planning and execution of technology transfers, the accumulation of invisible assets, whether manufacturing competence, market know-how, or global coordination capability, should be explicitly recognized as a value-enhancing activity. It is dangerous to act as if the existence of a partnership permits lowering commitment to the maintenance and expansion of core competencies. Such a strategy assumes that the partner is unwilling or unable to learn and thus unable to alter the long-term bargaining power regarding the appropriation of benefits. In the context of competitive collaboration, such an assumption is unsupportable.

It does not make sense to set up barriers to learning. Artificial constraints imposed on information flow in the partnership may hinder its ability to sustain its competitive edge and thus erode the competitive position of both parent companies. The only sustainable response is a proactive policy encouraging organizational learning that matches, if not surpasses, the learning ability of the other partner. Everything else is an inferior solution. In the longrun, the competitive advantage of a firm can be maintained only through the organization's capacity to accumulate invisible assets by a carefully planned and executed process or organizational learning.

REFERENCES

Abegglen, J. C., and Stalk, G. Jr. (1985). *Kaisha, The Japanese Corporation,* Basic Books, New York.

Cole, R. E. (1985). "The macropolitics of organizational change: A comparative analysis of the spread of small-group activities," *Administrative Science Quarterly,* 30, 560–85.

Contractor, F., and Lorange, P. (1988). "Why should firms cooperate? The strategy and economics basis for cooperative ventures," in F. Contractor and P.

Lorange (eds.), *Cooperative strategies in International Business.* Lexington, Mass: Lexington Books.

Hamel, G., and Prahalad, C. K. (1988). *When Competitors Collaborate.* Unpublished manuscript.

Harrigan, K. R. (1984). "Joint ventures and global strategies," *Columbia Journal of World Business,* 19 (2): 7–13.

Hedberg, B. (1981). "How organizations learn and unlearn," in P. C. Nystrom and W. H. Starbuck (eds.), *Handbook of Organizational Design,* New York: Oxford University Press.

Hergert, M., and Morris, D. (1988). "Trends in international collaborative agreements," in F. Contractor and P. Lorange (eds.), *Cooperative Strategies in International Business,* Lexington, Mass.: Lexington Books.

Itami, H. (1987). *Mobilizing Invisible Assets,* Cambridge, Mass.: Harvard University Press.

Johnson, C. (1982). *MITI and the Japanese Miracle,* Stanford, Calif.: Stanford University Press.

Johnson, H. T., and Kaplan, R. S. (1987). *Relevance Lost: The Rise and Fall of Management Accounting,* Boston: Harvard Business School Press.

Killing, J. P. (1983). *Strategies for Joint Venture Success,* New York: Praeger Publishers.

Kobrin, S. J. (1988). "Expatriate reduction and strategic control in American multinational corporations," *Human Resource Management,* 27 (1): 63–76.

Mowery, D. C. (1988). "Collaborative ventures between U.S. and foreign manufacturing firms: An overview," in D. C. Mowery (ed.), *International Collaborative Ventures in U.S. Manufacturing,* Cambridge, Mass.: Ballinger.

Nonaka, I., and Johansson, J. K. (1985). "Organizational learning in Japanese companies," in R. B. Lamb (ed.), *Advances in Strategic Management,* Greenwich, Conn.: JAI Press, 3, pp. 277–296.

Ohmae, K. (1985). *Triad Power: The Coming Shape of Global Competition,* New York: Free Press.

Perlmutter, H. V., and Heenan, D. A. (1986). Cooperate to compete globally. *Harvard Business Review,* 64 (2): 136–152.

Porter, M. E., and Fuller, M. B. (1986). Coalitions and global strategy, in M. E. Porter (ed.), *Competition in Global Industries,* Boston: Harvard Business School Press.

Prahalad, C. K., and Doz, Y. L. (1987). *The Multinational Mission. Balancing Local Demands and Global Vision,* New York: The Free Press.

Pucik, V. (1983). "Management practices in Japan and their impact on business strategy," in R. B. Lamb (ed.), *Advances in Strategic Management,* Greenwich, Conn.: JAI Press, 1, pp. 103–131.

Pucik, V. (1988). "Joint ventures with the Japanese: Implications for human resource management," in F. Contractor and P. Lorange (eds.), *Cooperative Strategies in International Business,* Lexington Books: Lexington, Mass.

Reich, R. B., and Mankin, E. D. (1986). "Joint ventures with Japan give away our future," *Harvard Business Review,* 64 (2): 78–86.

Root, F. (1988). "Some taxonomies of international cooperative agreements," in F. Contractor and P. Lorange (eds.), *Cooperative Strategies in International Business,* Lexington, Mass.: Lexington Books.

Teece, D. J. (1986). "Profiting from technological innovation: Implications for integration, collaboration, licensing and public policy," in D. J. Teece (ed.), *The Competitive Challenge: Strategies for Industrial Innovation and Renewal,* Cambridge, Mass.: Ballinger.

Tung, R. (1984). *Key to Japan's Economic Strength: Human Power,* Lexington, Mass.: Lexington Books, D. C. Heath.

Westney, D. E. (1988). "Domestic and foreign learning curves in managing international cooperative strategies," in F. Contractor and P. Lorange (eds.), *Cooperative Strategies in International Business,* Lexington, Mass.: Lexington Books.

Wright, R. W. (1979). "Joint venture problems in Japan," *Columbia Journal of World Business,* 20 (1): 25–31.

THE PRACTICE OF INTERNATIONAL TECHNOLOGY TRANSFER IN THE PACIFIC RIM

Reviewing the record of technology transfer between the developed and the developing countries in general, and between the United States, Japan, China, and Korea in particular, is like observing groups of blind people trying to establish contact in a foggy night. Much depends on chance, and all the parties involved lack crucial information about the real needs and real constraints of each other. The fact that much technology is successfully transferred, and that international business alliances are formed, is testimony to the dire human need for these processes to take place.

One reason for the problems associated with international technology transfer, problems that are amply documented in the next seven chapters of this book, is that technology is not something that is easy to transfer or to trade in an open market. Beyond some simple cases where technology is no more than the information necessary to design and to produce a certain good; technology is: ". . . firm-specific information concerning the characteristics and performance properties of production processes and product design, . . . it is tacit and cumulative in nature, . . . recipients, (and transmitters), would normally be obliged to devote substantial resources to assimilate, adapt, and improve upon the original technology" (Rosenberg and Frischtak, 1985, p. viii). The need to transfer rather vague information that is embedded in the organization makes the organization-embodied technology transfer the prime goal of international technology transfer. Communicating and transferring information and behavior so intimate to the transmitting organization, and therefore often alien to the receiving organization, is complex and sometimes ambivalent both to the transmitter and to the receiver.

The complexity and multifaceted nature of the process of technology transfer, as well as its relationship to international business, is expressed in the final part of this book. The following seven chapters represent seven independent studies on various cases and dimensions of technology transfer. In addition to their value as independent studies, they provide a multidimensional view of the process of international technology transfer as it is practiced in the Pacific Basin (including the United States). There are three major dimensions to the process of international technology transfer: the first is the nature of the technology, the second is the nature of the client and its goals, and the third is the nature of the process itself (Agmon and Agmon, 1989). In the first dimension, we can differentiate between a product or a single-design technology, a production process technology often expressed by a turnkey project, and a capability technology. Extending the definition of Gee (1981), the first is associated with product-embodied technology, the second with person-embodied technology, and the third with what we have defined earlier in this book as organization-embodied technology. The second dimension makes the distinction between macroorganizations, such as state agencies, which typically have political and societal goals, as well as economic objectives; microorganizations (firms) that have financial and organizational goals; and individuals who are motivated by personal utility considerations. The third dimension measures the environment, both the institutional aspects and whether the environment is friendly or hostile. Cultural considerations fall under this dimension. The studies included in the third part of this book deal with these dimensions. They also provide commentary on the nature of the process of international technology transfer, and the managerial and policy lessons of the cumulative experience embedded in the seven studies. In this, the third part of this book (indeed the whole manuscript), is an example of international technology transfer in the field of international management.

In Chapter 9, Harris provides an analysis of the environment for technology transfer between the United States and Japan. In our terms, the focus of the chapter is on the third dimension, the environment, and on the macroorganizations both in Japan and in the United States as the clients and contributors to the process of international technology transfer between these two countries. Focusing on the environment and the macroorganizations makes this chapter akin to a discussion of international trade, particularly those issues of political economy such as the balance of trade and the balance of power between the two countries. Although Fischer transfers the location of the analysis from Japan to China, and the focus from the macroorganizations (state agencies) to microorganizations, he still shares the concern about the environment in Chapter 10. His analysis emphasizes the role of culture and of value judgments with regard to alternative growth paths as the essential factors in the selection of a successful mode of international technology transfer. The two chapters taken together (Chapters 9 and 10), set up and demonstrate the importance of the environment and the main actors in it, in determining the success of the specific attempts in technology transfer between Japan and the United States, and China.

How to measure success in the multidimensional space of international technology transfer is the subject of Chapter 11. Von Glinow, Schnepp, and Bhambri used their extensive research experience in technology transfer between the United States and China to draw an intricate map of different stakeholders who operate in two distinctly different environments. Expectations, measures of success and rewards are different, and they have to be considered to make the transfer a success.

Whereas Von Glinow and associates are looking at general criteria for success for different actors, Grow's contribution in Chapter 12 focuses on the firm-specific characteristics and their role in determining the success of a particular attempt of technology transfer. From the firm-specific case studies of United States and Japanese competition for the market of technology transfer in China, Grow generalizes the requirements for a transmitter to receiver fit. A micro-organizational fit is the necessary condition for a successful technology transfer. The production aspects, the marketing of the output to be produced by the Chinese firm, the receiver of the technology, as well as the structure of the relationship between the two firms involved in the transfer, are all elements in the specific fit or its absence. The various expressions by which technology transfer can be effected are discussed from a receiver point of view in the Chapter 13 by Linsu Kim. Kim argues that there is more than one way to affect technology transfer. Technology can be transferred by direct investment by the transmitting firm, by licensing initiated by the receiving firm, and in case of need by what is euphemistically called reverse engineering. If there is a real need for a technology transfer it will be effected, and different functional fields of management and economics may be used as vehicles in different environments and times.

Managements of both transmitters and receivers should be realistic enough to realize that a transfer will take place, and flexible enough to find the most opportune way to effect it. Any attempt to block technology transfer, or even to control it, will end up with higher costs for everyone involved.

Technology is related to time and place. It can flow from one country to another in some given form in one period, and reverse its direction and change its form in a later time period. This trait, as it applies to the process of technology transfer between Japan and the United States, is documented and analyzed in Chapter 14 by Bela Gold. Technology transfer from the United States was a major factor in the rebuilding of Japan after World War II. A reverse transfer of technology from Japan to the United States might be as important in what some call the "reindustrialization" of America. Operations management and production policy are both affected and determined by technology transfer. Economic growth and, therefore, the magnitude and the composition of the trade balance of the United States and Japan, are affected by the production policy of the two countries; which means that technology transfer, through its expression in the functional fields of management, contributes to the dynamics of the trade balance.

Wes Johnston's contribution in Chapter 15 deals with a seemingly straightforward subject of the institutional structure of one province in China, and its effect on the ability of the foreign corporation to transfer or sell technology to Chinese firms. However, this detailed analysis provides us with more than just information. It highlights the importance of the specific environment in the attempt to create the "fit" discussed earlier by Grow. It also highlights the relationship between the technology itself, and the organizational vehicles in which it is transferred. Last, it emphasizes the process of international technology transfer as organization-embodied and capability-oriented.

REFERENCES

Agmon, O., and T. Agmon. (1990). "International Technology Transfer and Organizational Development Interventions: Effective Partners in International Business," USC Working Paper (April).

Gee, S. (1981). *Technology Transfer, Innovation and International Competitiveness,* New York: John Wiley and Sons.

Rosenberg, S., and C. Frischtak. (1985). *International Technology Transfer: Concepts, Measures, and Comparisons,* New York: Praeger.

8
Technology Transfer and Sino-Japanese Relations*

MARTHA CALDWELL HARRIS

Japanese technology transfer to China is a case of the half-full glass. Japan remains China's largest trading partner,[1] providing China with a large share of its machinery, transport, and telecommunications equipment needs. Japan is also China's largest aid donor and an important provider of external financing. Japanese firms, like Mitsui, are on the ground in China, with offices in most major cities and representatives in even distant regions.

However, the Chinese have repeatedly criticized Japan for being much more interested in selling products than transferring technology.[2] Foreign investment is a case in point. In Shanghai, for example, Japan's share of total investment has in recent years been half that of the United States.[3] When Prime Minister Nakasone visited Beijing in January 1987, he was greeted with complaints about Japan's lackluster investment in China. Later in the year, in the wake of the Toshiba affair, Chinese officials called on Japan to increase imports from China and to concentrate more on high technology exports.

Japan is thus criticized in China for being stingy with its technology, while in the United States there are lingering suspicions that Japan is too quick to sell to China and other communist nations. These differing perceptions reflect Japan's unique position vis-à-vis China. As the country with the most extensive trading relationship with China, Japan's industry leaders also strive to maintain their competitiveness vis-à-vis China and

*Background research for this chapter was conducted in the course of a study by U.S. Congress, Office of Technology Assessment, where the author was a senior analyst. The views expressed here are the author's and not necessarily those of the Office of Technology Assessment or the National Research Council.

The views expressed here are those of the author and not an official position of the National Research Council, or the National Academies of Sciences or Engineering. This chapter was written in the spring of 1988 and does not reflect the important changes that occurred in 1989 which resulted in a much less conducive climate for technology transfer from Japan and other Western countries to the Peoples Republic of China.

other Asian countries, while continuing to rely on the United States for military security.

This chapter examines the pattern of technology transfer from Japan to China in recent years, analyzing factors that variously stimulate and impede the process. The literature on technology transfer suggests a number of general motivations for technology transfer, including opening markets, developing lower cost production facilities overseas, raising revenues through licensing, and cementing political relations with technical assistance. During most of the past 9 years since the reestablishment of normal relations between the two countries, Japan's technology transfer to China has been governed by two major goals: (1) expanding sales in the Chinese domestic market and (2) providing China with aid and financial assistance to minimize political conflicts between the two countries. While these motives are not so different from those affecting other suppliers of technology, Japan has developed a characteristic style of technology transfer to China in conjunction with large infrastructure projects, factory renovation, and sales of standardized consumer product manufacturing lines.

Nonetheless, there have been signs of change in recent months. New Sino-Japanese joint ventures in high technology fields, expanded science technology (S and T) exchanges, and Japanese plans for equity investment in export-oriented facilities were announced in 1988. This chapter examines some of the forces stimulating past patterns in technology transfer and discusses the implications for Japan, the United States, and China if Japan's technology transfers are deepened and focused more in high technology fields.

THE BILATERAL CONTEXT FOR JAPANESE TECHNOLOGY TRANSFER TO CHINA

International politics, particularly China's relations with the U.S.S.R. and the United States, have shaped the context for Sino-Japanese technology transfer during the past 15 years. The Nixon shock of the early 1970s provided a strong impetus to groups of influential Japanese politicians and businessmen, who had already begun to push for a more positive stance toward China.[4] As China came to see the Soviet Union as the major threat to Asian security in the 1970s, and as United States–Soviet relations moved from a period of detente to confrontation under the Reagan administration, China became a more attractive trading partner for Japan. These developments made it possible for Japan to expand economic interaction with China without jeopardizing security commitments with the United States.

Japanese observers track political–economic cycles in trade with China, where trade has boomed in periods of closer bilateral relations and tapered off in times of heightened political friction. Beginning in the late 1970s when Japan and China signed a long-term trade agreement and a peace treaty, bilateral trade generally expanded until 1986 when China's exports to and imports from Japan took a downturn.[5] This downturn followed Chinese student demonstrations in late 1985. Chinese resentment over Japan's "economic invasion" of China surfaced: Japan's trade surplus with China reached more than $6 billion in 1985 while overall bilateral trade grew $19 billion. The student demonstrations also focused criticism on Japanese Prime Minister Nakasone's visit to a shrine honoring Japanese war dead, illustrating the interrelationship of trade and politics in the Sino-Japanese relationship. A fundamental tension continues between the benefits of growing economic interdependence and persisting fears on both sides that the long-term result will be to limit sovereignty.

During the first half of the 1980s, a number of other factors contributed to the expansion of technology transfer from Japan to China. Leaders on both sides have emphasized the complementary relationship of China's potential energy exports and Japan's energy needs, and between China's requirements for machinery, equipment, and factories, and Japan's export strengths. Through long-term trade agreements, the two countries formally committed themselves to these exchanges.

Despite the principle of balanced trade adopted in the long-term agreements, however, Japanese exports of machinery and equipment grew much more rapidly than Chinese exports of oil and other types of energy, contributing to a growing trade imbalance. The formula of a balanced swap of "oil for machines" sounded good in theory, but almost immediately foundered due to lagging Chinese oil exports, the unattractiveness of waxy Chinese crude oil to Japanese industry, and the softening of the worldwide oil market that made supplies from other sources readily available to Japan, not to mention Japanese tariffs on commodities that China traditionally exports.[6]

Another important impetus for Japan's expanding economic relationship with China has been an emerging new style of Japanese international leadership in science technology. Pressed by the United States to take on a larger international role not defined simply in economic terms, and reluctant to embark on a military buildup that would be seen as threatening to other Asian nations, Japan has opted for a strategy of expanding contributions in science and technology as the earmark of a new form of international leadership. China, an Asian neighbor with a huge population and well endowed with natural resources and an ambitious modernization program, offers a prime test case for Japan. Japan has the know-how to assist China in modernizing its factories and upgrading the capabilities of technical and managerial personnel, and in so doing can demonstrate a new willingness to assist other nations in their overall economic development.

These stimuli notwithstanding, other factors have acted to limit technology transfer. While Japanese businessmen tend to downplay the likelihood of a "boomerang effect," transferring technology to China will certainly contribute to the emergence of a formidable trader and a potential competitor in some areas. (Japanese experts typically stress the fact that Chinese enterprises are not yet capable of assimilating the most advanced technology, due to regulations that limit the discretion of foreign managers in employment decisions, sourcing components, repatriating profits and selling in the local market.) To the extent that Japan concentrates its technology transfers on large energy and infrastructure development projects, on renovating factories using standardized technologies and producing less sophisticated consumer goods, Japan may avoid the boomerang, or deflect it toward other Asian countries. As more fully discussed below, such a strategy is not without its problems since recent experience shows that it runs the risk of provoking a strongly negative reaction on the part of China.

Another unstated but important concern is with transfers that contribute to building China's military capability. Until quite recently, Japan has tended to define such transfers narrowly to encompass export of weapons and equipment designed for military conflict. For Japan, where public opinion runs counter to direct exports of weapons and where strategic concerns dictate caution, there has been little thought of Japan becoming a major supplier of weapons systems. When it comes to technologies with civil as well as military applications (computers, telecommunications, precision instruments), however, there is more ambiguity. A general desire to go slow with transfers that directly and significantly improve China's military capability or competitiveness vis-à-vis Japan in high technology industries has limited the scope of technology transferred. Related to these factors is a desire not to move so quickly in aiding China that other Asian countries feel threatened.[7]

During the late 1980s, a number of new factors have emerged that affect Japan's technology transfer in sometimes conflicting ways. First, due to a decline in the value of the yen against the dollar, the price competitiveness of Japanese firms has been challenged. In addition, smaller Chinese enterprises found it difficult to utilize loans from private Japanese banks, due to comparatively high interest rates. A major factor, however, is policy determined. China adopted a "selective import" policy in 1986, with the goal of using foreign currency more efficiently by increasing the local content of imported plants. As a result, Japan's plant exports to China dropped 30 percent in 1986 over 1985 to a level of $1.1 billion.[8] While Japan's foreign direct investments in the United States and Europe grew quickly, investments in China declined in 1986.

In 1987, however, a countertrend emerged in the form of the repercussions of the Toshiba affair. China repeatedly complained about Japan's 1-year ban on exports by Toshiba Machine Company to communist bloc countries, claiming that the ban effectively froze 25 contracts with $16 million in China.[9] Contracts with other Japanese companies were also allegedly delayed, due to a tightening of the license review process in Tokyo.[10] A number of Japan's largest manufacturers and trading companies asked the government to ease restrictions on trade with China and to permit Toshiba Machine to follow through with exports contracted before the ban.[11]

In late October 1987, the Japanese government announced that it would permit the company to fulfill previous commitments and that the Japanese Ministry of International Trade and Industry (MITI) would expedite licensing of exports to China, in a strained attempt to reconcile commitments to take a harder line on companies that violate coordinating committee for multinational export control (COCOM) rules and the need to placate China. This represented a compromise—exports contracted before the official ban were permitted, but Toshiba Machine could not receive any cash payments for them until the 1-year ban was ended. At about the same time, the United States tabled plans to approve some higher technology exports to China, in retaliation for what the Reagan Administration called continuing sales by China of silkworm missiles to Iran.[12] (The U.S. freeze on higher technology exports ended during a visit to the United States by the Chinese Foreign Minister in early 1988, and in July 1988 COCOM member countries loosened some restrictions on exports of computers to China.) The overall, long-term impact of the Toshiba affair on Japanese technology transfer policy is to differentiate China more clearly from the Soviet bloc and to raise expectations that more advanced technology will be transferred.

By 1988, there were signs of significant change developing in Japan's technology transfers to China. For the first time in years, Japan's trade surplus with China shrank to under $1.3 billion in 1987.[13] The question is whether Japan will move toward more extensive technology transfers to China as the only way to retain market share in China. To understand the implications of such a change, it is important to understand the patterns of technology trade that emerged in the past decade since the signing of the long-term trade agreement in 1978.

JAPAN'S APPROACH TO TRANSFERRING TECHNOLOGY TO CHINA

Institutions and Organizations

Japan's government sets the general policy context for economic relations with China, and furnishes important incentives such as aid and official financing, but it is the private sector that is the driving force in technology transfer. The Foreign Ministry has determined that helping China modernize will contribute to China's peaceful integration in Asia. Official policy is to assist China in line with three principles: (1) preserving good relations with Association of Southeast Asian Nations (ASEAN), (2) providing no military aid, and (3) cooperating with Western aid donors. The Japan International Cooperation Agency, which provides grants and technical assistance, is responsible for the Foreign Ministry. MITI is also heavily involved by virtue of its role in setting policy on plant exports and working with private firms to coordinate work on large energy and infrastructure projects in China. On a number of occasions, MITI has disagreed with the austerity-minded Ministry of Finance and other ministries over financing for projects in China. The Export-Import Bank of Japan, the Overseas Economic Cooperation Fund that administers aid loans, and the Science and Technology Agency are also involved in various aspects of science and technology exchange.

Members of the ruling Liberal Democratic Party and the opposition parties also make frequent trips to China and continue to play key roles in mediating relations with China and other Asian nations. In late 1986, Prime Minister Nakasone passed a formal request to China to participate in talks to ease tension on the Korean peninsula. The Japanese press reported that an LDP Dietman acted as an intermediary between China and South Korea while visiting the latter in early 1987.[14] Sympathies for Taiwan continue among some Japanese politicians, despite the break in official relations that occurred in the early 1970s.

Differences between Japanese supporters of China and Taiwan have at times cast a pall over technology transfer prospects. In 1987, when a Japanese court ruled that Taiwan was the rightful owner of a disputed dormitory in Japan, the Chinese reaction was swift and negative—with threats to break off trade.

A distinguishing feature of Japan's approach is the important role played by informal and "unofficial" interactions. Japan and China have established a committee for the twenty-first century, which includes eleven representatives from each side who exchange views on bilateral issues. While the Japanese side, which includes former high-ranking government officials as well as businessmen and academic leaders, is staffed by the Foreign Ministry, the talks are considered unofficial. The committee offers a unique mechanism for frank and significant dialogue between the two countries. With the committee's sponsorship, a youth center has been constructed in Beijing and a number of youth exchanges from both countries have occurred. The low-profile, informal approach to resolving problems, however, has not been without its problems. Hu Yaobang, considered to play a key role in moderating criticism of Japan after the student demonstrations, was himself castigated for working outside of normal diplomatic channels in bringing Japanese youth to China, and in private consultations with former Japanese Prime Minister Nakasone.[15]

Another organization that illustrates Japan's approach to technology trade with China is the Japan–China Association for Economy and Trade (JCAET), a bridging organization that links business and government.[16] The association includes many retired government officials, most of them from MITI, as well as businessmen and China experts from other organizations. Individuals are frequently rotated in and out, thus enhancing information exchange. The association provides a range of services to Japanese firms interested in trade with China, including the sponsorship of missions, studies of Chinese market conditions, and numerous publications. As such, it is an informal "window" (madoguchi) for Japanese firms and Chinese counterparts. The association works with Japan Economic Trade Organization (JETRO) and other key Japanese groups watching the

Chinese market to provide in-depth, informed analyses. JCAET staff travel often to China, providing authoritative reports to its membership upon its return.

Trading companies have for years been major players in trade with China. C. Itoh and company tops them all and has been actively involved in technology transfers. In 1985 alone, C. Itoh did more than $2 billion worth of business with China. The trading house had been active in China before the war and was the first Japanese firm to reestablish formal trading links in 1972. Over the past 15 years, C. Itoh has exported a variety of plants to China—steel, petrochemical, electronics—while also participating in large joint ventures in offshore oil exploration. With eight offices in China, the firm has a formidable presence there and has participated in most of the large projects supported with Japanese government aid. The firm is also facilitating intermediary trade between China and other parts of the world, such as Southeast Asia, the Middle East, and Europe.[17] Trading firms, such as C. Itoh, bring global market networks and expertise in barter and commodity trade across a wide range of industries. Mitsui, another Japanese trading company, is a joint venture partner in a company that leases equipment made around the world to more than 70 different Chinese enterprises.

Scope and Nature of Japanese Technology Transfer

Nineteen eighty-six can be seen as the year that marks the beginning of important changes in Sino-Japanese trade. In 1986, other trading partners began to make inroads (if only slightly) into Japan's market share in some sectors. Japan's whopping lead ($19 billion in two-way trade with China compared with about $8 billion for the United States in 1985) began to decline in machinery and transport equipment, office machines, and telecommunications. As a result, Japan's trade surplus with China declined, but remained substantial.

Nonetheless, there were major continuities with the past. Japanese exports to China remained strongly concentrated in machinery and equipment, as well as steel. Machinery and equipment made up more than half of Japan's exports to China, although exports of automobiles dropped after illegal sales and defective parts came to light in 1985. As a result of China's import controls on finished products such as automobiles and televisions, exports of components from Japan increased significantly. Exports of parts for washing machines and refrigerators, for example, increased markedly in 1986.

Exports of products, of course, do not constitute "technology transfer." But the traditional concentration of Japan's exports in plants and heavy equipment has been a point of contention. Chinese officials charged that Japan has pursued an "equipment-first" sales strategy.[18] The quarrel is thus with the content of the exports from Japan, although the volume has also been troublesome in the sense that exports up until 1987 far exceeded imports. By some accounts, Japan has consistently ranked first in terms of both number and value of technology import contracts.[19] One of the problems with this debate over the hardware/software content of Japanese technology and equipment imports is that the data do not take into account provision of software and technical services often offered free of charge by Japanese firms.[20] Japanese businessmen, for their part, often complain that the Chinese demand that feasibility studies be provided gratis and that they consistently undervalue the software component of contracts.[21] Even Chinese critics have begun to acknowledge cases (such as the Hitachi Shipbuilding Company) where Japanese firms have beat out rivals by offering more favorable technology transfer terms. Nevertheless, the perception continues that Japan has been much better at selling equipment than at providing training, technology, and related services needed for an effective transfer of know-how.

Despite the ambiguities inherent in the official trade and technology transfer data, Japan's approach has generally emphasized plant exports (especially for machinery production facilities and consumer product manufacturing), assistance in renovation of Chinese industries, and the provision of standardized manufacturing technologies to produce consumer products. This should not be interpreted to mean that there has been no transfer of advanced technology, but rather that it has typically occurred in the context of large projects. The prime example, of course, is the Baoshun Steel complex outside Shanghai. Nippon Steel has transferred state of the art technology, with Japanese government support. Thousands of Chinese engineers and technicians have been trained in Japan in conjunction with this project alone. The experience of JCG, a Japanese company that has exported dozens of large plants to China, illustrates that significant technology transfer has occurred in this way.

By looking only at aggregate data on commodity and plant exports, it is easy to overlook the other types of technology transfer underway. NEC, for example, is training thousands of Chinese software engineers and is a partner in the Japan–China Software Center. It is important to note that NEC has developed a sophisticated technology transfer strategy designed to address its shortage of software personnel. Many Japanese businessmen, technicians, and specialists are involved in exchanges with Chinese counterparts. The Industrial Bank of Japan and the Bank of China cooperate in seminars on Chinese financing and there is a constant movement of specialized personnel between these and other financial, industrial, and technical organizations in the two countries. The Japan International Cooperation Agency's projects on factory renovation in China are another dimension of Japan's technical assistance; in this case the Japanese government is supporting studies of industries to identify opportunities for Japanese firms to assist with transfers of standardized technologies.

Investment is another important dimension of the technology transfer picture. Japan's booming direct foreign investment is causing some concern in certain quarters in the United States, in contrast to China where lagging Japanese investment is a major source of friction. By most accounts, Japan ranks third behind the United States and Hong Kong in investments.[22] While the level of Japanese investment increased in 1985, it fell sharply in 1986. For their part, Japanese investors in China claim that operational costs are high due to labor regulations, high cost and low quality of locally produced components, power shortages, requirements to balance foreign exchange expenditures, and arbitrary implementation of laws. Japanese investors have clearly judged that China offers an uncertain investment climate in comparison to competing opportunities in the United States and the newly industrializing countries of Asia.[23]

It is noteworthy that Japan and China signed an investment agreement in August 1988 when Prime Minister Takeshita visited China. Japanese investment in China rose during the first half of 1988, and MITI studied plans to boost investments in China. In addition to changes in export insurance, there are indications of experimentation with new approaches such as special incentives for smaller Japanese firms to invest in China. While the United States and China have yet to sign an investment agreement, Japan signaled a new willingness to promote deeper involvement in the Chinese economy.

To summarize, the general pattern of Japanese technology transfer to China over the past decade has been heavily oriented toward transfers in conjunction with large infrastructure and energy projects, as well as transfers of standardized consumer goods production technologies. Japanese business in the past pursued a cautious strategy, stressing product exports and participation in projects (particularly government-supported projects), studiously avoiding direct equity investment. This is not to say that Japanese firms have transferred no advanced technology—cases were noted earlier that tend to be obscured by overall aggregate trade data. But given the choice, that they usually have, Japanese firms have preferred to transfer standardized, or older technologies no long central to their own corporate sales strategies—technologies which they argue are more "appropriate" for China.[24] There are, however, some indications of change.

Aid, Finance, and Facilitating Mechanisms

If the Japanese private sector is the driving force in technology transfer to China, the government is the go-between or facilitator. The extensive financing and aid provided by the Japanese government indicate the salience of a political calculus. Such support is extraordinarily extensive in the case of China, a strategically important neighbor.[25] Interrelated are desires to define a more constructive international role, beginning in Asia.

In recent years, Japan has been the major provider of aid to China. In 1985, for example, Japan provided more than $387 million in official development assistance (ODA) to China.[26] Japan's program dwarfs that of

West Germany, the country with the next largest program of about $96 million during the same year.[27] Since 1979 Japan has committed well over $4 billion in ODA to China, in two large multiyear packages.

The bulk of this aid has been in the form of low interest loans denominated in yen to support large infrastructure projects such as railroads, ports, and hydropower plants. By and large, these projects have been efficiently administered and both sides consider them successful.[28] Among the projects currently underway is one to develop a digital communications network between Shanghai, Tianjin, and Canton.

Grant aid and technical assistance make up a relatively small share of Japan's aid to China, compared with the yen loans described previously. Grant aid of $20 million has been used to build a hospital in Beijing. In conjunction with the project, medical equipment has been provided, 130 Chinese have been trained in Japanese medical institutions and a small number of Japanese doctors and nurses have been sent to work at the hospital.[29] Other grant aid projects include a telecommunications training center, a fish research center in Shanghai, and an agricultural research center in Mongolia.

The Japan Internal Cooperation Agency (JICA) has been responsible for assisting China in renovation of industries. The JICA program is designed to support factory surveys that identify opportunities for technical assistance carried out by private Japanese companies. JICA explicitly concentrates on projects that involve transfers of standardized technologies. Another type of technical cooperation can be seen in the nuclear field. Japan and China are cooperating on research to develop a high-temperature, gas-cooled reactor and on nuclear safety. MITI is also involved in projects in the rare metals area, and in others to develop export-oriented factories. The Japanese government decided in 1987 that yen credits can be used for factor renovation and for export-oriented plants.[30]

Japan's ODA loans for projects in China are in principle "untied," meaning that other countries can participate. In the early 1980s, however, despite the fact that bidding was formally open, Japanese firms clearly won the lion's share of the contracts. Japan has also combined aid with official financing (mixed credits), as have other countries such as Britain, Belgium, and Sweden.[31] Major infrastructure projects supported by Japan in China have involved both types of credits, drawing criticism from the United States that this runs counter to the basic notion of what aid should be. More recently, the Foreign Ministry effectively resisted efforts to use mixed credits in the case of bidding on a coal-fired power plant in Tianjin. In addition, the Organization for Economic Cooperation and Development (OECD) countries, finally with Japanese concurrence, agreed in 1987 to regulate the use of mixed credits.

While Japan's aid programs have been significant and much larger than those of other countries, the official financing offered by Japan has arguably been even more particularly important as a lubricant for Japanese trade and technology transfer. To take one example, supplier credits worth

$2.4 billion have been used to finance oil and coal development projects in China. Much of the credits have been used to purchase equipment and services for these large projects. The bank has also provided funding to assist smaller Chinese businesses importing machinery from Japan.[32] In most cases, such projects would be unattractive to Japanese firms without the ExIm credits. Private Japanese financing of Chinese projects is also, of course, quite substantial, but there is no doubt that government-supported official financing has helped to advance Japan's commercial interests in China, and to encourage some types of technology transfers.

Japan's lead in China depends on more than cheap financing, of course. Japanese private firms, specialized associations, and government-supported JETRO have thousands of representatives on the ground in China who are fluent in Chinese and good analysts of market trends. Mitsui alone reportedly has 120 employees fluent in Chinese, and C. Itoh another 150.[33] According to a European observer, Japanese firms work hard to develop personal relations with their Chinese counterparts and take a long-term view toward the market.[34]

In July 1988, the Japanese government announced a $7 billion 5-year aid program for China. In contrast to previous aid packages, regional development and assistance to smaller Chinese firms have been emphasized as targets.

Broader Implications and Future Prospects

Japan's trade lead in the years past has been coupled with a cautious approach to technology transfer. This "strategy" (whether conscious or ad hoc) has brought with it serious liabilities or risks. Vehement criticism by China is only an embarrassment to internationalist Japanese bureaucrats, but also an ill omen for Japanese traders and politicians.

For a number of reasons, a sales-first approach to technology no longer appears viable. First, China has already demonstrated that it is ready and willing to use import controls to limit imports of Japanese finished products, particularly consumer goods not considered to be necessities. The sharp decline in finished product imports from Japan in 1986 brought on a shift to Japanese components imports, a shift that was precisely the aim of Chinese policy. Second, the appreciation of the yen means that imports from other countries have become more attractive. Third, the Chinese repeatedly emphasize that they prefer the American style to the Japanese: U.S. firms have been more willing to invest, and have gained a reputation as less reluctant to transfer advanced technology. The fact that other suppliers are willing to transfer technology puts added pressure on Japanese firms.

The broader implications of Japan's approach are worth noting. Japan was able to carve out a mighty market share in China, at the same time limiting imports from China into its home markets. This effectively increased pressure on the U.S. market to accept Chinese imports. U.S. insistence that Japan open its markets increasingly reflects these larger realities. During the late 1980s, there has been growing concern in the United States that Japan should expand imports from other Asian nations.

Second, Japan has traditionally been able to follow the lead of the United States on export controls. By taking a low-profile role, Japan avoided making waves. Indeed, export control policy vis-à-vis China was rarely specified in detail in public statements, as it was always assumed that Japan's policy would be consistent with that of COCOM. Japan thus eschewed a visible role in setting Western export control policy, thus shifting the onus to the United States for controls unpopular in China.

While Japanese firms committed themselves to the Chinese market in the sense of sending representatives, they minimized potential investment risks by limiting equity participation in production facilities in China. In so doing, however, they opened themselves up to strong criticism by the Chinese. It seemed safe to focus on selling automobiles, for example, rather than setting up production facilities in China. But illegal sales and defective products created a scandal that will be long-remembered in China as another Japan problem, even if Chinese officials were themselves directly involved. Japanese business leaders thus managed to avoid the "boomerang effect"—a direct competitive challenge from industries in China to which Japan transferred technology—but incurred strong resentment in China.

While Japan's traditional approach to technology transfer to China may seem "safe," it will be difficult, perhaps impossible, for Japan to pursue it in the years ahead. Some of the reasons are suggested in the implications noted above. The United States and other industrialized countries in the West, not to mention Asian countries, have come to recognize that Japanese restrictions on imports from Asia have negative spillover effects on their own bilateral balances. Reluctance to take a blatant hard line on trade with Japan has diminished in the context of the current U.S. debate over a trade bill that includes a number of measures widely seen as "protectionist" and directed against Japan.

In the wake of the Toshiba affair, there has been a reevaluation of COCOM and the Western export control system. In the process, the export control policies of Japan have come under closer scrutiny. From a U.S. and allied perspective, a major result appears to be new vigilance on the part of the Japanese government and major Japanese corporations in limiting illegal exports.[35]

Important, but less noticed, have been changes in Japan's export control policies vis-à-vis China. As Chinese officials and Japanese exporters alike complained about trade-limiting effects of limits on sales to communist countries by Toshiba Machine and a more careful licensing process in Tokyo, the Japanese government searched for a formula that would permit Japan to respond to complaints from both the United States and China. The result has been publicly to differentiate China from other communist countries in Japan's official policy. In addition, the Japanese government has devised ways to allow Toshiba Machine to carry through on major exports. The stage appears to be set for expanded Japanese exports of higher technology products to China. In January 1988, for example, Hitachi announced plans to export video tape recorder manufacturing technology to China. The deal was widely reported as representative of a new type of "high tech" cooperation with China.[36]

The appreciation of the yen and other policy-related factors are, moreover, pushing Japanese industry to move plants offshore. To date, the greatest impacts have been felt not in China but in other Asian countries; the recently signed Sino-Japanese investment agreement may pave the way for expanded investment in China. Japanese business is developing a global production strategy that may well be extended to China. During the past year, Japanese and Chinese leaders have discussed ways to promote Japanese participation in export-oriented firms in China. The Japan Trade Council is now arranging training for Chinese traders at some of Japan's largest trading houses.[37] Two Sino-Japanese groups have already made the first exports of color televisions from China. Initial exports are going to the Third World, but exports to Western Europe are projected to begin shortly.[38] Such signs indicated a shift in Japanese strategy toward one focusing on a teaming of Japanese firms with Chinese counterparts, using China as a platform for exports.

Another factor that may be changing concerns perspectives on Chinese political stability. After the fall of Hu Yaobang, viewed in Japan as a proponent of reforms and understanding of Japan, the party pledged to deepen reforms and in early 1988 Chinese officials announced that foreign businesses would be permitted full authority in managing joint ventures. These steps have served to buoy Japanese confidence that Chinese reform policy will remain in place, despite leadership changes. This could increase investor confidence in China.

Japan may be embarking on what will be seen later as a significant shift to higher technology exports, more extensive science and technical exchange, and joint ventures for export. On the one hand, such a shift could occur gradually, building on some of the more extensive technology transfers that have already occurred. On the other hand, publicity and official blessing for such a shift could mark the beginning of a new and deeper technology relationship between the two countries. Regardless, it will be the decisions of Japanese businessmen themselves, rather than the government of Japan, that will be the most important determinants.

With Japan's assistance, China could get a critical boost in its plans for modernization. Some Western analysts have forecast that China will become a superpower—a major military as well as economic force—in the early part of the next century.[39] What Japanese leaders will have to weigh carefully is the prospect that a closer Sino-Japanese technology transfer relationship would enhance Chinese military might. Leaders in China and Japan have consistently viewed the other's military aspirations with the alarm. Should Japan's leaders commit themselves to a new style of technology transfer to China, it would also be necessary to consider what kind of security relationship would be appropriate. Could Japan play a special role in helping to integrate China more fully into the Western market and security system, or would a closer technology transfer relationship with China raise new problems for the Western alliance? These are questions that deserve careful consideration.

As Japan's aid program grows to dwarf that of the United States and other Western countries, resentment is likely to grow on the part of American businessmen who see Japanese aid as a tool of commercial policy. For years the United States has been encouraging Japan to beef up its aid program, but few considered the full implications. From a Japanese perspective, the danger is that the aid program will be criticized by Western countries as too heavily centered in China and too transparently supportive of business interests. Japan will need to make unusual efforts to expand technical assistance and untied assistance to avoid potential criticism from other OECD countries and from China.

A careful look at Japan's approach to technology transfer suggests the importance of perceptions in Sino-Japanese relations. While Japanese firms and organizations have concentrated on transfers of standardized technologies, high technology transfers have already occurred. Regardless, Chinese remain critical that Japan has been a most reluctant partner.

Should Japan decide to publicize and focus more on high technology transfers, the Chinese may well continue to pressure Japan for increased technology transfer. If commercial and market factors push Japan toward more investment and deeper technology transfers, the question remains as to how Japan will evaluate the strategic calculus and play a larger role in aid and economic assistance without incurring the resentment of other OECD donor countries. The answers will have important implications for the security environment in Asia and for the Western alliance. As Japan shapes its role in transferring technology to China, observers will form impressions of what kind of global leadership Japan is likely to exercise in the years ahead.

NOTES

1. Excluding Hong Kong.
2. See Office of Technology Assessment (OTA), Technology Transfer to China, 1987, Chapter 5.
3. *Japan Economic Journal*, "Japanese Firms Lag Behind in Investment in Shanghai," March 7, 1987, p. 10.
4. See Chae Jin-Lee, *China and Japan* (Stanford: Hoover Institute Press, 1984), p. 9.
5. Ma Juyniei, MOFERT, "Sino-Japanese Trade," *Intertrade,* October 1987, p. 51.
6. Silk, satin, carpets, honey, chestnuts, dried persimmons, rice straw, litchi nuts, and Hami melons are among the high tariff items mentioned by the Chinese.

7. The principle has been formally embodied in Japanese aid policy.
8. "Local Content Becoming Issue in Plant Exports," *China Newsletter,* 69, July–August 1987, p. 1.
9. The ban was instituted by the Japanese government after evidence came to light that the company had sold sophisticated advanced machining equipment to the Soviet Union in violation of COCOM (The Coordinating Committee for Multilateral Export Controls) rules.
10. Noel Fletcher, "Japan Seeks to Speed Exports to China," *Journal of Commerce,* December 29, 1987.
11. See "Japanese Exporters Request Easier Rules for Trade with China," *Wall Street Journal,* September 16, 1987.
12. Adi Ignatius, "Yeutter Will Press China to Open Markets Wider to American Goods," *Wall Street Journal,* February 1, 1988.
13. Japanese Ministry of Finance data. During 1987, Sino-Japanese trade ($16 billion on a bilateral basis) fell 13.7 percent from the level of 1986.
14. See "Nakasone Take Seoul Plea for Talks in Peking," *Financial Times,* November 10, 1987 and Mainichi Shimbun, January 20, 1987.
15. "Dormitory Hubbub," *Far Eastern Economic Review,* May 21, 1987, p. 39.
16. Nitchu Keizai Kyokai, established in 1972 with partial financing from the Japanese government, the association was to play a "private role" in trade with China. Japan's largest trade associations (Keidanren and the Keizai Doyukai) cooperated to form the organization.
17. See "Itoh a Big Partner in Trade Deals," *China Daily,* September 29, 1987.
18. In 1986, according to Chinese analyses, 85 percent of the technology and equipment imported by China was in equipment (hardware rather than software). See *China Daily News,* September 7, 1987.
19. Chinese statistics record imports of "items of technology and equipment." For a review of trends in the period 1973–1986, see *China's Foreign Trade,* issue 3, 1987.
20. See Deborah Diamond-Kim, "The Power of Commitment," *The China Business Review,* November–December 1986, p. 43.
21. The "software" component of technology and plant imports to China has been increasing, according to Chinese statistics. See Keisuke Odagawa, "A Japanese View of China's Plant and Technology Market," *China Newsletter,* 69, July–August 1987, p. 9.
22. See, for example, Nai-Reunn Chen, *Foreign Investment in China: Current Trends,* U.S. Department of Commerce, 1986 and National Council for U.S.–China Trade, *U.S. Joint Ventures in China: A Progress Report,* 1987. Note that data cover a number of categories, including cooperative ventures, joint resource development projects, and processing arrangements. Data on investment in China vary greatly and should be treated with caution.
23. In 1985, Japanese investors had pledged more than $12 billion in ASEAN and about $100 million in China. *China Business Review,* November–December 1986, p. 37.
24. This conclusion is based on careful examination of the aggregate date on trade, investment, and technology transfer as well as reading of the Japanese-language and English-language press.
25. For an excellent analysis of the background security factors that led Japan to reevaluate aid policies toward China, see William L. Brooks, "Japanese Economic Assistance to China," paper for Center for Strategic and International

Studies Conference on Japan and the United States in the Third World, May 19, 1987.

26. Figures on a net disbursement basis, from the Overseas Economic Cooperation Fund.
27. The United States has no formal aid program for China, but the government does provide limited assistance in the form of feasibility studies carried out through the Trade and Development Program (TDP). TDP programs in China were funded at about $4.6 million in 1986. See OTA, *Technology Transfer to China,* 1987, p. 234.
28. China suspended some contracts with Japanese firms in 1979 and 1981 due to foreign exchange shortages that made it difficult to cover the local costs of projects. Some OECF funds were eventually used to provide commodity loans to support the completion of the Baoshun steel complex and a petrochemical facility. See Brooks, p. 13.
29. Hiroko Asami, "A Symbol of Friendship," *China Medical,* Spring 1987, p. 68.
30. "Looking for Tokyo," *China Trade Report,* April 1987, p. 4.
31. See, for example, Ian Harper, "China's Loan Menu Offer Takeaway Profit for U.K.," *Electronic Times* (London), May 22, 1986, concerning a British plan to provide 300 million pounds in soft financing for China.
32. See Hong K. Kim and Richard K. Nanto, "Emerging Patterns of Sino-Japanese Cooperation," *Journal of Northeast Asian Studies,* Fall 1985.
33. Kim, p. 41.
34. Nigel Campbell, China Trade Strategies: The Inside Story.
35. Observers in the U.S. Congress, however, remain anxious to see how the new programs and policies will be implemented before they draw the conclusion that Japanese export controls have been effectively strengthened.
36. "Hitachi, Chugoku e VTR Gijutsu" [Hitachi to Export VTR Technology to China], *Nihon Keizai Shimbun*, January 23, 1988, p. 1.
37. "Foreign Trade Council to Train Chinese," reported by Kyodo on January 28, 1988 as reported in FBIS-EAS-88–020, February 1, 1988, p. 3.
38. Bob King, "Japan–China Link in TV Drive," *Financial Times* (London), August 6, 1987. p. 4.
39. DOD report, 1987.

9
China and Opportunities for Economic Development Through Technology Transfer

WILLIAM A. FISCHER

Technology, be it hardware or software,[1] is value-laden. It reflects, in design, operation, and inherent expectations about its utilization and advantages, the culture in which it was conceived. Sometimes this is an important factor and sometimes it is not. The significance is determined by the scale of the transfer and the cultural, environmental, and economic differences between the originating society and the employing society. Nonetheless, one consequence is that the process of technology transfer is an inherently contradictory process. Although the objective of any technology transfer is to benefit the recipient by upgrading its capabilities in some fashion (in market-regulated transfers the supplier of a technology also expects to benefit from its participation), any such improvement is usually accompanied by adjustments, accommodations, and often concessions, among individuals, institutions, and practices in the receiving nation, that are necessitated by new requirements introduced into the economic/social system by the alien technology.[2] Sometimes these changes are minor or positive and result in an almost "painless" and generally popular improvement in the local situation. On other occasions, however, the dislocations in institutional and/or value regimes in the recipient country may be quite dramatic and lead to significant disadvantages or destabilization among negatively affected segments of the society. The societal context into which technology is transferred may be more important to the ultimate success or failure of that transfer than the technology itself.

Despite anticipated cultural contradictions and the costs and dislocations involved, the aggressive upgrading of local skills and capabilities through some form of technology transfer remains a common policy of choice in most developing countries, including a growing number of previously politically isolated nations.[3] For a variety of reasons, these nations appear to believe that the potential advantages of rapid industrial growth through the acquisition of existing foreign technology outweigh the costs and fears associated with a degree of foreign influence over product design, process development, product utilization, and organizational design and management that would otherwise not be present. Often, however, the policy decisions that are made regarding the acquisition of foreign technology, and/or the analyses of these decisions, fail to consider the cultural, social, economic, and political context in which the transfer occurs. For example, these decisions are frequently made by agencies responsible for technology transfer in a legalistic sense and nothing more. Furthermore, such agencies tend to be preoccupied with the immediacies of their own situation and are often oblivious to the surrounding international arena for technology flows. The purpose of this chapter is to consider an active and ongoing program of economic modernization in the People's Republic of China, which is heavily dependent on the acquisition of foreign technology, and to consider this experience in terms of other economic and social concerns as well as international competition for markets and development resources.[4]

GROWTH PATHS FOR ECONOMIC DEVELOPMENT AND THE ROLE OF TECHNOLOGY TRANSFER

The Traditional Growth Path

The demand for industrial science and technology, be it foreign or indigenous in origin, is derived from demands for other things. As I have noted elsewhere, "the ability to develop new industrial products and processes is associated with the process of economic development. In fact, often it is not the products or processes themselves that are desired, but the industrial capabilities embodied in them."[5] These industrial capabilities are seen as the means to such ends as a better standard of living and a higher quality of life for the citizens of the developing country. At the industrial level, the acquisition of foreign technology is often seen as a means of achieving foreign exchange by facilitating access to international commerce. Therefore, the pursuit of foreign exchange to satisfy other national objectives is often seen as an important rationale for transfer of foreign technology that will improve the developing nation's export potential. Accordingly, a national policy geared toward the generation of foreign exchange has traditionally meant an initial adoption of a "growth path" that emphasizes increased exports of high-volume, commodity-type products; the production of which relies heavily on low-wage, unskilled labor: the developing country's primary comparative advantage. In such instances, the exporting industry seeks to compete on the basis of flow-shop assembly processes exhibiting a high division of labor. Here, the considerably lower wages in the developing nations allows the industry to offer a comparative advantage to potential customers from the developed world. The products have tended to be almost exclusively high-volume, low-variety, no-fashion, mature products, as these require little of the manufacturer other than acceptable (but not necessarily "better than acceptable") quality, and low production costs. Design (to the extent that there is any), distribution, and marketing, tend to be the province of the developed world buyers, who then typically market the products under their own label, within their own system. The maturity of the product, and the lack of fashion, ensure that there will be few if any "surprises" in terms of market demand and, consequently, little if any "responsiveness" is needed by the developing country factory. This is further reinforced to the extent that the production process can be segmented, thus allowing the decoupling of the activities performed in the developing country from vertically dependent preceding and succeeding activities. This removes any reason for integration or infrastructure development on the part of the foreign buyer and reduces the risk of production disruption due to faulty or inadequate interorganizational linkages.

In short, it is possible to characterize the traditional growth path for development through manufactured products as having been through the subcontracting of cheap labor resources, by developing country industries, for the production (or a portion thereof) of simple products for buyers from the developed world. In this manner, the developing country industrial enterprise enters into the realm of international business, exports product, and earns foreign exchange but, nonetheless, still remains somewhat detached from the global market place. Some observers, in fact, see this as an affirmation that a new stage in capitalism has been reached, with developing country production being incorporated into a "system of production geared to retaining competitiveness for firms in developed countries after a product has entered the down side of the product cycle."[6] The choice of this model also represents the perpetuation of the traditional center-periphery relationship between the developing country industry and the developed world.[7] Needless to say, such views run counter to the aspirations for national economic and political sovereignty that many in the developing world have hoped would come as a result of their entrée into international commerce.

Technology transfer under such conditions has tended to be restricted to the the movement of older, labor-intensive equipment and complete production processes that are exchanged either as outright sales or as portions of compensatory contract arrangements. Only incidental production management skills are transferred (if any are transferred at all) and the institutional relationships are neither assumed to be necessarily durable nor intimate. Such circumstances are suitable in those situations where a degree of market "closeness" is being retained as long as the products to be exported remain simple ones. As the exported products become more sophisticated, however, the need for increased and freer relations with foreign economic actors becomes necessary. Only in those nations where the domestic market has been opened up, however, can there be greater reliance on technology transfer mechanisms that involve a more durable and dependable presence on the part of developed country firms, such as franchises, joint ventures, and even direct foreign investment into wholly owned subsidiaries. These types of transfers introduce greater degrees of foreign technology and expertise into the society but also greater foreign cultural and political influence.

Alternative Growth Paths

The traditional growth path for the generation of foreign exchange through increased exports is one that is extremely manufacturing oriented and, in fact, is based on the "brute force power" of the economies of scale associated with the highly repetitive mass production of simple products. It cares little for the development of market sensitivities or distribution systems and, as we have seen above, leads the developing nation to rely on agents of firms in the developed world to account for such matters. In the event, however, that such a growth path is blocked, an alternative growth path that produces foreign exchange must be developed or else the policies of economic reform and modernization may very well come to a screeching halt. Christopher Bartlett, writing in the global strategy literature, suggests the basis on which alternative growth paths might be developed (Fig. 9.1: path 1 represents the traditional growth path described above).[8]

The "natural" competitive reaction to overwhelming cost advantages tends to be the development of a "market niche" strategy that emphasizes some sort of particular responsiveness to customer needs, usually either in terms of product design or development or else in terms of a willingness to serve the customer promptly despite very short notice. Hayes and Wheelwright have suggested that in mature markets such responsiveness means positioning the manufacturing process somewhere "above" mass production in the "high customization–low customization" continuum.[9] This is de-

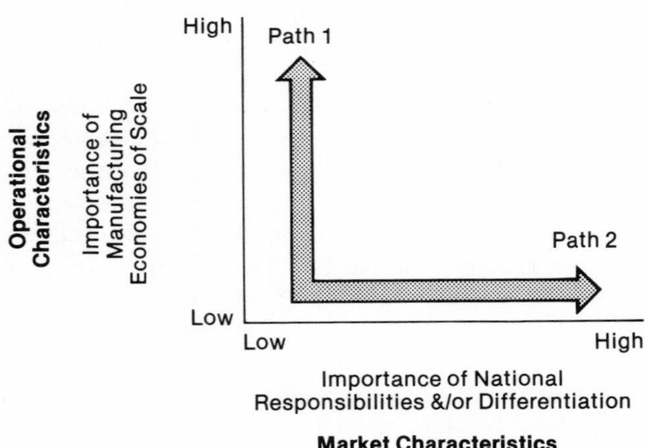

Figure 9.1 Market characteristics.

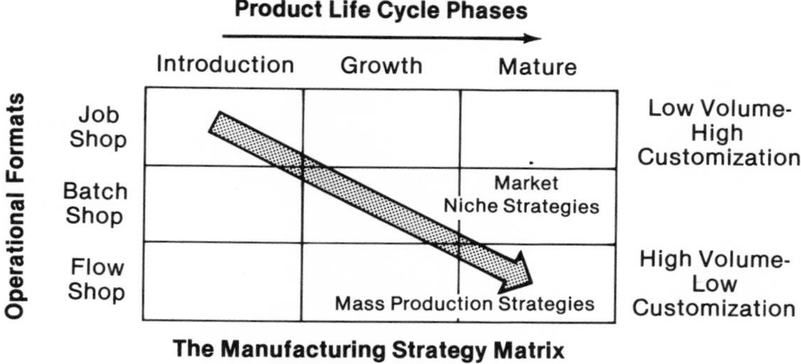

Figure 9.2 The manufacturing strategies matrix.

picted in Figure 9.2. The managerial implications of such a position are profound and often difficult for a firm from a developing country to master. First, and foremost, is the degree of market understanding necessary to be not only responsive to changing customer desires but, frequently, to be able to anticipate them to quickly "gear up" for the production of new or altered products, along with high levels of support from the firm's vendors, who also must be able to respond quickly. Needless to say, the quality of such products must be high (to justify the premium that can be commanded) and access to and dependability of distribution systems must be guaranteed. One way of dealing with such requirements is to locate manufacturing operations close to, or in, the target market to better serve it. This has led to so-called "franchise sourcing," through the establishment of highly autonomous affiliates or subsidiaries in the target market.[10] Growth paths that emphasize a high degree of local responsiveness and/or differentiation are depicted in Figure 9.1 as path 2.

National Policy Prerequisites for Growth Path Exploitation

The successful choice of a particular growth path from Figure 9.1 requires not only industrial capability but can require significant government policy support as well. Often, this relates to policies governing the presence of imports and/or the encouragement of exports and policies regarding the degree of "openness" in the domestic market. For the past decade or more, a wide following (although not complete consensus[11]) has developed among students of economic development around the idea that the outward-looking, export-led economies, such as those that characterized the recent economic growth within Southeast Asia, are now accepted, if not "preferred," "models" for national economic and social growth.[12] It is argued, for example, that these trade regimes force the exposure of local industries to international competition and that such competition not only raises the sophistication of the local industries but also stimulates entrepreneurial and innovative vitality. Developing nations that have adopted more insulated, import-substitution regimes, on the other hand, have tended to grow less rapidly and have exhibited a poorer sense of "responsiveness" to changing world market conditions. At the same time, it is important to note that the relationship between external orientation (i.e., export promotion (EP)) versus import substitution (IS) is not the same as, but is related to, national policies regarding domestic market orientation. Domestic market orientation addresses degrees of market openness to foreign economic interests and while the external and domestic orientations are related, they are potentially two very different and separate policy choices. In considering external orientations, "import substitution" refers to situations where the government encourages foreign trade relations to move *away* from a neutral laissez-faire position regarding the sourcing of products toward conditions favoring indigenous sourcing of items (by local firms or local agents of select foreign firms) to conserve foreign exchange, protect domestic industries, or reduce foreign influence.[13] "Export promotion," on the other hand, refers to those economies where government policy has moved *toward* the neutral free-trade position, through the encouragement of exports: "Thus the EP strategy does not imply any subsidization of exports beyond the level that restores equality between the effective exchange rates on imports and exports."[14] The second dimension, which describes market openness, can be conceived of as a range of situations bounded at one end by those relatively open societies, where the government is neutral on the question of sourcing, allowing international market prices to determine the origin of an item, to those societies at the polar opposite end of the spectrum, where access to the domestic market is significantly constrained by government policy, that is, relatively "closed" societies.[15] A simple matrix portraying various combinations of export/import emphasis and the openness of the domestic market is provided in Figure 9.3.

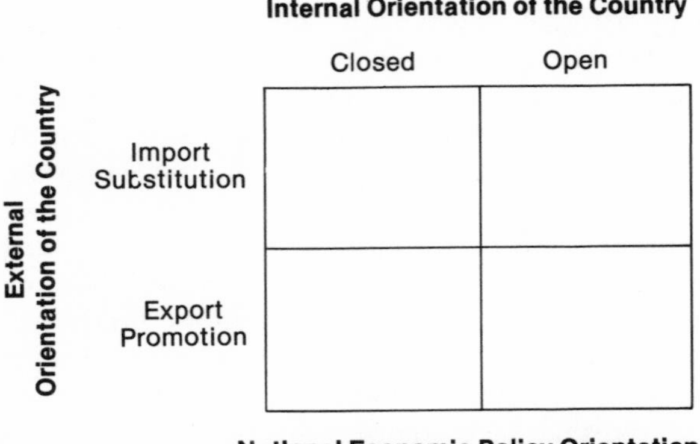

Figure 9.3 National economic policy organizations.

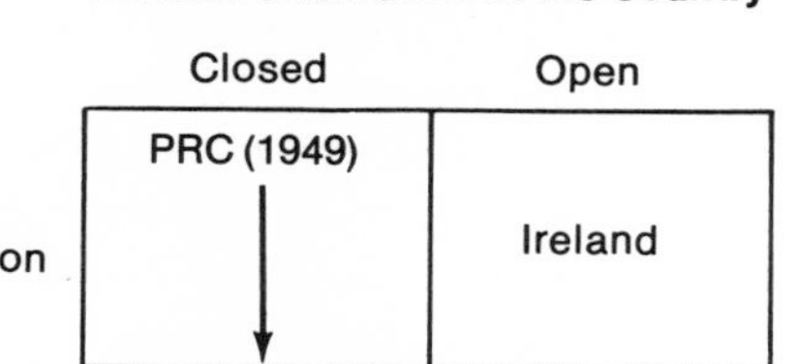

Figure 9.4 National economic policy orientations.

It is, in fact, possible to cite examples of the various combinations of trade regimes that are possible (Fig. 9.4). The People's Republic of China, between 1949 and 1979, was essentially a closed economy emphasizing policies of import-substitution. Present-day Korea appears to be a relatively closed economy favoring export-promotion, as was Japan during its period of rapid economic growth in the 1960s and 1970s. Hong Kong has apparently always been both open and export-promotive, whereas Ireland, with its access to the European economic community (EEC), suggests an example of a relatively open economy that has attracted foreign investment chiefly because of the advantages associated with import-substitution.[16]

The choice of a foreign economic regime, considering both the primary orientation of foreign economic relations and the openness of the domestic market, is a reflection of government policy and local infrastructural conditions. The autarky that characterizes closed–IS economies is primarily determined by government policy and serves to isolate the national economy from the rest of the world's advances in science and technology, fashion, and managerial practice. Closed–EP economies, on the other hand, represent attempts to generate foreign exchange to acquire needed technologies, but at the same time attempt to protect local industry from foreign economic and/or cultural encroachment. Such economies, to compete through exports, must have access to foreign technologies and designs. Because of their desire to insultate their economy from foreign exposure, technology transfer is typically achieved through such "arms-length" technology transfer mechanisms as licenses, reverse-engineering and imitation, and some contract services. For such arms-length mechanisms to work, however, the nation must possess sophisticated absorptive capacities because the actual assimilation of the foreign experience is being consummated in a nonintimate situation. The importance of such a sophisticated absorptive capacity was quite evident in the case of Japan.[17] Considerable time is also required for the achievement of international standards in many industries under such a closed–EP regime of foreign economic relations. The idea of open economies that emphasize import substitution policies, on the other hand, is somewhat contradictory. Nonetheless, Ireland's access to the EEC market, and the IS policies that were evolving within the EEC, suggest just such a regime. In most cases, this type of economic policy will work to attract desired foreign technology only when the market to be served is a large one. The primary disadvantage of the open–IS regime is that it is not an effective generator of hard currency, as exports are not encouraged. In the case of an economy where the prevailing local infrastructure is undeveloped (thus ruling out of closed–EP regime), and foreign exchange is desired (thereby eliminating an open–IS regime), it becomes important to arrange technology transfer mechanisms that ensure both intimacy and durability in the relationship between the foreign technology supplier and the recipient nation. Such mechanisms include franchises, co-production, joint ventures, and even direct foreign investments. Figure 9.3 would suggest that this means a combination of export promotion (to generate foreign exchange) and access to the domestic market (to attract an intimate and durable presence by the foreign technology supplier): the open–EP position. The choice of one of these four foreign economic relations regimes creates the surrounding policy environment in which industrial decisions take place.

CHINA: TECHNOLOGY AND ECONOMIC DEVELOPMENT

In the case of China, the debate over the wisdom and advisability of fueling economic growth through increased participation of foreign technology, investment, and influence has been a topic of serious debate for a considerable time. For at least several hundred years, the Chinese have had to consider the merits and demerits associated with Western science and technology. The record of post-war China has been one of alternating periods of great interest in and almost total rejection of foreign technology. Central to the present set of economic reforms initiated by Deng Xiaoping is an explicit and dramatic endorsement of the virtues of "opening up" to the outside world and a recognition of centrality with regard to the role that foreign technology will play in China's modernization. What is not quite as clear, however, is the nature of the mechanism by which foreign technology will influence China's economic development post-Tianamen Square in 1989. The specific path by which China hopes to modernize is not yet totally apparent and the lessons of other nations' developmental experiences, particularly in Asia, are obscured by differences in the international commercial environment that suggest changing motivations and practices on the part of technology suppliers as well as newly emerging competition for development resources among a set of simultaneously modernizing major nations—China, the Soviet Union, and India—not to mention a host of newly industrializing (Hong Kong, Taiwan, Singapore, and South Korea) and neo-newly industrializing (e.g., Thailand) countries (NICs) and regions. In sum, the opportunities for economic development in China, through technology transfer, will grow or contract in direct response to the dynamics of forces both internal and external to the Chinese economy, which relate directly to the calculus of the suppliers' and recipient's needs, perceptions, and adjustment capabilities.

For most of its existence, the People's Republic of China has exhibited a relatively close, import-substitution foreign trade regime. For a variety of reasons, ranging from foreign-imposed economic blockades to the chaos of the Cultural Revolution, China has expended relatively little energy on external foreign economic relations. The one notable exception was the massive transfer of Soviet technology that marked the first 10 years of the People's Republic's life. Ironically, in the 1960s, fear of Soviet military intentions led China to continue adherence to a philosophy (and policies) of "self-reliance," at the national and regional levels, that further frustrated any inclinations toward increased foreign economic contacts as a result of the now institutionalized structural deficiencies within the Chinese economy. In fact, even if such inclinations did exist, China, during the period from 1949 to 1979, was ill-prepared to enter into competitive international markets. It not only faced the numbing requirements of rebuilding a war-devastated economy and attending to the domestic needs of one-quarter of the world's population, but its economic infrastructure, management sophistication, and operational assets were inadequate to meet the demands that would be made by almost any level of international economic intercourse. Of course, continued isolation from the international marketplace did very little to alleviate this situation and probably exacerbated China's inability to compete when prevailing government policies changed in the late 1970s.

The reascension of Deng Xiaoping and the supporters of economic and political reform in the late 1970s brought with it a new attitude toward the role of foreign economic interests in developing China. "Opening-up" to the outside world became an explicit goal of the new modernization effort. Progress in each of the "Four Modernizations" has become dependent on foreign technologies and expertise to an almost critical level. The reformers have, in return, seen significant growth in the interest of foreign industries in developing a presence in China. In 1987, China's total foreign trade amounted to U.S. $82.7 billion, of which exports amounted to U.S. $39.5 billion, and imports U.S. $43.2 billion. At this level, exports amounted to 13.5 percent of the gross national product in 1987, compared with 9 percent in 1981.[18] In addition, U.S. $7.57 billion were actually invested in China in 1987 by foreign interests, of which U.S. $2.24 billion represented direct investment.[19] By the end of 1987, there were 10,008 joint ventures with foreign partners operating in China, representing a total contract value of U.S. $21.96 billion since 1979, with U.S. $8.47 billion paid-in as of that date. Although the numbers are quite difficult to define precisely, the Chinese government has "confirmed" 226 of them as being "technically advanced" and 608 as being "export-oriented."[20]

Despite these rather impressive numbers, few (either Chinese or foreign) would maintain that the present extent of foreign participation in the Chinese economy is totally satisfactory. In fact, many would probably state that it is actually disappointing. The reasons for this are many and complex, and the fault lies on both sides, but the implications are significant for continued Chinese economic development. In brief, China has not attracted either the numbers or the type of foreign investment and trade that it had hoped for. Its foreign trade balance has been a deficit (albeit lately a declining one) since 1984,[21] and it continues to lag behind the rest of the world in both technological innovation and commercial practice.[22] Nonetheless, it remains the clear intention of the present Chinese leadership to rely on foreign economic relationships to power the development of the nation's economy, and one can expect continued policy initiatives to emanate from the very highest levels of the Chinese government in an attempt to effect a more suitable environment with regard to foreign economic interests.

CHINA: THE LIKELY DEVELOPMENT SCENARIO

Potential Problems with Growth Paths 1 and 2

As noted earlier, the traditional development scenario for many developing countries is characterized by a reliance on cheap labor to produce commodity-type articles in mature markets (Fig. 9.1; growth path 1). These products are typically sold to well-established distribution systems based in the developed world. This scenario is not unfamiliar to Chinese policymakers and, in fact, has been the growth path relied on within the Chinese textile and apparel industries. Such a growth path would be attractive to the Chinese because it would generate foreign exchange earnings by exploiting China's clear competitive advantage: cheap labor. It would also allow China to preserve an essentially closed or protected domestic economy, free from foreign competition and cultural influences (Fig. 9.3; closed–EP). However, a simple linear extrapolation of the initial growth path of exportation of low-cost, mass-produced, commodity type items is likely to encounter significant economic and/or political problems in a reasonably short time and, in the case of China, these problems appear to have the potential to short-circuit or divert export (and hence economic) growth from the originally conceived plan (Fig. 9.5).

There are several reasons why it is unlikely that China will continue along the closed–EP growth path that it has recently adopted after moving from nearly three decades of closed–IS behavior. Possibly the most potent of these reasons is the potential for automation that is inherent in the very sectors of developed country markets targeted by Chinese exports. The simplicity of the products involved, their low fashion content, and the large

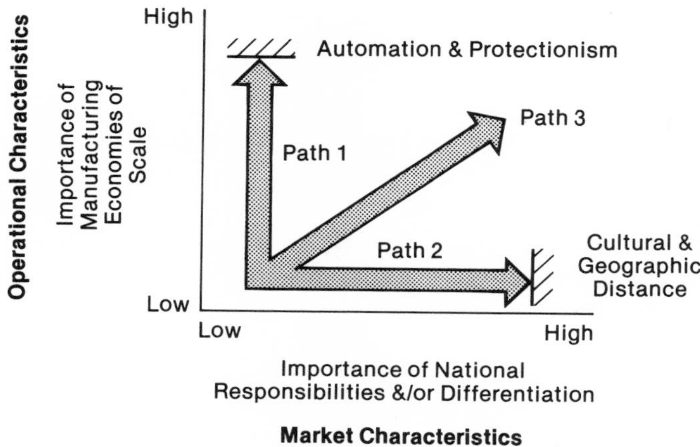

Figure 9.5 Market characteristics.

production volumes involved argue for increased automation within the besieged firms in the developed country industries. Recently, in fact, many such industries in the United States have invested heavily in automation, resulting in a return to the United States of a number of assembly processes that had previously moved offshore to co-opt low-wage foreign labor. Continued investment in capital equipment also reduces the importance of the direct labor component of the cost of goods sold, making offshore production that much less compelling.[23] In addition, competition in the commodity-end of mature markets, based on low price advantages, leads to low profit margins, making these products somewhat unattractive to the manufacturers. A further threat to the continued growth of low-wage Chinese exports is the rising tide of protectionist sentiments in the developed world. Nearly 60 antidumping actions have already been taken in developed countries against Chinese products in a variety of industries where increased exports have led to unemployment of older, unskilled, and less mobile citizens of the developed country.[24] Finally, the Chinese themselves have a tradition of preoccupation with their own domestic market. Not only is it easier for a Chinese manager to serve the domestic market than it is to export, it is frequently more profitable as well. This lack of inducement, and even disincentive, saps the enthusiasm for exports at the level of the firm and diverts industry from supporting government policy. Finally, the prevailing policies of autonomy and decentralization work against the need for the coordination and integration that would be needed to maximize a strong economies of scale strategy. Chinese managers, intent on maximizing the fortunes of their own enterprises in what they perceive to be a zero-sum game, resist the sort of cooperation and direction that would maximize the gains to China that might result from this sort of strategy.

One possible variation on this theme is for Chinese industries to serve other developing country markets with products that can be mass-produced with labor intensive operations without fear of retaliation through automation or protectionism. Denis Simon has labeled such a strategy an "intermediate market,"[25] but it carries the burden of logistical difficulties involved in serving culturally and geographically diverse, often small and always poor markets, that have inadequate distribution systems. Furthermore, such markets are not demanding, consequently even the seller, successful there may not be prepared to enter the much richer and more demanding cosmopolitan markets in the "first world."

Similarly, there are strong barriers to increased exports, and the generation of foreign exchange, through the choice of a strategy based on local responsiveness and/or differentiation (growth path 2). In this case, the Chinese are too distant, both geographically and culturally, and have been isolated from the advanced industrial societies of the West for too long to be effective providers of customized products. The Chinese understanding of Western fashion, design, quality expectations, and distribution systems is presently totally inadequate for the high level of responsiveness that a high-customized strategy requires.[26]

Participation in Global Networks: An Alternative Growth Path

A third possible growth path, and one that is distinctly nontraditional, is for the developing country firm to insinuate itself into a global manufacturing/distribution network, organized by a transnational firm from the developed world. In this case, the operational characteristics that heretofore were limited to manufacturing economies of scale (Fig. 9.1), are now expanded to include the economies attendant to coordination and integration into a common network of raw material suppliers, component manufacturers, producers of finished products, and distributors. The benefits from such an arrangement appear to be considerable. Participation in a global manufacturing/distribution network would provide Chinese firms an entrée into international trade as a collaborator rather than as a competitor. This should work to increase greatly Chinese access to market information, managerial skills and knowledge, new manufacturing technology, and a host of other essentials required to support fully the network's mission.[27] As a member of a global manufacturing/distribution network, the Chinese firm guarantees a durable and intimate presence by the more sophisticated foreign partner, so that the costs and frustrations of arms-length technology transfers no longer have to be incurred. In short, participation in such global networks allows China to compete on the basis of its primary comparative advantage—cheap labor—but in a fashion that does not necessarily lead to a blunting or diverting of this growth path.

Requirements for Growth Path 3

Despite its apparent attractiveness, growth path 3 requires the adoption of economic policies by the Chinese government that represent significant departures from what has been seen in China during the period of the People's Republic. To be responsive to the needs of a network, the member Chinese firm must allow a degree of intimacy and involvement by its foreign partners in matters such as product design, vendor selection, process technology choice and investment, manpower skills and workload planning, that heretofore have been the province of bureaus within the industrial structure, or even various mechanisms of the Communist Party. Furthermore, significant improvements are needed in the ambient Chinese infrastructure to assure the manufacturing responsiveness and organizational agility needed to participate in sophisticated international markets. Clearly, the close and continuing involvement of transnational corporations will be necessary to achieve such conditions. However, there must be inducements for such involvement if it is to be forthcoming. Primarily, these inducements involve some promise of eventual access to the domestic Chinese market, some promise of being able to serve that market in a relatively unfettered manner, and some hope of being able to repatriate the profits generated by such activities. Anything less will reduce the interest that such transnational firms might have for establishing a long-term, reliable presence in China; without such a presence, China will be forever consigned to be a bit player on the periphery of the world market. Essentially, China must adopt an open–EP regime to secure the type of technology transfer intimacy required to obtain advanced technology and managerial sophistication *and* generate foreign exchange.

Alternatives to China

The "Eldorado" promise of China that attracted so many foreign suitors in the 1970s has dimmed over the years, as many have withdrawn from the market with little but horror stories to relate. At the same time, new entrants have appeared, some from unlikely corners of the world community, and offer practical alternatives to China for foreign investment, technology, and managerial involvement. In particular, India, the Soviet Union, and some of the neo-NICs, have grown in relative attractiveness over the past few years and have consequently reduced China's bargaining leverage.

Each of these alternatives has elements that make it more attractive than China at any particular point in time, and disadvantages that detract from its suitability. India, for example, represents a large pool of low-wage labor that is suitable for inclusion into global sourcing networks and its domestic market is not only large but perhaps potentially "richer" than China's. The English language is one of India's basic languages and its legal and commercial traditions are Western in origin. On the other hand, India suffers from images left over from the 1970s when it established a closed–IS regime and drove firms as prominent as IBM and Coca Cola out of its market. In addition, despite the recent philosophical changes under Rajiv Ghandi, the Indian governmental bureaucracy remains one of the most formidable in the world.

Perhaps the greatest uncertainty recently introduced into the calculus of global business is the Soviet Union under Mikhail Gorbachev. While in many ways more removed from the international community for a longer period of time than even China, and clearly underdeveloped in terms of civilian industrial capabilities and managerial skills, the Soviet Union, with its large population and commercial access to Eastern Europe, presents an attractive opportunity for Western investment. Anyone who doubts this should consider the recent observation by Donald M. Kendall, former Chairman of Pepsi Co. (which plans to add 21 bottling plants to the 19 it already franchises in the Soviet Union): "You can't stay out of a country the size of the Soviet Union and stay a major international marketer."[28] With such thoughts being bandied about, it is not entirely out of the question that new corporate investment in the Soviet Union might compete with similar investments in China. Nonetheless, despite the promise and allure of *perestroika,* it seems unlikely that the Soviet Union will, in the relatively near-term at least, pose a major threat to continued investment in the Peoples Republic of China.

Finally, there remains the potential of the NICs and the neo-NICs. These economies, including Taiwan, Hong Kong, South Korea, and Hong Kong, as well as Indonesia, Thailand, Malaysia, Brazil, and a number of other nations poised for economic take-off, may represent the real, continued threat to China's ability to pursue growth path 3. Already possessing reasonably good infrastructures, skilled work forces, and a tradition of responsiveness, these economies are not terribly threatened by competion from low-wage Chinese labor in a world where the relative importance of direct labor costs appears to be continuous. Perhaps their principal disadvantage lies in their own small (although rich) domestic markets and the consequential inability to compete with China as a source of investment if access to domestic markets ever becomes a "bargaining chip."[29]

CONCLUSIONS

The argument has been made throughout that technology transfer is as much a political and social phenomenon as it is an economic one and that strategies that involve the utilization of foreign technology for economic development also require accompanying social and political policy changes that can be quite contradictory to the initial rationale for the technology transfer. In the case of China, it appears unavoidable that benefits to be gained from the acquisition and utilization of foreign technology will come at the cost of increased foreign participation in Chinese economic and social systems. This will occur because the growth path appears most likely for China to follow will require a degree of commercial partnership between global manufacturing and distribution networks and Chinese enterprises that transcends the traditional prerogatives of both the Chinese state and Communist Party. Without a significant relaxation in these two entities, control over management of the Chinese enterprise, and the Chinese domestic economy, it is quite possible that potential suppliers of foreign technology will look elsewhere for partners. At a time when other sizable nations, such as India and the Soviet Union, are reentering the world economy, such threats are not idle ones.

NOTES

1. Throughout this paper, the term *software* is employed to represent the practices that are associated with a particular technology. These practices may pertain to work styles, managerial skills, or commercial behavior.
2. The late Frank Bradbury observed that one of the characteristics that differentiated technology transfer from other "transfer processes in technological change" is that in order for technology transfer to be successful, changes had to occur in either the technology or the recipient.
3. While China is the most obvious and most significant example, Vietnam, Laos, and North Korea are other recent examples of countries attempting to break their isolation from Western technology by making overtures to potential foreign investment.
4. This chapter will address issues of economic development from the perspective of corporate strategy rather than from the more traditional macroeconomic perspective. There are two reasons for this:

    1. The author agrees with the argument advanced by Kim Clark that an understanding of international economic competition requires both a knowledge of markets and a knowledge of what goes on within the organizations in those markets: ". . . from the standpoint of policy, whether public or private, on international competition and innovation, a greater understanding of the role of management in competition seems essential." Effective executive decisions and action depend on the competitive environment as well as on what happens inside the firm. Similarly, public policy on innovation and international competition will work its effect through firms, where behavior is strongly influenced by the internal structure and processes that govern decision and action. [Kim B. Clark, "Managing Technology in International Competition: The Case of Product Development in Response to Foreign Entry," in A. Michael Spence and Heather A. Hazard (eds.), *International Competitiveness* (Cambridge, MA, Ballinger, 1988), p. 29.]; and
    2. The role of institutions is so important in China, in terms of understanding possibilities and defining constraints, that it is necessary to craft development strategies at the industry level to explore these issues at a meaningful and practical level. Consequently, this chapter continues to develop a theme recently presented by the author in William A. Fischer, "China as a Player in the World Economy," prepared for the 1988 Montgomery Lecture on

Marxism and Captialism in the People's Republic of China, The University of Nebraska at Lincoln, Lincoln, Nebraska, March 3, 1988.

5. William A. Fisher, "Trade Policy and the Impact of Foreign Technology," in Richard D. Robinson (ed.), *Direct Foreign Investment* (New York, Praeger, 1987), p. 153.
6. Joseph Grunwald and Kenneth Flamm, *The Global Factory,* Washington, D.C., The Brookings Institution, 1985, pp. 6–7.
7. Robert Heilbroner, "Hard Times," *The New Yorker,* September 14, 1987, pp. 96–109.
8. Christopher A. Bartlett,"Building and Managing the Transnational: The New Organizational Challenge," in Michael E. Porter (ed.), *Competition in Global Industries* (Boston, MA, Harvard Business School Press, 1986). The material that follows is based on the premise that Bartlett's work provides a useful means of conceptualizing various industrial strategies at the firm level. These strategies then suggest implications for a developing country, whose industries opt to pursue such strategy.
9. Robert H. Hayes and Steven C. Wheelwright, "Link Manufacturing Process and Product Life Cycles," *Harvard Business Review,* January–February 1979, pp. 133–140.
10. M. Therese Flaherty talks about "franchise sourcing" in "International Sourcing: Beyond Catalog Shopping and Franchising," Working Paper, Harvard Business School, March 1988. The choice of foreign affiliates to serve target "host" markets is discussed in Jack N. Behrman and William A. Fischer, *Overseas R&D Activities of Transnational Companies* (Cambridge, MA, Oelgeschlager, Gunn & Hain, 1980).
11. Deepak Lal and Sarath Rajapatirana, "Foreign Trade Regimes and Economic Growth in Developing Countries," *The World Bank Research Observer,* 2 (2), July 1987, pp. 189–218.
12. John B. Sheahan, *Alternative International Economic Strategies and Their Relevance for China,* World Bank Staff Working Papers, Number 759, 1986.
13. Lal and Rajapatirana, ibid.
14. Ibid., p. 197.
15. Ibid., p. 210.
16. The choice of Ireland for this last category was suggested by comments made by Richard Robinson in "Government Policy Options vis-a-vis Foreign Business Activity," paper presented at the Chinese Academy of Social Sciences–Sloan School of MIT conference on The Role of Foreign Investment in Economic Development, Hangzhou, China, March 1985.
17. William A. Fischer, *Japanese Postwar Industrial Innovation: A Review of the Literature* (Washington, D.C., The Program of Policy Studies in Science and Technology, George Washington University, 1974).
18. Xinhua English Service, February 23, 1988, as reported in Foreign Broadcast Information Service, *China: Daily Report,* FBIS-CHI-88–035, February 23, 1988, p. 12; GNP figures for 1987 from Xinhua English Service, February 23, 1988, as reported in Foreign Broadcast Information Service, *China: Daily Report,* FBIS-CHI-88–035, February 23, 1988, p. 11. Statistics for 1981 as reported in John B. Sheahan, *Alternative International Economic Strategies and Their Relevance for China,* World Bank Staff Working Paper #759, Washington, D.C., The World Bank, 1986, p. 42.
19. Xinhua English Service, ibid., p. 12.

20. Shen Feiyue, "Foreign Capital Ventures Top 10,000," *China Daily,* January 23, 1988, p. 1.
21. Elizabeth Cheng, "Reforms Could Lead to Larger Deficit," *Far Eastern Economic Review,* March 24, 1988, pp. 72–73.
22. William A. Fischer, "China's Industrial Innovation: The Influence of Market Forces," in Merle Goldman and Denis F. Simon (eds.), *China's New Technological Revolution* (Cambridge, MA, Harvard University Press, in press).
23. Flaherty, ibid., p. 13 and Table 2.
24. Xue Rongjiu, "The Causes of Protectionism and How to Deal With It," *Guoji Maoyi Wenti,* 3, 1987, pp. 1–9, as translated in Foreign Broadcast Information System, *JPRS Report,* JPRS-CAR-87–050, October 7, 1987, pp. 30–43.
25. Denis F. Simon, personal communication.
26. William A. Fischer, *The Transfer of Western Managerial Knowledge to China,* report prepared for the Office of Technology Assessment, Congress of the United States, May 1986; William A. Fischer, "Assessing Chinese Manufacturing Capabilities," paper presented at the National Meeting of the Academy of International Business, Chicago, October 1987.
27. Flaherty observes that "It appears that the potential for transferring knowledge among previously independent internationally franchised operations is enormous." ibid., p. 22.
28. Leslie Wayne, "Taling Deals—Joint Ventures in the Soviet Union," *The New York Times,* November 19, 1987, p. 30.
29. Hong Kong, of course, is already open, but the others are not totally so.

10

Assessing Success in the United States–China Technology Transfer

MARY ANN VON GLINOW, OTTO SCHNEPP, AND ARVIND BHAMBRI

Technology transfer is a process by which expertise or knowledge related to some aspect of technology and operations is passed from one group of individuals to another, and thereby from one firm to another (Schnepp et al., 1987). The process includes (1) the dissemination of documentation describing the technology, (2) the transfer of "know-how" for converting documentation to product, and (3) the transfer of hardware such as equipment and components. The typical technology transfer process evolves through a series of stages. Initial contacts evolve into negotiations. Once a formal contract is negotiated, there is a start-up phase for the actual transfer of technology. After the initial problems of start-up are overcome, the technology transfer settles into an ongoing process of feedback and exchange that continues until the relationship is terminated. The objectives and requirements of key stakeholders vary from stage to stage and provide the overall framework for assessing the success of the technology transfer process.

THE KEY STAKEHOLDERS

The primary stakeholders in a technology transfer project are obviously the affiliates directly involved in the project, namely the supplier(s) of the technology and the recipient(s). In some cases, financial institutions or Chinese government development corporations that set policy or provide resources are also stakeholders in the venture. Finally, the governments of the contractual participants serve as stakeholders as they also have an interest in, and can affect, the success or failure of the project. The interests and aims of the U.S. government are generally limited to policy level concerns centered around defense, security and political issues, but on the

Chinese side, the government agencies are often part of the actual decision-making process surrounding the technology transfer and the management of the industrial enterprise.

Stakeholder Profile

To define a frame of reference for evaluating success from the perspective of each stakeholder, a profile is presented that describes each key stakeholder's goals, resources, and decision-making processes.

The U.S. Technology Supplier

The typical U.S. technology supplier is a public corporation and, for the American observer, the most easily understood entity. Increased revenues and profits are primary goals for the company and entry into the potentially lucrative China market is one of the strategies toward this end. Since the most important resources contributed by the U.S. affiliate are technology and management expertise, the successful American company has frequently had an established record of international technology transfer and a reputation as a world leader in a specialty required by China for its modernization program. An implicit corporate goal, therefore, is for the U.S. firm to reinforce its image of technological leadership.

Although cooperative technology transfer projects in China have usually had strong support from the corporate office, decision-making authority has typically been vested in one key individual during most stages of the often protracted negotiations and implementation. This individual is typically a professional manager with experience in the company's international operations. Since these managers operate in the spotlight of attention from the corporate office during Chinese negotiations, one of his (her) personal goals typically is to achieve visible results as early as possible through the exercise of individual initiatives.

The Chinese Recipient

The Chinese technology recipient(s) have mostly been large- or medium-sized enterprises with employee populations frequently in excess of 2,000 workers. These enterprises often have a sizable, experienced, and competent engineering and technical workforce, but they have little emphasis on the management function. The primary aims of the Chinese affiliate(s) are centered around the acquisition of new and cutting-edge technology, updated expertise, and capability in design, manufacturing, as well as management. As a result, there is great concentration on maximizing training for the company's personnel in as much technology as the foreign affiliate can be convinced to include.

The decision-making process in Chinese enterprises is typically not obvious and information concerning it is not easily available to foreigners.

Typically, the enterprise is controlled or "led" by a central ministry bureau or a provincial (or municipal) bureau. Responsibility for negotiations has in the past been delegated to "trade corporations" reporting to the Ministry of Foreign Economic Relations and Trade (MOFERT), but more recently, the "leading department" has been in charge through its own trade corporation. Decisions are based on consensus among a number of agencies involving a relatively large number of individuals. This decision-making procedure is seen by Westerners as cumbersome and unnecessarily time consuming. From the Chinese representative's point of view, however, obtaining as much information as possible and going through the consensus and approval process is essential to protect him/herself from subsequent criticism and recriminations.

OVERALL INDICATORS OF SUCCESS

Technology Supplier Criteria

Studies have revealed a number of criteria that U.S. firms wish to optimize upon entry into the China market via technology transfer. Among these, the financial aspects of the project typically head the list (Clare, 1987) since profitability is uppermost among U.S. company aims. In the short term, revenues can be generated by direct sales or by the sale of technology and components as part of a licensing agreement. Profit and revenue volume are direct criteria for success. Since Chinese currency is not freely convertible, the portion of earnings that can be repatriated represents an additional, obvious and measurable, indicator. Most recently, the Chinese government has announced regulations under which such conversion may be facilitated.

An additional aim of most foreign companies is penetration of the Chinese domestic market. Access to the internal market is controlled by the government and any gains in this direction are important markers of success. There are two levels of market access, depending on whether the product source is located inside China or abroad. Locally produced products are likely to achieve market success as government approval of the project in the first place was based on domestic requirements. Direct access for the sale of foreign manufactured products is harder to achieve since it necessitates foreign currency allocations by the appropriate authorities. These sales, therefore, represent a high level of achievement and success.

Probably the most important criterion for commercial success in China is the degree of success in the management of the foreign exchange resources and demands of a joint venture. Often, critical components or materials, or both, have to be imported for local assembly or manufacture and the product is then sold to the internal market. To overcome the unavoidable foreign exchange deficit, the government encourages at least partial export of product to generate foreign exchange. In a number of cases the U.S. affiliate has been able to buy back components manufactured in

China to achieve balance. Thus, a key indicator for success includes the extent to which products or components made in China are exported and earn foreign exchange. In addition, the Chinese government has given permission to a joint venture to receive part-payments in foreign exchange from Chinese customers, if the customer has disposable foreign currency. Another indicator, therefore, is the extent to which the joint venture has been successful in negotiating with Chinese customers to receive payment in foreign exchange. Also, permission may be obtained to buy foreign exchange from other foreign investment enterprises with foreign exchange surplus.

Because one of the strategies of U.S. companies is to develop local sources for components to minimize foreign exchange expenditure, the extent of such local development is one more criterion. Some companies have even encouraged their U.S. suppliers to link up with potential component suppliers in China, and thus help develop the local infrastructure.

Competition between the U.S. firm and its technology recipient/affiliate, for example, in bidding for the same contract is a concern of technology suppliers and the successful technology transfer agreement must minimize the potential for such an adversarial posture. Clearly, such occurrences are negative indicators since they adversely affect the supplier–recipient relationship. The rate at which the technology in question is expected to become outdated relative to the agreement period and the rate at which the Chinese affiliate may develop and become a producer of new technology are both indicators of the potential for such competition. At present, the technical manpower resources of China are such as to expect a low level of competitive innovation for the near future while technology absorption capability is high (Schnepp, 1988). Foreign companies have also been concerned with successfully protecting of proprietary technology and restricting it to the designated recipients. China has enacted a patent law as of 1985, but its effectiveness is yet to be tested.

Technology Recipient Criteria

On the Chinese side, it is, to some extent, difficult to differentiate between the success criteria of the Chinese enterprise and the Chinese government, particularly on the macrolevel. Both are first and foremost interested in the acquisition of new and modern technology, as well as Western management skills. As a result, the enterprise is preoccupied with training Chinese personnel, since it is recognized that this is an essential prerequisite to successful technology absorption. In addition, the Chinese recipient of the technology gains status as a result of its access to up-to-date technology. The number of employees who obtain training and the depth to which these trainees become conversant with the supplier's technology represent important indicators of success for the Chinese affiliate.

The enterprise is also interested in earning foreign exchange and there is a great deal of recognition that comes with success in this direction. This goal can be achieved by exporting the product of the acquired technology. Ultimately, the Chinese recipient enterprise strives for self-sufficiency or independence from the technology supplier. Relevant indicators include the localization of production, including the proportion of local materials and components in the product and the level of absorption of the foreign technology. The latter is measured, in the final analysis, by the suitability of components manufactured by the recipient for incorporation in the original product. Thus, the level of exports of components from the Chinese enterprise to the U.S. technology supplier is an important indicator.

Chinese Government Criteria

The criteria for success for the Chinese government are similar to those of the enterprise on the macrolevel. For example, the government is concerned with the contribution that imported technology will make to the achievement of major economic objectives and industrial development. To that end, there is emphasis on cutting edge technology that will help China narrow the gap that separates it from the industrialized world. Preservation of foreign exchange by obtaining technology at the lowest possible price is another major concern. Observers have consistently maintained that the major criterion for the selection of suppliers in China is the cost factor. The concept of self-sufficiency is also a valid criterion at the state level. China wishes to minimize dependency on foreign sources and, therefore, stresses rapid localization of imported technology. The relevant indicator is the time taken to accomplish this aim and the degree to which it is accomplished. The amount of capital invested in China by the U.S. firm also represents a key indicator of success since attracting foreign investment is another prominent aim of the Chinese government.

An important overall criterion of success from the Chinese government's point of view is the conservation of power consumption. Much has been made in the Chinese press of the need to conserve power and the need to modernize the industrial plant to achieve this end (Li Peng, 1988; Bai 1985). This criterion has been quantified in terms of power consumption per unit product and comparisons with the norms of industrialized countries have been discussed. Another criterion is the rate at which production costs can be reduced from the start-up levels by increasing labor productivity using acquired management skills. Regional distribution of enterprises is another state-level concern with an emphasis on development of rural and border areas. The accelerated development of the coastal regions, as a goal of the country's economic policy, has also been emphasized in recent official announcements, although this policy has been most recently called into question. Presumably, the decision to locate a technology recipient enterprise in rural areas would depend on the level of the technology concerned, since the availability of technically skilled manpower decreases rapidly as the distance from major urban centers increases.

The creation of new jobs as a result of the technology transfer is certainly also a concern. However, sometimes this aim is only achieved in the long-run as the foreign partner to a joint venture has a competing aim—the reduction of the number of employees of a typically overstaffed factory with low productivity.

SUCCESS INDICATORS IN THE NEGOTIATION PHASE

During this phase, each of the stakeholders is concerned with overcoming barriers caused by cultural and language differences as well as differences in accepted procedures and management styles in both technical and commercial arenas (Schnepp et al., 1987). Successful communication and resolution of these differences is usually judged by the prevailing atmosphere during contacts, and the time required to discuss and settle any particular agenda item. The total time taken to reach an agreement and to sign a contract is a measure widely used to assess success, but several other more subtle indicators can be used to gauge progress while negotiations are still underway.

Technology Supplier Criteria

The criteria for the success of a foreign business venture in China are not standard and the evaluation of many accepted indicators cannot be accomplished by conventional methods. A major criterion for successful operation in China, as elsewhere, is access to information on local conditions available to the U.S. firm. In China, however, the barriers to information gathering and to its verification are particularly formidable (Mayer et al., 1986). As a result, the recipient's willingness to provide access to his own plants and to mediate access to the installations of his suppliers and of potential customers represents a major indicator of success. Furthermore, the provision of such access and openness to discussion of technical and administrative difficulties on the Chinese side indicate the development of greater than usual trust between the affiliates, an essential condition for a successful relationship. Openness regarding the Chinese company's plans for future development and its role in the development plans of the region and the country are also important.

Penetrating the protective screen surrounding the decision-making process and the identity of decision makers represents additional key success indicators. Success in gaining an understanding of the Chinese negotiating team and of all personnel present in the room can provide important clues to the identity of secondary stakeholders. A further step would be actual contact with the leading personalities and the opportunity to lobby them, even though the effectiveness of lobbying a "decision maker" may often fall short of expectations based on U.S. models; the decision-making power, or the willingness to accept responsibility for decisions, is often limited and strong reliance on consensus is common, even among officials of reasonably high stature. The appearance of ranking "leaders" at social functions is significant and also provides opportunities for initiating some level of management of the Chinese decision-making process. In particular, the level of the bureaucratic hierarchy's representation during a visit by a senior American executive and the amount of publicity given to such a visit provide important clues to the success of the interaction.

Since the development of trust and confidence toward the foreign company and its personnel is a major goal of the Chinese side during the initial phases of the project, the atmosphere between the parties provides a good indicator of progress toward an agreement. A relaxed discussion, an absence of tensions, and a lowering of the level of formality are all positive signs. Admittedly, serious difficulties may be encountered in the evaluation of many of the above described indicators. The degree to which the success of a technology-transfer project can be assessed is, therefore, subject to sensitivity to the subtleties of Chinese verbal and nonverbal signals. The ability to gain perspective regarding the progress of negotiations in itself becomes an indicator of success.

Technology Recipient Criteria

The primary aims of the Chinese side during the initial and negotiating phases of the technology transfer process are the development of trust between the parties and assessment of the prospective foreign partner's suitability for the future relationship. Indicators of relevance include the extent to which the U.S. company demonstrates openness to change and a willingness to adapt its practices to suit the needs of the Chinese partner and the local environment. U.S. firms sometimes receive conflicting signals since one of the avowed aims of Chinese enterprises is to learn U.S. management procedures and to increase efficiency. However, Chinese negotiators almost universally abhor the use of standard contracts and legalistic style. They favor a give and take attitude toward everything, including the breadth and depth to which foreign technology will be accessible to the Chinese side. Patience on the part of the foreigners is appreciated but quiet persistence is accepted in good grace.

The Chinese side also measures success in the budding relationship in terms of the level of involvement of U.S. corporate executives. A visit by the company president or the CEO is seen as an important expression of interest and commitment. Though open confrontation has sometimes occurred during the negotiation phase of technology-transfer projects, the Chinese officials are sensitive to such occurrences and prefer to confine them to the lower ranks. As already stated, the cost of the technology is a premier criterion for the selection of a foreign technology supplier. Other success indicators include considerations of appropriateness of the technology for the targeted markets and its suitability for local manufacture and eventual localization. The level of the technology available relative to industrialized world standards is also important. The reputation of the supplier as a dominant source of modern technology is important to the recipient.

By being designated as a foreign technology recipient the Chinese enterprise has already achieved a measure of success. However, the Chinese enterprise must also assess the progress of the continuing interactions with the foreign company and demonstrate this success to the supervisory government agency. The relevant indicator, which will be monitored by the "leading" agency, is the opinion formed by the supplier of the technology recipient. The qualities by which the judgment will be made include technical competence in understanding the technology, production capability, and managerial efficiency. The potential for absorption of the new technology will be judged in these terms and successful demonstration of such capability to both the foreign company and to the government agency is critical.

Chinese Government Criteria

During the negotiating stage of the technology-transfer process, the Chinese government becomes heavily involved. Generally, one of the central or regional government agencies, depending on the scale of the project, is charged with responsibility for negotiations with the technology supplier, while other entities play a secondary role. The performance of the negotiating team is closely monitored and the outcome of the negotiations reportedly is assessed almost daily. The criteria for success are assumed to center around cost, quality of technology, and stature of the supplier company. The desire to modernize and to close the technology gap is ever-present in the minds of officials and, therefore, the technology transfer project is judged in terms of its contributions to this macroobjective. The final agreement must also guarantee the updating of the technology transferred during the lifetime of the agreement and, therefore, dynamic transfer agreements are considered superior to static agreements that contract for a frozen stage of the technology. More detailed criteria of interest, such as payment schedules and training program requirements in terms of foreign travel of personnel, are also of interest.

SUCCESS INDICATORS IN THE IMPLEMENTATION PHASE

The implementation stage begins after the contract has been signed and signals the onset of the actual software and hardware transfer. During this stage, the content of the agreement is tested against its actual implementation; performance results can be used to determine if the agreement is an effective vehicle for technology transfer. For example, tests of the suitability of the content of the agreement include the following questions:

Can the companies meet the agreed-upon schedules? The first problem faced by the U.S. supplier is the procurement of the necessary export licenses. Next, the

Chinese recipient has often pressed for fast delivery of documentation and the U.S. side has had difficulties in collecting and expediting the vast quantities of required paper on time. Planned training schedules are tested by the capacity of the Chinese recipient to select and send the personnel and the U.S. supplier's ability to plan and implement effective training programs.

Are the training programs designed to suit the Chinese trainees in terms of their level of technical training and experience and in terms of content required for implementation of the agreement? Often, time is wasted and ill will aroused by assuming that Chinese engineers are inferior. Also, Chinese trainees have frequently arrived in the United States expecting on-the-job training, and have instead received classroom-type training, leading to early disillusionment.

Are disagreements arising between the technology supplier and recipients? Often the written agreement is not detailed enough and leads to misunderstandings. For example, the Chinese side has often assumed that all components of the company's product will be included in the transfer while, in fact, the U.S. company does not own the technology of many components that it out-sources from other manufacturers in the United States

U.S. Government Criteria

Immediately after the conclusion of the technology transfer agreement, the U.S. technology supplier must apply to the Department of Commerce for the necessary export licenses. One of the aims of the U.S. government is to protect U.S. technology from being used contrary to the country's interests. For example, if advanced electronic technology is transferred to China and then passed on to a third country that is considered an adversary of the United States, then the licensing process has failed since the U.S. security may be judged to have been threatened. Therefore, success of the licensing policy is judged by prevention of such incidents. The issue of balancing military and trade interests is far from being unambiguous and no absolute criteria exist; the extent to which strengthening China is in the long-term strategic interest of the United States is a matter of judgment. Somewhat arbitrary rules have been set by the U.S. government and these are subject to change according to high level policy requirements. Success or failure is judged by the implementation of these rules.

The interests of the U.S. government are also served by the expansion of trade between the two countries and the strengthening of political bilateral relations. Therefore, trade statistics including figures on the issue of export licenses are used as criteria to demonstrate commitment to the government level relationship. Figures on U.S. investment in China serve a similar purpose. Government leaders often make pronouncements in these terms (Schultz, 1988). On the other hand, the government is concerned with the protection of domestic U.S. manufacturers leading to intergovernment agreements on import quotas to the United States. For example, textiles are strictly regulated by such means. Success is judged by the efficacy of these quotas and their benefit to the U.S. economy. There is a trade-off between protective measures and allowing free competition to lower the prices that U.S. consumers have to pay for a commodity or product. While these are both national policy criteria, U.S. government representatives are also interested, in the short term, in the degree to which the specific technology-transfer agreement is consistent with stated national policy and aids in bilateral negotiations.

Technology Supplier Criteria

Barriers to information flow are well recognized as an impediment to doing business in China. As the U.S. firm becomes more involved, however, the technology transfer project becomes an experimental tool for learning about the Chinese industrial and business environment. In particular, the technology supplier has an improved opportunity to understand the Chinese enterprise's network of suppliers and end users of the product, and the lines of authority that link the technology recipient to local, regional, and central government agencies. The data so gathered help the Americans to assess realistically the technology transfer process and of the opportunities for future expansion of the company's activities in China. Success can be measured by the adequacy of information available to the company's management for making policy decisions about current and future commitments to the Chinese market.

On the operational performance side, the start-up phase requires four groups of operations: (1) paper dissemination, (2) training in the United States, (3) transfer of "hardware", and (4) follow-up consulting in China. Success in the first operation can be assessed based on the ability to keep to contractual time schedules. This task has often been difficult because of Chinese insistence on receiving the bulk of the documentation within a short time frame after the issuance of the required export permits by the U.S. Department of Commerce. Also, the supplier has encountered occasional difficulties in amassing the vast quantities of paper from different plants since many U.S. firms do not have a central technology information bank. Success can further be judged by the efficiency with which documentation transfer is accomplished and by the firm's ability to respond to the complaints and queries by the Chinese side.

The training program is tied to schedules as well, although less weight seems to be given to successful observance of agreed time frames. Here, the emphasis is on the efficiency with which skills are transferred to the Chinese trainees and this is where indicators of success must be defined. The ability of the trainees to perform the functions assigned to them once they return to their home enterprise provides a basis for assessing success, although the required information is not always available to the technology supplier. Apart from performing their functional tasks, the trainees must in turn train their own personnel and also train customers in application and maintenance of the product. Since the supplier–recipient relationship is still in its formative stages at this point, the level of satisfaction of returning Chinese trainees is an important indicator. Some companies have used debriefing sessions for this purpose. The cost-effectiveness of the training programs is also important.

An additional index for measuring the effectiveness of the training program in the United States is the amount of follow-up consulting that is necessary in China. Such support is very expensive and, depending on the terms of the agreement, one of the primary stakeholders must bear the cost. There have been occasions where the technology supplier has provided consulting services at its own cost when the budget of the recipient ran out, even though it was the responsibility of the recipient to pay for such services. This was done to ensure the success of the project since the U.S. company felt that its reputation in China was at stake.

Consulting has been the cause of some friction because the parties use different models for the function of a consultant. The Chinese often wish to limit the consultant to answering the specific questions that they initiate while the Americans tend to want to be fully informed on the process of absorption and of the problems encountered by the technology recipient. The degree to which agreement on the consulting function can be reached is a good indicator of successful cooperation between the parties. The subject merits serious attention at this stage by both sides, since consulting is likely to play a significant role over the lifetime of the technology transfer agreement.

The best criterion for successful transfer of hardware, including production equipment in the early stage and specialized materials and components later on, is the time that elapses before actual production begins. Obviously, the evaluation of the quality of the product serves a complementary function. These last two criteria actually serve to judge the overall success of the venture since production is, of course, a major goal of all concerned.

Technology Recipient Criteria

The recipient enterprise has one primary goal during this stage against which to gauge its success: the acquisition and absorption of the technology agreed upon during the negotiation stage. These aims are complementary to those of the technology supplier and cover paper, training, hardware, and consulting. Once more, the Chinese enterprise must again keep the relevant government agencies satisfied with the progress made.

With respect to the documentation disseminated by the supplier, the criterion for success at this stage is the timely and effective assimilation and adaptation for use. The second criterion parallels the sender's indicator for successful training—the trainees' ability to manufacture the final product. For optimal results, hands-on training in the United States is desirable but, in many cases, union rules limit or forbid the access of outside personnel to machinery on the shop floor. Also, training inadequacies have been reported, which required retraining either in China or in the United States. For example, in one case, Chinese design engineers were only trained to perform design calculations since this is the design engineer's function in America. In China, however, the design engineer performs the additional function of drafting the plans. For training to be effective, it must be geared to a level appropriate to the trainee's job context.

The aim of consulting assistance, from the point of view of the technology recipient, is complementary to that of the supplier. Occasionally, the recipient will encounter problems during implementation that can only be addressed by on-site consultation. Success will be measured in terms of the consultant's ability to determine the cause of a particular difficulty in a short time and the breadth of knowledge demonstrated.

Hardware transfer can be judged by the absence of defective parts and the absence of major hurdles to the installation and operation of equipment. Adaptation of documentation, training, and effective consulting, all contribute to the successful absorption of equipment.

Chinese Government Criteria

Often the Chinese government plays a major role since it is not uncommon for government agencies to demand that the documentation be channeled through them for purposes of initial processing and control. The success criteria are then parallel to those of the technology recipient, and the relevant agencies often keep close tabs on the progress of the project. On the macrolevel, the government judges the particular technology transfer project according to its contribution to the overall aims of modernization, energy conservation, job creation, and foreign currency savings or eventual earnings.

SUCCESS INDICATORS DURING THE ONGOING PROCESS

By the time the ongoing stage is reached, many of the imperatives and criteria for success of the primary stakeholders have already been articulated. As the evolution of the technology transfer project progresses, in analogy to the life cycle of a product or of an organization (Greiner, 1972), the primary stakeholders tend to settle into reasonable working relationships. Nevertheless, as the project matures, new issues and criteria for success emerge and previous issues reappear in changed forms.

U.S. Government Criteria

At this stage, the U.S. government functions primarily as a watchdog. Its agencies incorporate the project's results into their overall China trade statistics to help U.S. corporations make informed strategic decisions and to serve as a basis for government policy decisions. These policies are concerned with reciprocity in opening up internal markets in both countries and negotiating trade quotas in sectors where restrictions are imposed. The first criterion for success, therefore, is the overall success of the project in terms of the fulfillment of the aims of both the United States and China. This indicator feeds directly into the second criterion, which measures the benefit derived from the project to the U.S. economy as well as to the buttressing of the government's political objectives and the strengthening of the political bilateral relationship.

Technology Supplier Criteria

The first obvious criterion is the return on the substantial investment that has been made in terms of time, energy, resources, and capital. The second is the increase in direct sales by the U.S. company to China, attributable to its presence and visibility as part of the technology transfer project. For return on investment to be fully effective, the U.S. company must have been successful in repatriating an appropriate portion of the earnings. Profits in local currency are positive but not sufficient indicators of achievement. Long-term indicators include success in establishing a reputation as a competent and reliable supplier of technology and of high quality products. This indicator can be measured in terms of the success in expanding the U.S. side's activity in China, including the addition of further product lines to the original transfer project and the development of new technology transfer ventures.

Another indicator is the success in building a substantial data base on China's industry and market sectors, on the decision-making process and its lead personalities, and on the supplier—manufacturer end user networks that control essential transactions. The lines of authority connecting the targeted enterprises to governmental agencies represent an additional area where data are essential. The extent to which this data enables the company to make informed strategic decisions is the success criterion of the information gathering function.

Success in the transfer of management skills and the degree to which these skills have produced changes in the Chinese enterprise are critical indicators. It has been a common experience that it is harder to transfer management software than technical software and hardware and it is important to remember that the former skills are vital to the support of the technology transfer process. The management functions that must be in place to ensure efficient technology transfer include the basic organizational systems, procurement, inventory control, manufacturing planning and scheduling, accounting control, marketing, and, of particular importance, human resource management technology (Von Glinow and Teagarden, 1988).

The overriding indicator of success depends on the judgment of effective transfer of the selected technology. Despite the fact that this criterion is one of the major overall indices, it may not be assessed until the last phase of the technology transfer project. The criteria include product quality and the level of the recipient's technological independence.

The rapport between supplier and recipient and the ease of communication between them is again an important indicator of success in this stage of the transfer process. At this point, however, it must be fully addressed and evaluated, whereas during earlier stages it was easier to tolerate a lower success level in communication.

An additional indicator can be found in the success of the venture's foreign exchange balance management. This includes the availability of foreign currency to buy essential components from abroad and/or profit repatriation through government allocations, from export earnings or by means of government authorization for charging local customers partly in foreign currency. Most recently, the purchase of foreign currency from foreign investment enterprises that have a surplus has been permitted. The degree of localization of the product is another quantifiable indicator. The punctual adherence by the Chinese side to agreed upon payment schedules represents yet an additional key success factor that may often but not always be related to the foreign currency balance management.

Technology Recipient Criteria

Once more, many of the success criteria of the technology recipient parallel those of the supplier. The level of absorption of the imported technology and of management and infrastructural reforms represent significant success indicators. However, management reforms can be deemed beneficial only if greater efficiency can be demonstrated in terms of increased productivity, reduced energy consumption, and improved product quality. A survey of professionals has shown that Chinese educated personnel ("intellectuals") set great store by good relationships in the workplace (Chen Wei et al., 1985). Therefore, the social environment of the Chinese enterprise must also be measured according to increased enthusiasm and interest of the work force and improved interpersonal relations.

Product quality and the time taken to achieve technological independence are further important success indices. The degree of localization, measured in percentage of total value, is another index of interest. Often, significant support from government agencies on different levels is required to achieve maximum possible localization. The ability to mobilize such support can be used as another indicator of success that contributes to the overall localization index.

An important measure of success is the earning of foreign exchange by exports or savings by means of import substitution of products. The resulting ability to accumulate foreign exchange capital for investment is a useful index.

The availability of effective consultation by engineers and managers of the foreign affiliate during the entire term of the cooperative venture agreement is a significant indicator of the success of the cooperation and good communication between the parties. This activity persists since technical innovations usually continue to be introduced during the entire course of a dynamic technology transfer project. Also, there is a continuing need for experimentation with new management techniques.

The insulation from pressures by external agencies to produce short-term results that would inhibit the more important long-term achievements of the technology transfer can be used as a measure of success and should be an aim of the technology recipient. Support and recognition by government, rather than pressure for change, are further positive indicators of success. Recognition in China comes in the form of awards, and preferential treatment for the assignment of skilled manpower, and foreign currency allocation.

Chinese Government Criteria

During the final stages of the technology transfer project, the Chinese government has a vested interest in its successful completion. The ultimate goal here is for the enterprise to engage in independent manufacture of a high technology product that is competitive on the domestic and world markets such that it benefits the economy as a whole. Production should be cost effective, energy efficient, and highly localized. Again, the government's aims parallel those of the technology recipient in desiring foreign exchange earnings or savings.

A major concern of the Chinese government is increased foreign investment in China since the country is short of development capital. Therefore, the ultimate hope of the government is that a foreign company engaging in business in China will eventually engage in equity investment or, if it has already done so, increase its investment. The equity investment in the technology transfer venture or the investment resulting from the follow-up activities of the technology supplier constitute a success indicator of prime importance.

Paradoxically, the Chinese government is also concerned with achieving a state of minimum dependence on foreign companies and countries. It must walk a thin line between becoming overly dependent on one source for leading edge technology and acquiring the best technology suited to Chinese conditions and aims. The appropriate indicator for success of such a policy is the rapidity with which technical independence can be achieved by the technology recipient and the cost effectiveness of the technology procurement. Also, energy efficiency of the production is in the national interest and can be measured by comparison to international norms.

CONCLUSION

We have attempted to analyze the criteria for assessing success of technology transfer processes by focusing on the major stakeholders and on the stages of the process. While some of the criteria we have discussed are characteristic of one particular party to the transfer process, some are common to two or even more of the stakeholders.

The stages of the technology transfer process that we have defined are useful demarcations but they also often overlap. Likewise, the validity of the success indicators has been found in many cases to extend into successive stages. We find that the analysis presented here is useful to make evaluations of the progress of a transfer process and points to commonalities as well as genuine conflicts of interest of the different stakeholders. The most pervasive example of overt conflict is the foreign exchange aspect of the venture. The U.S. technology supplier wishes to maximize the return on its investment and repatriate earnings in foreign currency, while the Chinese technology recipient and government wish to earn or save foreign currency. The commitment by the two stakeholders to mutually exclusive success criteria frequently imperils the entire technology transfer project.

When stakeholders who have a great deal riding on the success of the process have different or even opposing goals, a significant dilemma results whose resolution is far from clear. Most stakeholders have little ability to "step outside" the immediate constraints of the dilemma and to collaborate to achieve success as judged from a multiplicity of perspectives. Maier (1967) and others (Kilmann and Thomas, 1975, 1978) have cautioned against overemphasis on strategies for winning individual goals at the expense of other important stakeholders. Instead, both sides can gain only by adopting more collaborative postures that emphasize commonalities, free interchange of information, and mutual problem identification. As in all collaborative processes, we propose that the success criteria of all major stakeholders must be identified and optimized to achieve overall success of the technology transfer project.

REFERENCES

Bai Yiyan (1985). "Evaluation index system (JXP System) for technological acquisition, digestion and assimilation," Working paper, Research Centre for Promotion and Development of Chinese Science and Technology, October 13.

Chen Wei, En Zhuguang, Gao Jing, and Zhang Jianxin. (November 1985). "The reactions of intellectuals to the salary reform," Survey Report, Social Psychology Research Group, Psychology Institute, Chinese Academy of Sciences.

Clare, Todd. (June 1987). Presentation on AMC at USC's Pacific Rim Management Program: Doing Business with China.

Greiner, Larry. (1972). "Evolution and revolution as organizations grow," *Harvard Business Review*, 50:37–46.

Kilmann, Ralph, and Thomas, Kenneth. (1975). "Interpersonal conflict-handling behavior as reflections of Jungian personality dimensions," *Psychology Reports*, 37:971–980.

Kilmann, Ralph, and Thomas, Kenneth. (1978). "Four perspectives on conflict management: An attributional framework for organizing descriptive and normative theory," *Academy of Management Review*, 3:59–68.

Li Peng. (1988). Speech made at the National People's Congress, March 25.

Maier, Norman R. F. (1967). "Assets and liabilities in group problem solving: The need for an integrative function," *Psychology Review,* 74:239–249.

Mayer, C. S., Han, Jing Lun, and Lim, Hui Fang. (1986). "An evaluation of the performance of the joint venture companies in the People's Republic of China." Presentation at the University of Manchester.

Schnepp, Otto, Bhambri, Arvind, and Von Glinow, Mary Ann. (1987). "U.S.–China technology transfer: Problems and solutions," paper presented at the symposium on U.S.–China Technology Transfer, held at Woodrow Wilson Center of the Smithsonian Institution, Washington, D.C., April 2.

Schultz, George P., Beijing Zhongguo Xinwen She. (March 8, 1988). translated in FBIS Daily Reports.

Von Glinow, Mary Ann, and Teagarden, Mary B. (1988). "The transfer of human resource management technology in Sino–U.S. cooperative ventures: Problems and solutions," *Human Resource Management.* 27 (2):201–29.

11

Comparing Japanese and American Technology Transfer in China: Assessing the "Fit" Between Foreign Firms and Chinese Enterprises

ROY F. GROW

Ed Adams was a contented man. He was flying back to corporate headquarters in the United States after closing an important deal in China. His company, United Food Products, would transfer food processing technologies to an enterprise near Dalian in Liaoning province. In return, United Food Products would purchase several kinds of vegetables grown in the province and later would help the Chinese enterprise introduce its own canned food products into the northern China market.[1]

The negotiations had not been easy. Japan's Ajinomoto had also been interested in a similar project and Adams had run into their negotiating team often during the past year. Ajinomoto had a slick operation and its food processing technologies were first rate. The Japanese firm's final proposal had been well framed.

Ed had envied many of the advantages the Japanese representatives seem to enjoy. Their project team was well financed, their market information was up-to-date, and their sales representatives knew China intimately. In contrast, Ed's had been a lonely undertaking; he had approval from company higher-ups to negotiate in China, but the American firm had not really developed a China marketing strategy. Ed knew that he would have a lot of talking to do back home simply to convince higher-ups that this new joint venture held a great deal of promise.

What had turned the trick for Ed? He knew that he had developed some good working relationships with the Chinese enterprise manager who would handle the new joint venture. He believed that the American technologies had impressed the Chinese technicians he had met. He also suspected that his offer to train several Chinese technicians and managers in the United

States may have been important. These factors, Ed believed, had tipped the scale in his favor.

Just up the road in Shenyang (Liaoning Province's capital city) a drama with a different ending was playing itself out. An American and a Japanese company were vying for an important contract from Anshan Iron and Steel—China's largest steel complex. The American firm, National Industries, was bidding on a project to replace a number of heating furnaces in the complex's rolling mills. National's proposal was detailed and promising, and pointed the way to the refurbishing of Anshan's entire rolling mill operation.

Japan's Mitsui had also entered the project competition in Shenyang. The company put together a detailed proposal to upgrade a number of furnace projects—including Anshan's—in different parts of China.

National's chief Asian marketing representative was even more envious of his Mitsui counterparts than Ed Adams had been of Ajinomoto's negotiators. Mitsui had been in China a long time, and a division of the Japanese firm had even helped build a part of the Chinese complex in the 1930s. Mitsui's personnel were well-trained and their negotiating team included individuals who had worked at the Anshan complex in the 1940s. How could National compete against this sort of expertise? When Mitsui received the contract for the new heating furnaces, it seemed to many at National that the Americans had been overpowered by Mitsui's numerous skillful marketing representatives, these representatives' knowledge of China, and the company's willingness to spend substantial resources to tie down a new project.

The scorecard in Liaoning was mixed: An American firm had landed the contract for one important project and a Japanese company had won the second. Why the difference in outcomes between the two projects? Why had Chinese managers chosen to work with an American firm in one case and a Japanese company in another?

Alternative models have been advanced to explain the managers' choices of technologies. One possibility is that the choice is an economic one—reflecting a need to manage costs in a system where competition is keen or resources limited. Another possibility looks at the appropriateness of the technology itself, and assumes that managers choose new technologies for "engineering" reasons.[2]

There is no question that a good part of the reason foreign firms succeed in China has to do with the "appropriateness" of the technologies offered by such firms—the ways that the new technologies they offer meet some important economic and engineering needs of the Chinese purchasers.

But my research shows that at least a part of the reason that some technology transfer projects are successful and that others fail has to do with the "fit" between the supplying foreign firms and the receiving Chinese enterprise. Some foreign firms (and their managers) and some Chinese enterprises (and their managers) are simply well suited to one another, whereas other foreign/Chinese relationships are "odd couple" partnerships that come together like oil and water, even when the foreign technologies fit particular needs of Chinese purchasers.

During the course of more than 10 years' work, I have investigated more than 150 Japanese and American firms that have been involved in technology transfer projects in China. I have also interviewed several hundred corporate executives and government officials who have been closely involved in these projects. Many of these interviews took place over a sustained period, and in a number of cases, I worked as a consultant for the companies or became involved in the corporate planning process. Altogether, the firms in my study were involved in almost 325 different projects with Chinese end users.[3]

Both the Chinese "demand" side and the Japanese/American "supply" sides of the technology transfer process are fascinating studies. Since the mid-1980s the bulk of Chinese decisions about foreign commercial relationships—commodities, turnkey projects, scientific processes, training for technicians—has come from Chinese enterprises and their managers, not Chinese government officials in the central ministries. How individuals in these Chinese enterprises decide to look for and accept foreign technologies and goods is a complex story. The wide variety of factors that shape a Chinese manager's decision to enter into a relationship with a foreign firm, even within the same industry, are intriguing. Two Chinese manufacturers of pharmaceuticals, for example, may decide that they need vastly different technologies with an enterprise in Liaoning, for example, deciding to do business with Suntory, whereas a firm in Shanghai decides that Upjon offers better equipment. My research suggests that a great deal of the process by which foreign technology flows to China is shaped by the *purchaser* of this technology—primarily by decisions made by managers within the local Chinese enterprises themselves. I have written elsewhere about how these Chinese decisions about foreign technologies are shaped by a number of factors that include the nature of the enterprise itself, its financial and technological underpinnings, the nature of its organizational decision-making processes, and the pattern of its planning and implementation procedures.[4]

What does a Chinese enterprise manager look for in a foreign firm when he is acquiring new technologies? The Japanese and American "supply" side is as complex as that of the Chinese side, and it has been fascinating to discover the factors that go into a foreign firm's decision to enter the China market. Two manufacturers of automobile parts, for example, may decide to organize their activities in China in startlingly different ways. Chrysler's decision to assemble engines in Northeast China is based on a much different set of calculations than Toyota's decision to sell truck parts in the same Chinese region. IBM's decisions to enter (and then leave) the China market were based on a much different set of factors than NEC's decision to become involved in the southern China market. I have written about how these Japanese and American decisions about the flow of technologies to China are shaped by factors that include product selection, pricing, selection of sales representatives, sales strategies, financial negotiations, characteristics of the firm, and the nature of the firm's relationship with outside governmental and private organizations.[5]

Virtually every study of technology transfer to China (including my own) focuses on *either* the enterprises and managers of the Chinese demand side or on the companies and managers of the foreign supply side. In this chapter, however, I will examine the "fit" between foreign firms and Chinese enterprises—how the characteristics of some kinds of Chinese enterprises might lead them to work best with certain kinds of foreign firms.

Two sets of questions guide my investigation. The first set involves the characteristics of the different kinds of foreign firms and Chinese enterprises that are involved in technology transfer projects: Is it possible to make certain judgments about some of the important characteristics that shape the actions of Chinese enterprises and foreign firms engaged in technology transfers? Are there characteristics that separate some of these firms from others? Is it possible to make a judgment about which foreign firms work best with the different kinds of Chinese enterprises?

The second set of questions involves the fabled "Japanese advantage" in Chinese trade activity. This set of questions revolves around the possibility of discovering whether or not there are peculiarly "Japanese strategies" that are different from the procedures employed by American firms. Are there basic characteristics—size, experience, type of involvement—that separate Japanese firms in China from their American counterparts? Are Japanese firms active in China managed in ways not found in American firms? Do Japanese firms rely on other firms and support agencies in ways that are not often found in the United States?

I will look at data from 75 American and Japanese firms that have been involved in technology transfers to 60 enterprises and agencies in China.[6] I will not examine *all* of the factors that might affect the relationships between foreign firms and Chinese enterprises since my data set is too extensive. Instead, I will isolate several prominent and interesting categories of factors about foreign firms offering technologies and juxtapose these factors against some significant characteristics I have observed in Chinese enterprises acquiring foreign technologies. Looking at the way that these two sets of characteristics—those of foreign firms and those of Chinese enterprises—come together will provide at least a partial explanation of the success or failure of foreign projects that transfer technologies to China.

JAPANESE AND AMERICANS IN CHINA: SOME SIMILARITIES AND DIFFERENCES

Explanations for the success of American and Japanese firms in the international marketplace tend to focus on three broad categories: the characteristics of the firm itself,[7] the attitudes of the firm's managerial leadership that affect the way these managers approach the international market,[8] and the ways that firms (and their managers) use outside support services provided by public and private organizations.[9]

I have chosen to examine several characteristics from each of these three broad categories. The attributes that I have included in the next several pages by no means represent an exhaustive list; the list is simply illustrative of some of the more important qualities of foreign firms that are active in technology transfer projects.

Characteristics of Japanese and American Firms

What sorts of firms are active in the China market? Anecdotal information suggests that large firms involved in joint ventures have the best chance of success. There is also a conventional wisdom, especially among American executives, that the sort of Japanese firm that succeeds in China is different from its American counterpart: Japanese firms are said to be larger, to be more concerned with direct sales, and to possess far more experience in international markets.[10] An examination of Japanese and American firms active in the China market provides some data to judge the validity of observations such as these.[11]

Size

The size of a foreign firm (as measured by asset value, sales volume, number of employees, or number of foreign branches) has little bearing on a firm's ability to transfer technologies to China or to establish a viable commercial relationship with a Chinese purchaser. Contrary to a good deal of the conventional wisdom that circulates in the Japanese and American business communities, many small firms are very active in the China market, and these small firms are often more successful than their larger counterparts. Japanese firms that are active in the China market tend to be either *very* large or very small. More American firms in China fall into the intermediate range (Fig. 11.1A).

Type of Involvement in China

The majority of foreign firms in China—Japanese and American—are heavily involved in direct product sales. More Japanese firms are involved in some form of assembly agreement, typically an agreement that involves the purchase of Chinese subassemblies for products destined for a non-Chinese market (Fig. 11.1B).

Firm Size and Type of Involvement

The size of the firm is related to the type of Chinese commercial activity engaged in by the firm. In general, for both Japanese and American firms, small companies concentrate most of their efforts in the direct sale of products and services. Larger firms engage more often in joint venture relationships, assembly operations, and licensing agreements (Fig. 11.2).

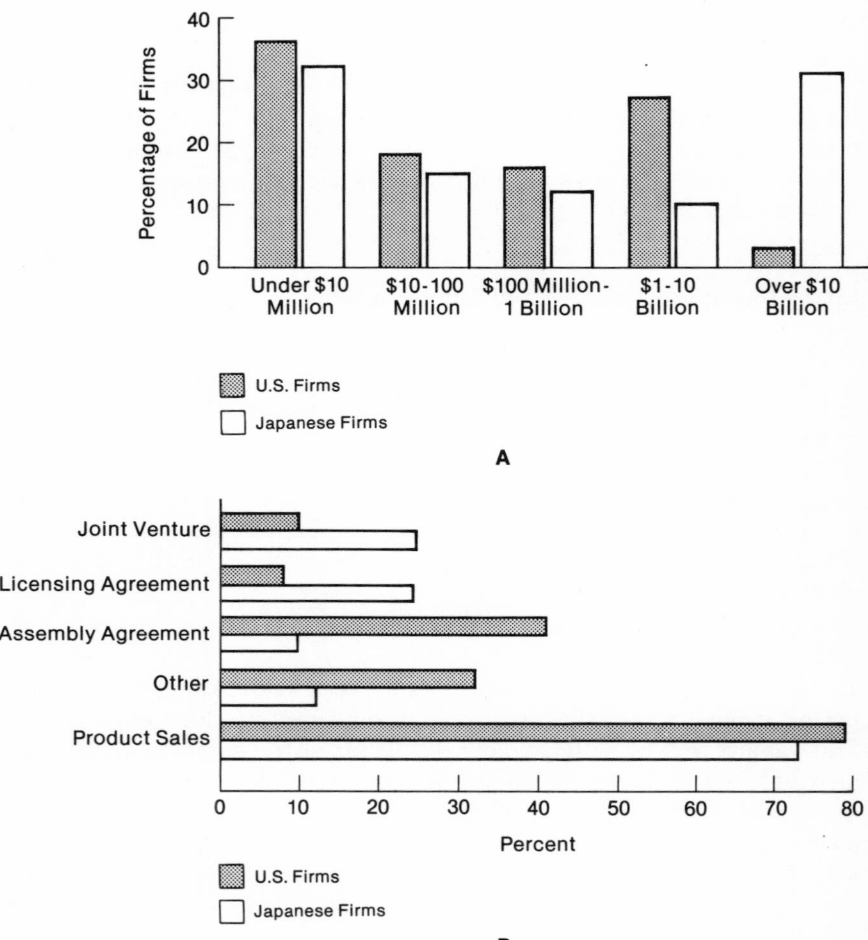

Figure 11.1 Size of foreign firms. A. Total annual sales. B. Type of involvement in China.

Piggy-Back Entry

Small Japanese firms tend to enter the China market by "piggy-backing" onto a project organized by a larger Japanese firm, typically a project organized by a trading company or a final-stage assembly operation. Small American firms more often use a "go it alone" strategy based on direct entry into the China market.

Manufacturing and Service Centers of Gravity

Many of the most publicized tales of success in the new China market involve service operations—hotel management, market consultants, travel brokers. Firms that are most successful in the China market, however, tend to be manufacturing operations.

Revenues From Exports

Large Japanese firms tend to receive a greater portion of their revenues from foreign sales and services than do American firms (Fig. 11.3). Small Japanese firms—even those more heavily involved in foreign commercial activities than their American counterparts—report smaller revenues from foreign activities. This discrepancy—greater involvement in foreign commercial activity by small Japanese firms but smaller revenues—occurs be-

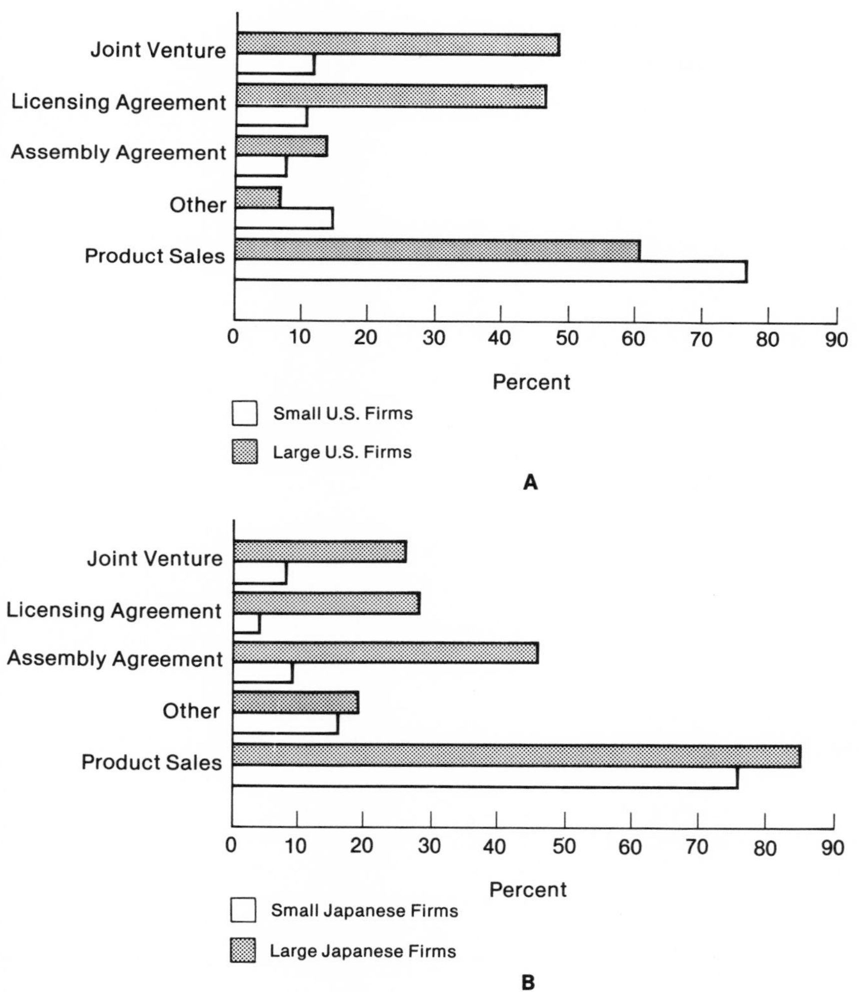

Figure 11.2 Firm size and type of involvement in China. A. U.S. firms. B. Japanese Firms.

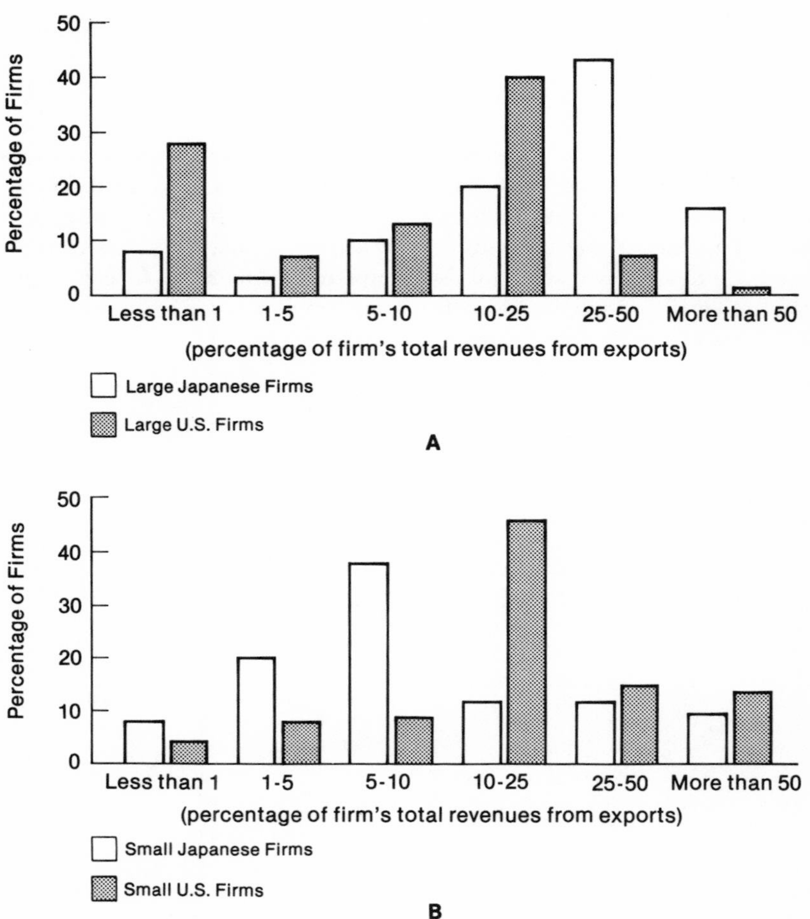

Figure 11.3 Revenue from foreign trade. A. Large firms. B. Small firms.

cause small Japanese firms tend to received their income from foreign commercial activity in the form of yen payments from larger Japanese firms.

Prior International Experience

China is not considered to be a good market for newcomers to the world of international trade, and this rule includes Japanese and American firms. Generally, firms that participate in the China market of the 1980s have had considerable experience in other parts of the world. Japanese firms tend to have slightly more experience than their American counterparts in foreign trade in general, and a great deal more experience in forming commercial relationships in other Asian markets (Table 11.1).

This cursory overview of some of the basic attributes of foreign firms suggests that there is a wide variety of companies active (and successful) in the China market. While size, by itself, is not an important factor in determining a firm's general level of success, size does become important in influencing the ways that a company becomes involved in this market: Small firms are most often engaged in direct sales, whereas large firms support a variety of operations that include joint ventures, licensing agreements, and assembly operations.

The most important factor separating Japanese and American firms involves the relationship between size and mode of entry into the China market: Small Japanese firms are much more likely to move into the China market in tandem with larger Japanese firms, while American firms of almost all sizes tend toward "lone wolf" strategies.

Attitudes of Japanese and American Managers

The talents and skills of Japanese managers are legendary and most American executives feel a bit of disdain (touched with a small tinge of envy) when hearing of the feats of their Japanese counterparts. Japanese managers, for example, are said by American executives to spend more time preparing to enter the China market, to conceive of China's role in the Asia market differently than do American executives, and frequently to take a longer-term frame of reference when plotting their overall strategies.[12]

Table 11.1 Prior International Experience (percent of firms involved)

	Small Firms (%)	Large Firms (%)	All Firms (%)
U.S. Firms			
None	14.3	0.0	7.3
India	42.9	66.7	51.2
Taiwan	57.1	88.9	69.7
Korea	57.1	88.9	70.7
Latin America	76.2	88.9	80.5
Other	33.5	66.7	46.3
Japanese Firms			
None	6.7	0.0	3.4
India	36.0	42.0	38.0
Taiwan	84.0	96.0	90.0
Korea	92.0	96.0	94.0
Latin America	16.0	32.0	24.0
Other	42.0	66.7	54.0

Question 7: With which developing countries besides China do you do business?

Table 11.2 Negotiating in China

	Expected Amount of Time (%)	Actual Amount of Time (%)
U.S. Firms		
3 months	5.3	0.0
6 months	21.1	18.9
1 year	28.9	32.4
2 years	31.6	13.5
3 years or more	13.2	15.1
Japanese Firms		
3 months	3.0	3.0
6 months	6.6	6.6
1 year	12.1	6.6
2 years	27.2	24.2
3 years or more	51.5	60.6

Time required between initial inquiries by American/Japanese firms and beginning to do business in China (percent of firms)

Question 13: How much time had you *expected* to invest between initial inquiries and beginning to do business?

Question 14: How much time was *actually* required between initial inquiries and beginning to do business?

Attitudes About Preparation and Negotiation

Perhaps the single most notable difference between Japanese and American managers lies in the willingness of Japanese managers to spend a considerable amount of time in preparation and negotiation (Table 11.2). Typically, Japanese managers expect to take 3.7 years to complete their preparation and negotiation phase (they actually take 4.4 years). As a result of the different amounts of time spent in project preparation, American managers expect to spend 8 months in the preparation and negotiation phase (they actually spend 1.4 years). Japanese managers "know their customers" much more intimately than do any American managers who participated in this study.

Attitudes About China's Relationship to Other Asian Markets

Japanese and American managers all tend to think of the China market in terms of some sort of overall corporate strategy and the market's growth potential. But Japanese managers tend to see China as a source of raw materials and subassembly parts; American managers tend to focus on "size of market" variables—in the fabled market of a billion customers (Fig. 11.4). Consequently, Japanese managers are much more able to see China as part of an increasingly integrated Asian market—a market in which Chinese purchasers of foreign technology are increasingly active.

Most American business people feel more comfortable with the idea of linkage in European markets than they do in Asian economies. The increasing integration of the European Economic Community allows business people to think in terms of production in one part of Europe, assembly in a second part, and entry into a distribution system in a third. Many Japanese business people think of China in much the same way, conceptualizing their marketing strategies in terms of China's increasing integration into the rapidly growing trade among Asian nations. Perhaps no more than 10 percent of American business people are capable of formulating their China commercial activities from this same perspective.

Attitudes About the Importance of Technology

Japanese and American executives are not in agreement about what constitutes a transfer of technology. Does it occur with the shipment of hardware such as machinery or scientific apparatus? Or is technology transferred when software—knowledge, formulae, and organizational strategies—are transferred? Most of the participants in this study indicated that their firms were engaged in the transfer of technology as part of the normal course of their business activity in China.

As Table 11.3 and Figure 11.5 indicate, respondents from American firms tended to believe that they transferred technology primarily through the sale of the product itself. Respondents from Japanese firms believed that their transfers of technology occurred more often as a result of licensing agreements, training sessions, and the working out of details during the formulation of proposals.

Clearly some of the differences between Japanese and American firms reflect the resources possessed by the firms themselves. Some firms have a greater depth of knowledge, scientific skills, and management expertise that make the more intangible sorts of technology transfer possible. They also have larger staffs, more complex divisions of labor, longer experience in

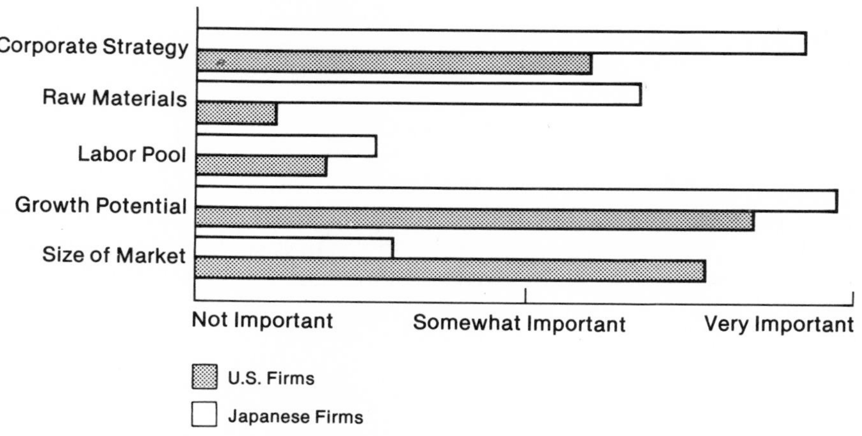

Figure 11.4 Factors involved in deciding to enter the China market.

Table 11.3 Methods of Technology Transfer (percent of firms)

Technology Transferred	U.S. Firms (%)	Japanese Firms (%)
Sale, lease, or lending of equipment	65.9	39.3
Training	41.5	57.5
Transfer of technical knowledge during presentations/proposals	36.6	51.5
Licensing of technology and proprietary information	24.4	18.1
Joint ventures	24.4	9.1
Direct sale of technical information	14.6	18.1
Coproduction	12.2	48.5
Other	4.9	30.3

Question 3: Which of the following ways of transferring technology, expertise, and/or scientific information have you used in your China venture?

training, and a greater ability to absorb indirect costs during the initial phases of new ventures.

But part of the difference in the kinds and amounts of technology transferred results from perception. Firms concerned primarily with direct sales often fail to appreciate the immense amount of knowledge they cover in preliminary work sessions. One representative of a small firm, for example, at first argued that he transferred technology only with the delivery of his product—a quality control testing system. But as he talked about the steps that he had moved through in making his sale—discussions, sessions in the Chinese end users' factory, working with Chinese engineers on final specifications—he finally concluded that he had transferred more knowledge in the working out of his final deal than he did with the shipment of the equipment itself.

Attitudes about Short-run and Long-run

In the early 1980s, a large number of American managers looked to China for some sort of quick hit. However, this philosophy has been changing. Even when their firms pushed them to "make their numbers every quarter," most American managers expressed their thoughts about China in terms of some sort of long-term framework. American parent firms, though, tend to be more driven by short-term and long-term cashflow considerations than Japanese firms (Fig. 11.6)

Attitudes About Future Opportunities

In spite of the gloomy forecasts regarding business activities in China currently found in the Japanese and American media, the majority of managers from both countries believe that business activity in China is likely to improve in the future (Table 11.4).

The attitudes of foreign managers about the China market are diverse and sometimes contradictory. Nonetheless, two general clusters of attitudes are evident. At one end of the continuum are managers who build their strategies around a series of analytic statements about the China market. This group of managers emphasizes the need to develop relationships with potential Chinese customers; they tend to look at these potential customers in terms of the increasingly active role of Chinese enterprises in the larger Asian economy, and act so as to focus their firm's strategic position

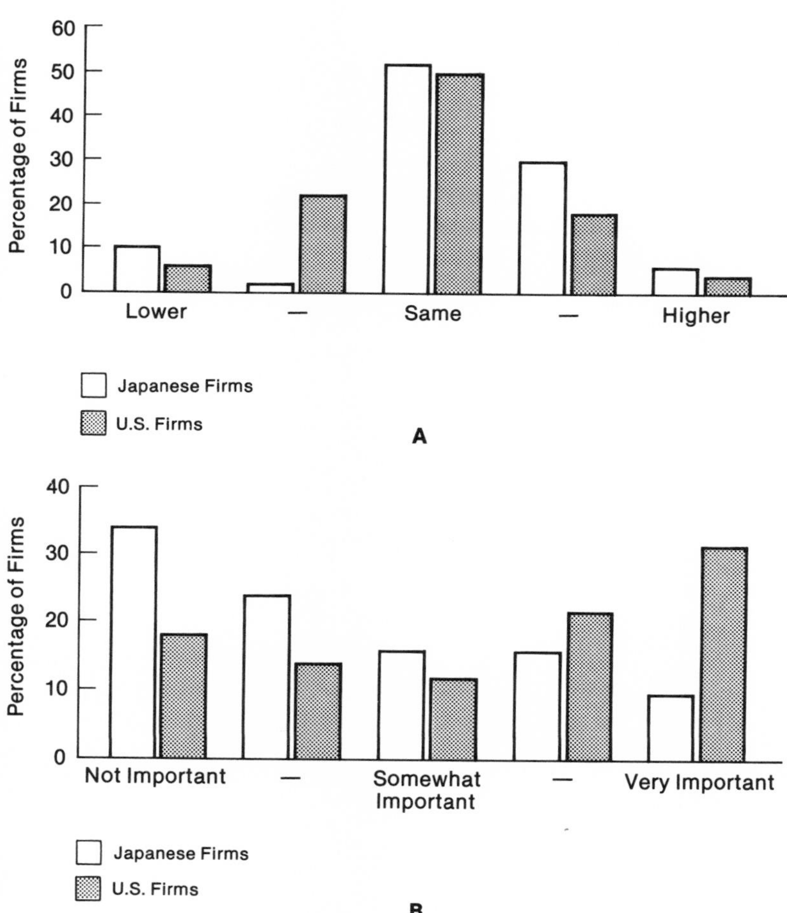

Figure 11.5 A. Managers who believe they transfer sophisticated technologies to China. B. U.S. managers who believe transferring technology is important for sales.

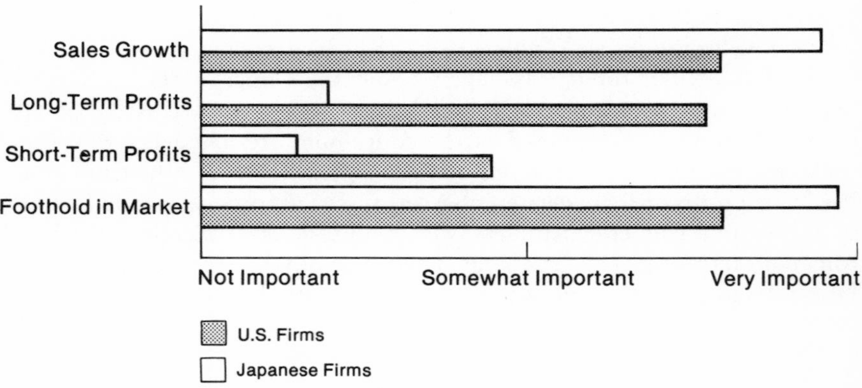

Figure 11.6 Objectives for China ventures.

on this developing trade activity. Another group of managers use more immediate financial criteria—the oft-noted "make-your-numbers" philosophies—to develop their China marketing strategies.

There are significant differences in the attitudes that Japanese and American managers bring to their China ventures. Japanese managers from both large and small firms tend to have attitudes about their China activities that fall on the "analytic" end of the continuum, whereas American managers tend to have attitudes that are often linked to more concrete financial criteria.

Table 11.4 Future Outlook (percent of firms)

	Small Firms (%)	Large Firms (%)	All Firms (%)
U.S. Firms			
Only a couple of transactions—unlikely to be repeated	11.5	6.7	9.8
Likely to continue at its present level	19.2	6.7	14.6
Likely to increase in the future	50.5	60.0	53.7
Don't know	11.5	20.0	14.6
Japanese Firms			
Only a couple of transactions—unlikely to be repeated	7.0	7.0	7.0
Likely to continue at its present level	20.2	7.0	13.0
Likely to increase in the future	66.6	80.0	74.0
Don't know	7.0	7.0	7.0

Question 2: Which of the following characteristics apply to your China business?

Links to Outside Organizations

All Japanese and American firms active in China make use of some sort of support service. Business people from both nations state that the most important support services provide the specific kinds of knowledge needed to make decisions about the China market. Managers are quite outspoken about the kinds of information they consider important. These managers also change their views about the sort of information they need as they gain experience in China. As Table 11.5 indicates, the kind of information that managers thought they needed *before* entry was often quite different from the kind of information they thought *after* they had entered it.

The following stand out as most important:

Information About Market Degmentation

American managers almost always focus on China as a "large market." Consequently, they tend to look at something they label as "China's needs"—aggregating demand on a national level. Japanese managers are more likely to segment the China market, focusing on five or six major urban complexes with populations that range from 70 to 130 million people apiece. As a consequence, Japanese managers are less likely to focus on "Chinese

Table 11.5 Needed Information About China (percent of firms)

Types of Information	U.S. Firms Before Entering	U.S. Firms After Entering	Japanese Firms Before Entering	Japanese Firms After Entering
China's needs for products and technology	88.9	61.1	47.1	52.9
Particular end-users of your product	38.9	61.1	94.1	100.0
Chinese decision making	27.8	66.7	88.2	94.1
Chinese law and practices	33.3	61.1	70.5	82.3
China's ability to purchase equipment from abroad	27.2	50.0	70.5	88.2
Competition	27.8	61.1	64.7	82.3
Likely market share	0.0	50.0	70.5	82.3
Labor costs	16.7	38.9	47.1	52.9
Availability of raw materials	16.7	27.8	35.2	52.9
U.S. (Japanese) law and regulations	55.6	44.4	35.2	29.4
U.S. (Japanese) governmental assistance for exports	33.3	16.7	47.1	47.1

Question 18: In *preparing* to enter the China market, was the following information readily available to your company?

Question 19: Which of the following categories of information did you find important *after* entering the China market?

demand" and are more likely to look at smaller market segments, such as Shanghai's growing population of women industrial workers or Canton's changing youth market.

Information About End-users

Most American managers in China begin their China ventures by working the "Beijing Ministry circuit" or relying on "whom-do-you-know" contacts. Americans thus have real trouble locating the end-users of their products and services. Japanese managers in China almost always begin their China ventures by asking "who is the *real* user of my products or services likely to be?" and then searching for information about this particular group of end-users. Japanese managers usually wait until *after* identifying Chinese enterprises likely to use their products before contacting Chinese officials in the central ministries or in the local bureaucracies and agencies.

Information about Chinese Decision Making

Most American managers have trouble seeing that the actual Chinese end-user of their products or services exists within a context of upstream suppliers and downstream users, and these Americans often do not understand the factors linking the decisions made by one Chinese unit with the decisions made by others. Japanese managers are more likely to focus on the decision-making *relationships* between various Chinese enterprises in a production system and attempt to discover who makes decisions about what.

Information about Chinese Law and Practice

The body of commercial law that governs the flow of products and technologies into and across China is still in its infancy. American managers often disregard this developing body of law, assuming in many cases that some sort of administrative decree or bureaucratic fiat will untangle the Chinese web of rules and regulations. Japanese managers are much more willing to work within the Chinese legal system and—through an understanding of the regulations—make the system work for the interests they represent.

Information about China's Ability to Purchase From Abroad

American managers report almost universal frustration about their ability to bring material and equipment into China from abroad and to expatriate earned income. Japanese managers better understand the relationship between importing and exporting both goods and capital, and they know more about the cross-cutting nature of the Chinese agencies and bureaucracies that affect these procedures.

Information about Competition

Japanese managers are keenly aware of sources of competition for their products and services, and surveying this competition is considered a vital part of their decision to enter the China market. American managers more frequently base their decisions about entering China on their perception of demand in the China market and the quality of the products and services they might offer to meet this demand. Most American managers have very little idea about the activity of non-American firms competing in the China market, and these American managers have even less of a feel for the ways that Chinese producers of the same products operate.

Where is it possible to obtain good information about these factors? Managers tend to have different views about the usefulness of the various sources. Among the more prominent differences between Japanese and American firms that use support services in their China marketing activities are the following:[13]

Attitudes about Sources of Information

In comparing the abilities of Japanese and American firms to search for needed information and subsequently use it, two points stand out: American managers look to a much different group of organizations than do Japanese managers (Table 11.6); and Americans are more often disap-

Table 11.6 Sources of China Support Services (percent of firms *using* these sources)

	Small Firms (%)	Large Firms (%)	All Firms (%)
U.S. Firms			
U.S. Department of Commerce	61.9	72.2	63.4
National Council U.S.–China Trade	42.9	71.4	53.6
Private consultants	52.4	61.1	53.6
State agencies	52.4	53.6	51.2
Chinese government agencies	57.1	50.0	51.2
Trade associations	52.4	44.4	46.3
Regional/local China organizations	47.6	55.6	48.7
Chamber of Commerce	33.3	28.9	34.1
International accounting firms	28.6	30.9	31.7
Other	13.8	5.6	7.3
Japanese Firms			
Banks	78.5	94.1	87.0
MITI	85.7	94.1	90.3
Ministry of Finance	78.5	88.2	83.8
Trading companies	71.4	94.1	83.8
Other firms	71.4	88.2	80.6
Trade associations	57.1	76.4	67.7
Chinese government agencies	42.8	41.1	41.9
International accounting firms	21.4	23.5	22.5
Prefectural agencies	14.3	5.8	9.6
Private consultants	0.0	5.8	3.2

Question 20: Check the sources you used and evaluate the usefulness (accurate, timely, specific) for the information they supplied.

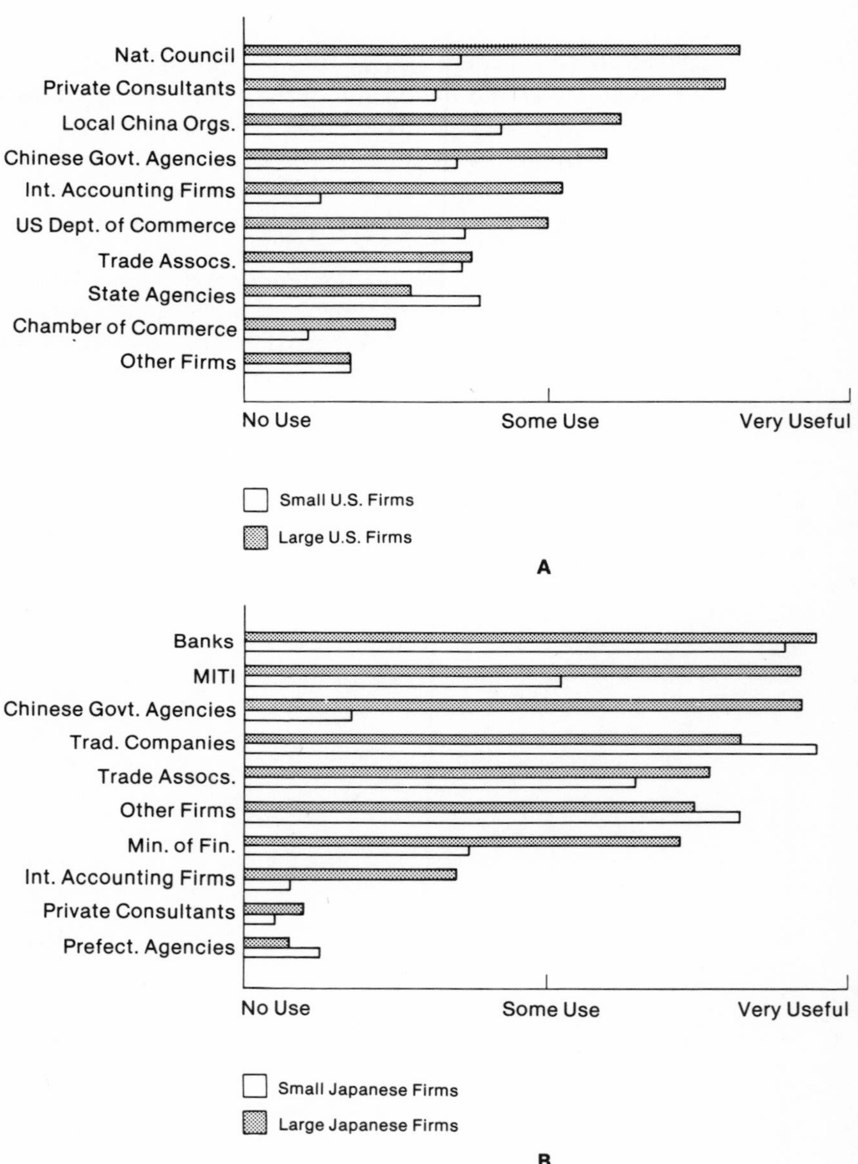

Figure 11.7 Usefulness of China support services. A. U.S. firms. B. Japanese firms.

pointed in the usefulness of the information they receive from these organizations (Fig. 11.7).

American managers report nongovernmental sources of information to be most useful. The organizations that Americans rely on most include the National Council on U.S.–China Trade, private consultants (Kamsky Associates, Technomics, Business International, etc.), and local China support organizations (especially in Seattle, New York, and Minneapolis/St. Paul).

Japanese managers rely on a more varied stable of information sources. This stable includes governmental sources such as the Japanese Ministry of International Trade and Industry (MITI) and, to a lesser degree, the Ministry of Finance. In addition, Japanese manager also have a highly developed network of private organizations that they rely upon for support: Banks (usually those that have some equity holding in the firm), trading companies, trade associations, and other firms (usually firms that are part of the same banking or trading company group).

Attitudes about the Helpfulness of Government

The fabled relationship between Japanese government and business is not without some severe problems. Japanese business people, like their American counterparts, engage in a love-hate relationship with government agencies. Managers from both countries prize their sense of autonomy and control while at the same time coveting the protection and assistance that government agencies offer. Japanese managers, however, differ from their American counterparts in the sorts of government activities that bother them most. Americans are most concerned about "uncertainty"—the rapid change in government policies that affect their foreign commercial activities—and what many managers consider to be the excessive paperwork burden imposed by these rapidly changing laws and regulations. Japanese managers, on the other hand, have become more concerned with formal and informal limits on exports imposed on firms by Japanese government bureaucracies and agencies. (Fig. 11.8; Table 11.7).

As in the previous sub-section, two clusters of activity suggest themselves here. There is a "go-it-alone" philosophy on the part of managers who see the attractiveness of their own products and services as the pri-

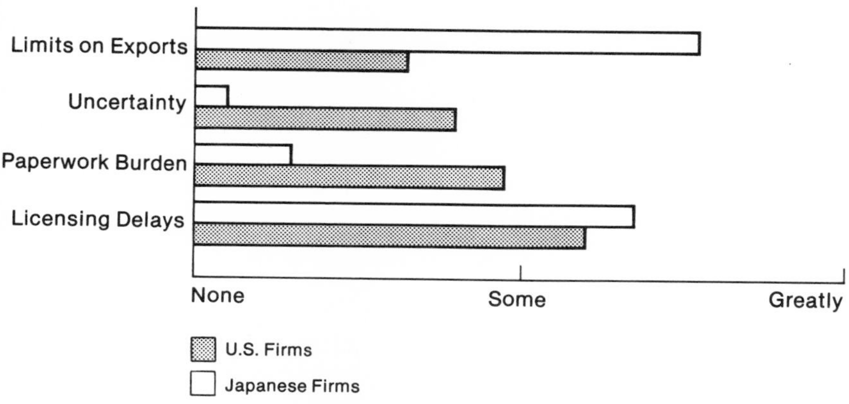

Figure 11.8 Managers who see government affecting their activities in China.

Table 11.7 Importance of Government Export Control Procedures (percent of firms)

		U.S. Firms (%)	Japanese Firms (%)
Question 23: Have government export control procedures substantially affected your business with China?	Yes	24	39.3
	No	46	39.3
	Don't know	14	18.1
Question 24: Are you able to get adequate, timely information on the status of your export license applications?	Yes	46	36.3
	No	22	30.3
	N/A	32	33.3
Question 25: Do export control regulations and their application reflect an adequate understanding of the technology and its military applications?	Yes	24	30.3
	No	42	30.3
	N/A	34	39.3
Question 27: Is the effort to obtain an export license a significant barrier to exporting?	Yes	22	21.2
	No	48	60.6
	N/A	30	18.1
Question 26: What fraction of your export licenses for China have gone to COCOM for evaluation?	<1%	29	—
	1–25%	12	
	25–50%	5	
	>50%	5	
	Don't know	20	
	No answer	29	

mary criterion of their success in the China market. Managers with this sort of outlook seldom look for information about the China market itself, adopting an attitude that seems to imply that potential Chinese customers will close a deal if they have sufficient information about foreign products and technologies. Another cluster of managers looks at their China activities in terms of the sorts of information they need about the market itself. This latter group tends to see success in terms of developing marketing strategies relevant to China's needs and in terms of a strategy that focuses on building relationships with potential end-users of these markets.

There are some clear differences between Japanese and American firms in the kinds of information that managers consider useful and the sources of support that they look to in providing this information. Japanese firms tend to (1) use much more detailed kinds of information in preparing to enter the China market and (2) search for this information among a greater number of sources in both the public and private spheres.

WHAT IS THE "RIGHT KIND" OF CHINESE ENTERPRISE?

By themselves, structural qualities, management attitudes, and relationships with support organizations do not explain why some firms are more successful in their China marketing activities than others. Success comes in many shapes and sizes: There are large American firms and small Japanese companies, firms that piggy-back and firms that go it alone, firms that use support services and firms that do not, firms that sell their products directly and firms that are involved in complex assembly operations.

Foreign firms succeed or fail in China because of "engineering" and "economic" factors. Successful foreign firms provide the right kinds of services, have production capabilities and management flexible enough to allow them to adapt to China's rapidly changing economic conditions, and pricing strategies that seem fair to Chinese purchasers.

However, another reason for transferring technologies has to do with the qualities of "fit" that go beyond the "mesh" of technologies (which is, of course, the most important factor). Some Chinese purchasers simply work better with certain foreign suppliers than with others.[14]

The Importance of Size

Chinese enterprises and agencies that are acquiring foreign technologies come in all sizes. Immense automobile projects look for ways to upgrade production capabilities and hydroelectric projects try to develop electrification grids. But even a small finite problem, such as finding a new type of metal lid for a canning operation or a necessary piece of equipment for a geological expedition, can become a major task for the Chinese enterprise looking for solutions.

Increasingly, the changing character of the Chinese economy gives the end-user—the production enterprises, service organizations, and distributors—the crucial voice in decisions about acquiring new technologies. While state agencies may promulgate general guidelines for technology acquisition projects, it is increasingly the end-user who has the expertise (as well as the strategic position in the decision-making process) to make technology decisions through their first cut. Will it be a Honeywell or a Mitsui machine? Del Monte or Suntory food processing equipment? General Electric or Matsushita CAT scanner? American motors or Nissan production equipment? The Chinese enterprise using new technologies has the largest say in most decisions.

Intuitively, it would seem that the size of the Chinese project would determine the size of the foreign firm that becomes involved in supplying the new technologies. Large Chinese projects would seem to need the capabilities that only a large foreign firm could provide. Could a firm smaller than Chrysler supply all of the equipment and expertise needed for the new Chinese automotive engine assembly operation in northeast China? Figure 11.9 shows that a correlation between size and foreign firms and degree of complexity of the Chinese projects does appear to exist.

Working with Partners

Further examination of the data in Figure 11.9 shows that the generalization about size is subject to some important qualifications. The first qual-

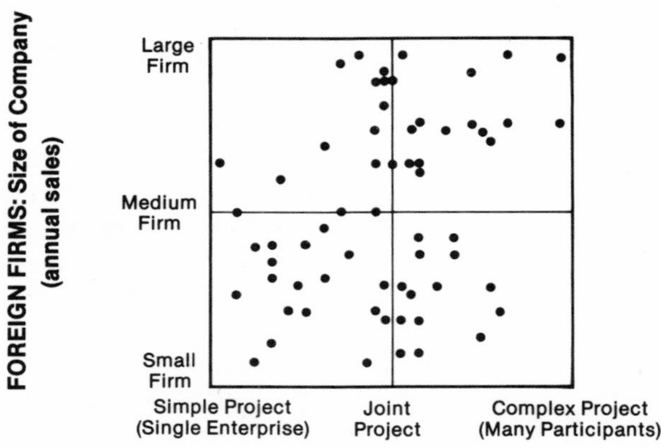

Figure 11.9 The importance of size: All firms.

ification has to do with the nationality of the firms: Are they American or Japanese firms? As Figure 11.10 suggests, American firms—large and small—tend to become involved in "simple" Chinese projects. Japanese firms—large and small—tend to work best with complex Chinese projects.

Why this relationship between place of origin of the foreign firm and the complexity of the Chinese project? The answer involves a number of different dimensions, and offers insights into the reasons that certain kinds of foreign firms work best with specific kinds of Chinese enterprises.

Part of the answer involves the attributes of Chinese large-scale projects. Many foreign firms involved in large-scale projects have found that such projects really involve a series of smaller and quite manageable decisions about energy sources, work rules, raw materials, and construction permits. Such large-scale Chinese projects involve a process of decision and ratification that frequently crosses jurisdictional lines and often involves a large number of unrelated Chinese enterprises and state agencies.

Such large Chinese projects require a special kind of management ability. Most important is the need for Chinese managers in these projects to work with a series of other Chinese managers, each of whom has different needs and requirements. Chinese managers in large-scale projects must make difficult choices that, if not handled correctly, can be costly for their own enterprise and careers, and those of their managerial partners.

Foreign firms that participate successfully in large Chinese projects are usually sensitive to the difficult pressures faced by Chinese managers who guide these projects. Some foreign firms simply have greater experience in handling these partnership relationships than others. Figure 11.11 indicates that foreign firms that are most successful at working with Chinese managers involved in complex partnership arrangements are those that have had considerable experience in forming such partnerships in their own countries. Sometimes such a partnership involves a "tandem" arrangement with other companies in a foreign market. The 3M Corporation, for example, has become quite adept at establishing production facilities in 80 different countries by bringing with them some of their most important suppliers of raw materials. The companies form a sort of "partnership among equals" in their market entry ventures. Other times, such a partnership involves a "piggy-back" strategy. Small Danei Electronics, for example, has moved into China by piggy-backing onto a larger project managed by Mitsubishi.

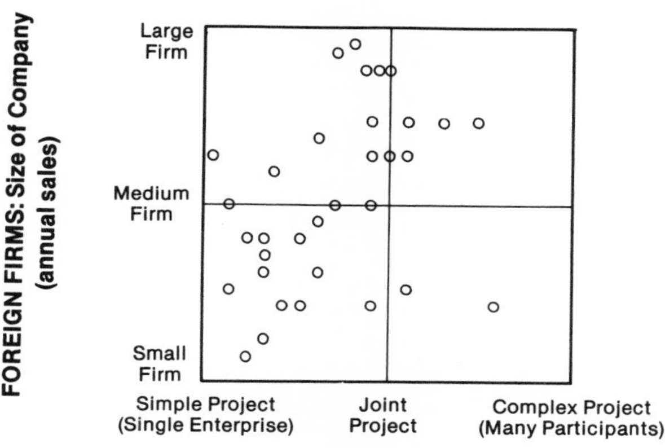

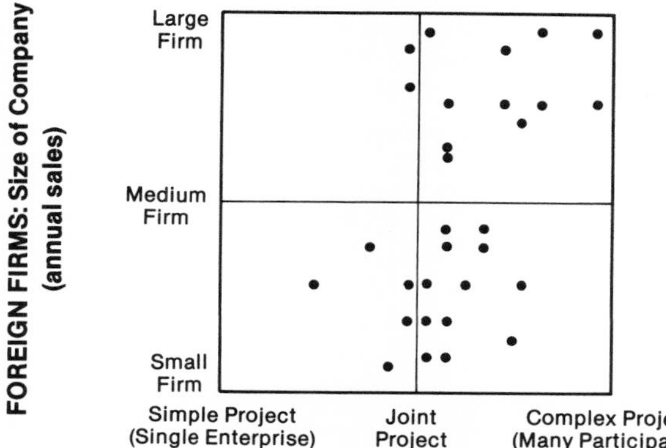

Figure 11.10 The importance of size: A. U.S. firms. B. Japanese firms.

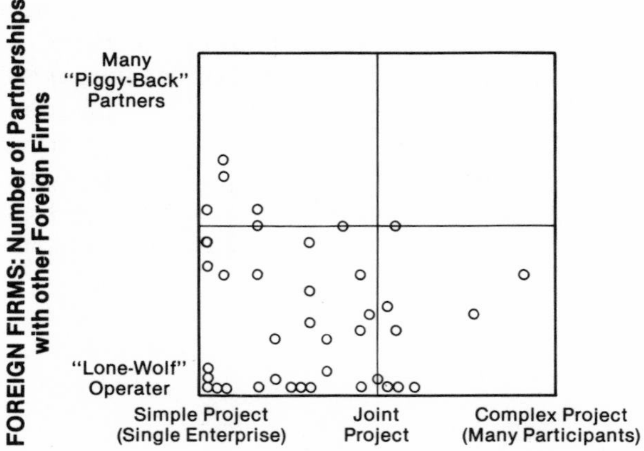

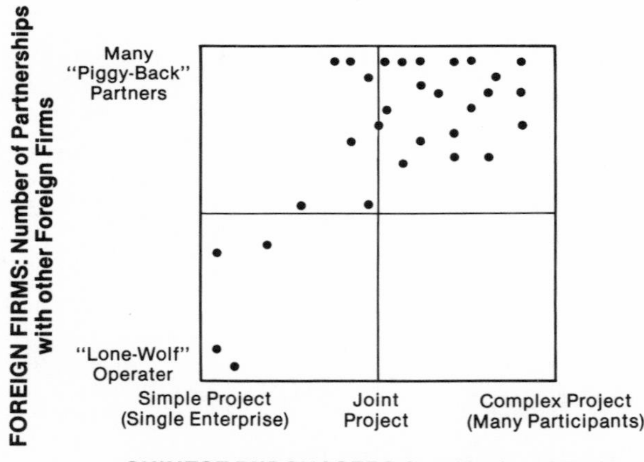

Figure 11.11 Working with partners. A. U.S. firms. B. Japanese firms.

Searching for Help

Another dimension that helps explain the preponderance of Japanese firms in complex Chinese projects has to do with the sorts of channels Chinese managers use to make their projects work. Lines of authority for Chinese managers have changed dramatically since the late 1970s. As central planning and allocation give way to a more diffuse system of operations, Chinese enterprise managers are facing a more fluid decision-making process. The most entrepreneurial managers have a multiplicity of contacts on the local, provincial, and even national levels. Many have established lines of communication with individuals and managers that in the past would have been out of bounds to them because such communications would have crossed jurisdictional lines. The broader the network, the better: If one channel is closed, others can be used.

Japanese and American managers live in an economic world that is changing just as rapidly—especially in relationship to China. Earlier, I described how some successful managers of foreign firms also use a multiplicity of sources of support for their China activities. These sources—both public and private—can provide expert information, guidance, and contacts in the new markets.

On both sides, then, we can see how important networks and access are. Some managers—both foreign and Chinese—rely heavily on outside sources of information and expertise; others choose to base their activities on information that comes primarily form within the firm itself. Figure 11.12 shows that foreign managers who are used to looking for information and support from a variety of different sources not only have better information on which to base their marketing activities, they also have a greater ability to interact with Chinese counterparts who have refined the same talents.

Mapping a Strategy

Looking for help is most important during the early phases of project design—when clear conceptualization can make or break the difficult negotiations that follow. Implementation requires a different set of skills.

Although the Chinese enterprise managers are most often responsible for overall coordination of a project that involves a foreign firm, many Chinese enterprises put a chief engineer in charge of technical decisions. A key variable in the success of foreign technology acquisition projects is the nature of the relationship between the enterprise's general manager and his chief engineer(s). When managerial and technical perspectives do not mesh, the possibilities of conflict within the Chinese enterprise can be magnified, and decisions within the enterprise can become fragmented and lacking in focus. When the manager works easily with department heads and technical personnel, the acquisition process tends to move more smoothly, regardless of the "mesh" of the new technologies.

Equally important to successful implementation are the ways that a enterprise manager works with "outside" support groups. Every Chinese enterprise exists in the context of a web of relationships with upstream suppliers of materials and services and downstream purchasers of finished products. New foreign technologies impose a strain on these relationships. Will new raw materials be available? At what price? Can transportation permits be obtained? Will pollution-control permits be issued? Will old customers like the new products?

For a manager to interact successfully with a network of suppliers and

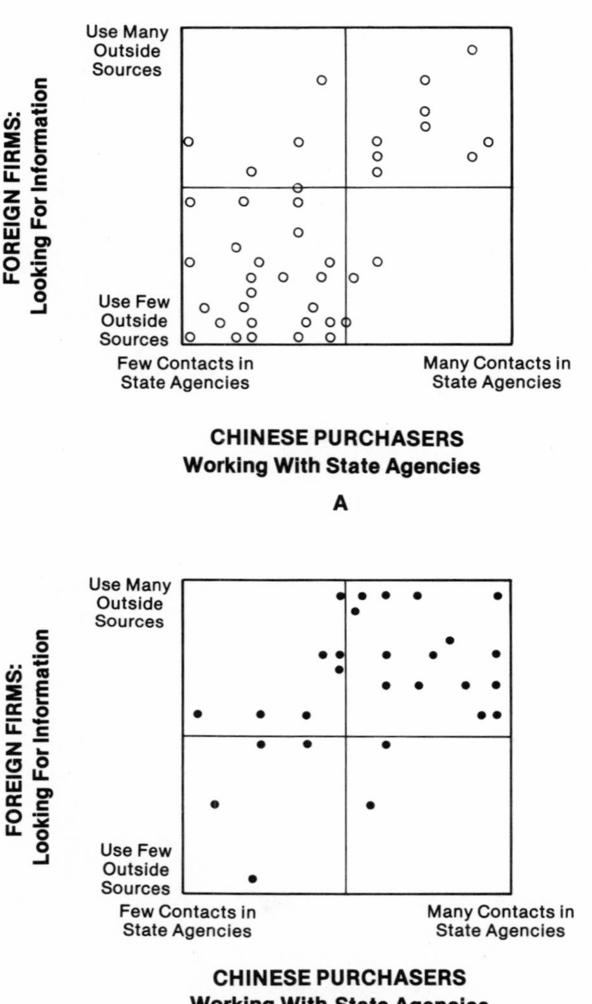

Figure 11.12 Searching for help. A. U.S. firms. B. Japanese firms.

users requires some strategic thinking—a sort of mapping out of alternative routings toward the successful completion of the project. Some Chinese enterprise managers have adapted to this new world by developing a sort of rough, individualistic style of management, moving in an almost brusque fashion through the complex maze of rules and regulations that have emerged during the past decade. Other managers have developed a more collegial work style, smoothing the way for their projects by working closely with peers who manager parallel institutions. The skills required for a

Chinese manager in this new world of increased autonomy are not at all the same as the skills required to survive in the old centralized system.

As Figure 11.13 indicates, foreign firms plug into these Chinese managerial styles in different ways. Interestingly, foreign firms that are "market sensitive"—who focus on end-users, segment markets, and examine Chinese decision-making processes—tend to work best with Chinese managers who have a somewhat collegial managerial style. Foreign firms that are product-

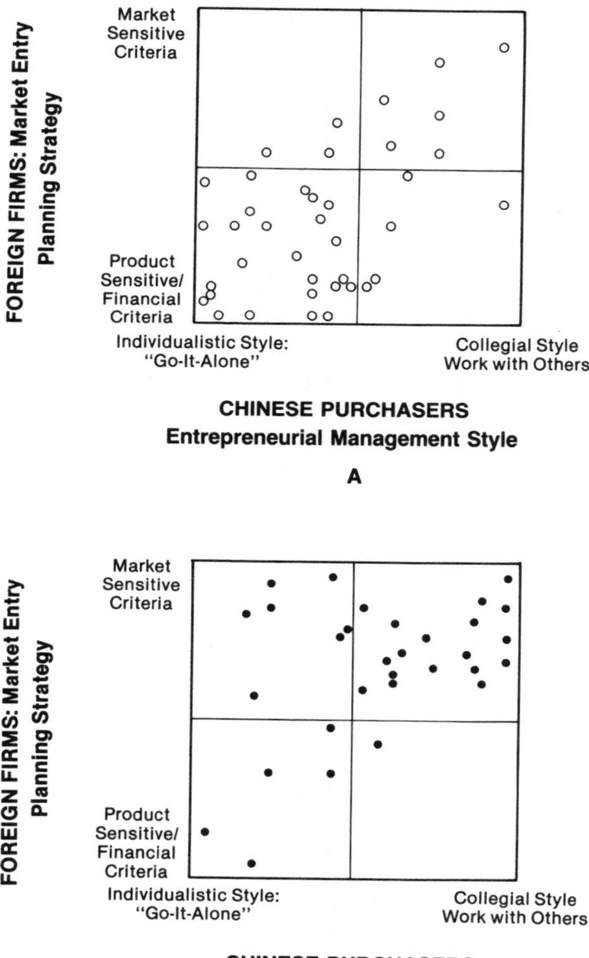

Figure 11.13 Mapping a strategy. A. U.S. firms. B. Japanese firms.

sensitive and price-sensitive—who focus on "bottom-line" factors and give presentations that emphasize "state of the art" bells and whistles—tend to work best with individualistic and "go-it-alone" Chinese managers.

WHY SOME FOREIGN FIRMS SUCCEED

United Food Products undoubtedly had the right sorts of technologies for the Chinese food processing project in Liaoning. In his presentations, Ed Adams emphasized technologies that mattered to the Chinese managers who would make the new project work: improved seed stock, upgraded canning machinery, improved quality control practices. These factors, Ed was convinced, had given him the advantage over Ajinomoto.

Equally important, but perhaps unrecognized by Ed, was the fact that United Food was the sort of firm that could work nicely with this particular Chinese enterprise. The Chinese manager was known to be a tough realist—even a bit of a maverick—who did not countenance interference from outsiders, whether these outsiders were from state agencies or party organizations. He liked to work alone, and he was proud of the accomplishments of his enterprise.

Similarly, United Food was a lone-wolf operation. The American firm kept its distance from government help and private consultants in the United States, and its top management prided itself on "making its numbers" every quarter, thereby maintaining its attractiveness in the eyes of New York financial analysts. United had never engaged in any sort of piggy-back operation with another firm. Over and above its technologies, United Food was a more natural fit for the Chinese enterprise than was Ajinomoto.

National Industries, in losing its competition with Mitsui, was playing a much different game. The heating furnace project—while involving about the same dollar amount of equipment and expertise—was very different in terms of the Chinese support networks that would be necessary for planning and implementation. The heating furnace project had to be a joint undertaking between a number of unrelated Chinese enterprises and the project was a cut across the jurisdictional boundaries of a half-dozen different economic agencies and provincial bureaus. Mitsui was ideally suited to the project—the Japanese firm not only had experience in China, it also had a long history of working with Japanese companies in other international markets. The company knew how to build support teams by working with different public and private organizations in Japan, and the company had a management style that stressed collegiality. National Industries, as experienced as it was in international marketing, simply did not work well in the complex China steel-making environment.

The most important finding in my study is that successful firms in the China market—both Japanese and American—possess specific kinds of organizational qualities, operational procedures, and managerial attitudes that distinguish them from their less successful competitors. I discovered no unique "Japanese strategy" of management or unusual organizational characteristics that were not also found in some American firms. There were, however, significantly more Japanese firms possessing the qualities requisite for success in China and using strategies appropriate to the situation than there were American firms.[15]

At no point can it be said that a foreign firm's success in the China market is simply a result of the possession of some sort of unique technology, adherence to a particular management style, or participation in a special relationship with government. Nor is it a function of the firm's national origin. Ultimately, the transfer of technology to China is a two-way street involving two sets of characteristics: (1) those of the foreigners and the firms that supply the new technologies and (2) those of the Chinese managers and the enterprises that seek them out. Neither can succeed without the other.

Obviously this "fit" between the nontechnology-related characteristics of foreign firms and Chinese enterprises is less important than the mesh of the foreign technologies with Chinese needs. Nevertheless, we are finding that it is "the fit" that occurs in these areas previously deemed nonessential that frequently makes the difference between a project that simply sputters along, and a project that thrives and grows.

NOTES

1. The names of the American firms have been changed.
2. See the discussion in Louis T. Wells, "Economic man and engineering man: Choices of technology in low-wage countries," *Public Policy,* (21, Summer 1973), p. 313.
3. I have analyzed Japanese and American firms in the China market in two separate studies. The first study examines the activities of over 100 Japanese and American firms entering the China market and is the basis of my *Competing in China: Japanese and American Businessmen in the Opening of a New Market* (forthcoming). A separate study analyzes an additional 50 firms: Roy F. Grow, *American Firms and the Transfer of Technology to China: How Business People View the Process,* a report for the Office of Technology Assessment (Washington, D.C., Contract No. 633-51550) February, 1987.
4. Roy F. Grow, "How factories choose technology," *The China Business Review* (May–June 1987), pp. 35–39; Roy F. Grow, "Acquiring foreign technology: What makes the transfer process work?" for Merle Goldman and Denis Simon (eds.), *China's Technological Revolution* (Cambridge: Harvard University Press), 1988; and Roy F. Grow, "Agents of change: The Chinese enterprise and foreign technology"; Roy F. Grow, "A Pharmaceutical Deal," *The China Business Review* (November–December 1987), pp. 40–43.
5. Roy F. Grow, "Japanese and American firms in China: Lessons of a new market," *Columbia Journal of World Business,* Volume XXI, Number 1 (Spring 1986); Roy F. Grow, "Reconsidering the China market," *Euro-Asia Business Review* (Paris, October 1987) pp. 9–14; and Roy F. Grow, "Managing entry into a new market; Japanese and American strategies in China," for the Academy of International Business Annual Conference, November 1987.

6. Data from 41 American and 34 Japanese firms. Data from the American firms has been reported in Roy F. Grow in *American Firms and the Transfer of Technology to China: How Business People View the Process,* op. cit.
7. As in works such as Michael Borrus, James Millstein, and John Zysman, *U.S.–Japanese Competition in the Semiconductor Industry: A Study in International Trade and Technological Development,* Policy Paper in International Affairs 17 (Berkeley: Institute of International Affairs, University of California), 1982; Hajime Eto and Konomu Matsui, *R & D Management Systems in Japanese Industry* (Amsterdam: North Holland, 1984); Charles McMillan, *The Japanese Industrial System* (New York: W. de Gruyter, 1985).
8. Carl Pegels, *Japan vs. the West: Implications for Management* (Hingham: Kluwer Boston, 1984); Toyohiro Kono, *Strategy and Structure of Japanese Enterprises* (New York: M.E. Sharpe, 1984); Tadao Kagono, *Strategic vs. Evolutionary Management: A. U.S.–Japan Comparison of Strategy and Organization* (Amsterdam: Elsevier, 1985).
9. Thomas McCraw, *American vs. Japan: A Comparative Study of Business–Government Relations Conducted at the Harvard Business School* (Boston: Harvard Business School, 1986); Michael Yoshino and Thomas Lifson, *The Invisible Link: Japan's Sogo Shosha and the Organization of Trade* (Cambridge: MIT Press, 1986); Sheridan Tatsuno, *The Technopolis Strategy: Japan, High-Technology, and the Control of the Twenty-First Century* (New York: Prentice Hall, 1986).
10. Note the questionnaire data in Nigel Cambell, "Japanese business strategy in China," in *Long Range Planning* (Great Britain: Pergamon Journals), Volume 20, No. 5, 1987, pp. 69–73. See also Deborah Diamond-Kim, "Japan's China trade," *The China Business Review* (November–December 1986), pp. 332–338.
11. Data from 41 American and 33 Japanese firms. In addition to the characteristics listed in this section, my research also suggests that the following characteristics are important to understanding the differences between American and Japanese firms that are active in the China market: production technology, vertical integration, marketing–production relationships, indebtedness, and production flexibility.
12. Data from 41 American and 33 Japanese firms. In addition to the characteristics listed in this section, my research also suggests that the following characteristics are important in understanding the ways that Japanese and American managers approach the China market: collegiality, method of pricing, selection of sales representatives, specific sales techniques, strategies of contract negotiation, attitudes toward financial institutions, importance of product satisfaction, ways of thinking about future orders.
13. Data from 40 American and 32 Japanese firms.
14. In past work, I have isolated clusters of characteristics that are helpful in understanding why some Chinese enterprises acquire foreign technologies and others do not. Bill Fischer and Denis Simon are now completing some of the most exciting work that analyzes the characteristics of enterprises that assimilate foreign technologies.
15. Why this is so is the subject of my book-length study.

12
Pros and Cons of International Technology Transfer: A Developing Country's View

LINSU KIM

Recently, international technology transfer has been a subject of debate in both developed countries (DCs) and less developed countries (LDCs). Many argue that international technology transfer from DCs to LDCs should be promoted because it is mutually beneficial. They claim that international technology transfer to LDCs allows enterprises in DCs (1) to prolong the life cycle of products that are becoming obsolete in the home market, (2) to find new, growing markets, and (3) to ensure its own survival by relocating production segments to LDCs where labor costs are lower. Likewise, international technology transfer from DCs benefits enterprises in LDCs by enabling them to generate and improve products and processes and to gain export markets.

On the other hand, others argue that international technology transfer should be restricted to protect national interests; that its long-term effect is rather negative. Opponents in DCs argue that technology transfer to LDCs has "boomerang" effects, ultimately damaging their own industries and employment. Those opponents in LDCs argue that technology transfer results in an economic and technological dependence of LDCs on DCs.

This chapter assesses the pros and cons associated with international technology transfer from an LDC perspective. It presents a conceptual framework that may be useful to identify and assess different forms and channels of international technology transfer. With Korea as the case in point, it examines how an LDC acquires foreign technology from DCs and discusses implications for both DCs and LDCs.

A CONCEPTUAL FRAMEWORK TO ASSESS TECHNOLOGY TRANSFER

Foreign technology transfer may be mediated by the market; the supplier and the buyer may negotiate payment for technology transfer, either em-

Table 12.1 The Mode of Foreign Technology Transfer

Market mediated	Direct foreign investment, foreign licensing, turn-key plant, technical consultancy, made-to-order machinery (Cell 1)	Standard (serial) machinery purchase[a] (Cell 2)
Nonmarket mediated	Technical assistance by foreign buyers, technical assistance by foreign vendors[b] (Cell 4)	Imitation (reverse engineering) observation, trade journals, technical information service (Cell 3)
	Active	Passive
	The Role of Foreign Suppliers	

[a]Except for small, standard machinery, foreign suppliers send their engineers to assemble and test-run machinery sold. Often, they teach local personnel how to operate it and provide after-sale services. In this sense, the supplier's role is not passive, but compared with those mechanisms in cell 1, this mechanism can still be classified in cell 2.

[b]The vendor's service mentioned here refers to technical assistance not directly related to the operation of machinery sold; rather, the suppliers provide technical information and consultancy on operations not related to the machinery sold in exchange to a long-term purchase agreement.

bodied in or disembodied from the physical equipment. Foreign technology may also be transferred to local users without the mediation of the market. In this case the technology transfer usually takes place without formal agreements and payments. The foreign supplier can take either an active role, exercising significant control over the way in which technology is transferred to and used by the local recipient, or a passive role, having almost nothing to do with the way the user takes advantage of available technical know-how either embodied in or disembodied from the physical item. The recipient may be a producer, attempting to generate new products for import-substitution, or a user, deploying foreign technologies to improve productivity and product quality. These three variables—the mediation of the market, the role of foreign suppliers, and the role of recipients—offer a useful eight-cell matrix (Table 12.1) to identify and evaluate different mechanisms of international technology transfer and to assess its pros and cons.

Most studies of technology transfer have devoted their attention to the examination of those modes in cell 1 (market mediated with active suppliers). These include technology transfer accompanied by direct foreign investment (DFI), foreign licensing (FL), technical consultancy (TC), and made-to-order machinery. Recipients of foreign technology in this cell are mostly producers, with only a few exceptions.

Technology transfer in cell 2 is market mediated, but foreign suppliers play a relatively passive role, not exercising much control over the way in which technical know-how embodied in physical items is transferred to and used by the buyer. The purchase of standard serial machinery that embodies new technologies serves as the major means of transfer in cell 2. Recipients of foreign technology transfer in this cell are mostly users.

Technology transfers that take place in cell 3 are nonmarket mediated, in which the foreign suppliers play a relatively passive role. Reverse engineering done by local firms for their product and process development, reverse engineering by public research and development (R&D) centers for localization of technology beyond the capacity of local firms, and technical information services provided by various public agencies are good examples. Both producers and users could be in this cell.

In cell 4, technology transfer per se is not negotiated and priced in the market, but the foreign partners involved play a relatively active role in transferring technological know-how. There are at least two distinct cases. First, foreign buyers of locally produced goods under original equipment maker (OEM) arrangements deliberately provide technical know-how to ensure that local firms manufacture products according to the end buyer's stringent specifications. Second, foreign vendors of components and equipment provide local buyers with important technical services related to a system, for which they sell their products.

In conclusion, besides such formal mechanisms as direct foreign investment, foreign licensing, and technical consultancy, which have been studied at great length in the literature, technology may also be transferred across national boundaries through the various informal mechanisms outlined above. A discussion of how an LDC uses these mechanisms follows using Korea as the case in point.

TECHNOLOGY TRANSFER IN PRACTICE: THE CASE OF KOREA

Korea is one of many LDCs that has developed comprehensive policies and measures to promote, enhance, and manage technology flows from DCs (Baranson and Roark, 1985). First, this section presents a brief discussion of Korea's public policies related to foreign technology transfer. Then Korea's experience in technology transfer under this public-policy environment is discussed. The Korea case illuminates further discussion of the pros and cons of international technology transfer.

Technology Transfer in Cell 1

Direct Foreign Investment

The Korean government took initial steps to organize national policies for technology transfer in the 1960s. Korea's direct foreign investment (DFI) policy was quite free at that time, allowing any form of bona fide foreign capital, including fully owned subsidiaries, with extensive incentives. However, not much foreign investment came in during the 1960s, primarily due to questions about Korea's political stability and the uncertain economic outlook.

The government reversed its DFI policy in the 1970s, tightening controls, fearing that unlimited flow of foreign investment might adversely affect the domestic economy. Joint ventures received higher priority than wholly owned subsidiaries. A general guideline was adopted setting three criteria: eligibility, foreign ownership, and investment scale. Therefore, competition with domestic firms was seldom allowed in both domestic and international markets. Export requirements were forced on DFIs. Foreign participation ratios were basically limited to 50 percent, except for high technology and entirely export-oriented cases, rendering Korea one of a few countries with very restrictive foreign investment regulations.

In September 1980, the Korean government reversed its position, substantially liberalizing foreign investment guidelines. Another important reform was made effective from July 1984. The major change was a switch from the system of a "positive list" (listing which industries are open to DFI) to that of a "negative list" (listing those that are prohibited). The government's open policy for DFI is aimed at inducing the transfer of sophisticated new technologies and at promoting market competition for domestic firms, even within the domestic market, to intensify their innovation activities.

Under such a public policy environment, Korea has drawn an increasing amount of DFI through 1986 (Table 12.2), excluding the 1977–1981 period, which reflects an economic recession in Korea stemming partly from domestic political and social instability and partly from the global economic recession. Over 48 percent of the total DFI took place in the last period (1982–1986). Japan accounts for over 68 percent in the number of cases and 55 percent of the value, followed by the U.S. (20 and 26 percent, respectively). However, the average size of the American DFI is more than twice that of the Japanese. Chemicals, machinery, and electrical/electronics account for over 72 percent of the total DFI in the manufacturing sector and over 46 percent of the total DFI in Korea. Its proportion has steadily increased over time, as Korea has undergone a structural change from labor-intensive industries to relatively more knowledge-intensive industries.

The size of DFI and its proportion to total external borrowing are significantly lower in Korea compared with other newly industrializing countries (NICs) such as Taiwan, Singapore, and Brazil. One report (KEB, 1987) shows that Korea's stock of DFI in 1983 was only 7 percent of that in Brazil, 23 percent of that in Singapore, and less than half the size of that in Taiwan and Hong Kong. The proportion of DFI in Korea to the country's total external borrowing is only 6.1 percent, far below the levels of Singapore (91.9 percent), Taiwan (45 percent), and Brazil (21.8 percent). This figure appears to be the outcome of the nation's DFI strategy, under which Korea favored loans as a source of foreign capital and relied on other mechanisms to gain foreign technology.

Unlike other NICs, the contribution of DFI to economic development has not been significant in Korea. A recent study (Cha, 1983) shows that DFI's contribution to the growth of the gross national product (GNP) in Korea in the period from 1972 to 1980 amounted to only 1.3 percent, while its contribution to total and manufacturing value added was only

Table 12.2 Foreign Technology Transfer to Korea

(unit: U.S.$ million)

Source	1962–1966	1967–1971	1972–1976	1977–1981	1982–1986	Total
Japan	8.3	89.7	627.1	300.9	875.2	1,901.2
U.S.	25.0	95.3	135.0	235.7	581.6	1,072.6
Others	12.1	33.6	117.3	184.0	309.7	658.7
Total	47.4	218.6	879.4	720.6	1,766.5	3,632.5
Foreign licensing						
Japan	—	5.0	58.7	139.8	323.7	527.2
U.S.	0.6	7.8	21.3	159.2	602.7	791.6
Others	0.2	3.5	16.6	152.4	258.5	431.1
Total	0.8	16.3	96.5	451.4	1,184.9	1,749.9
Technical Consultancy						
Japan	—	12.1	7.7	20.8	89.2	129.8
U.S.	—	3.1	6.0	16.7	159.1	184.9
Others	—	1.6	4.8	17.2	84.0	107.6
Total	—	16.8	18.5	54.7	332.3	422.3
Capital Goods Imports						
Japan	148	1,292	4,423	14,269	20,986	41,118
U.S.	75	472	1,973	6,219	12,394	21,133
Others	93	777	2,445	7,490	53,338	64,143
Total	316	2,541	8,841	27,978	86,718	126,394

Sources: Ministry of Finance for data on direct foreign investment and foreign licensing, Ministry of Science and Technology for technical consultancy data, and Korea Society for Advancement of Machinery Industry for capital goods data.

1.1 percent and 4.8 percent, respectively, in 1971, and 4.5 percent and 14.2 percent, respectively, in 1980. Its contribution to employment was only 0.2 percent and 1.5 percent, respectively, for 1971 and 1980.

Foreign Licensing

Korea's policy on foreign licensing (FL) was quite restrictive in the 1960s. General guidelines stipulated that royalties should be set within 3 percent of sales and contract duration within 3 years for the manufacturing sector, and that no export restrictions were allowed. In the early years, such a restrictive policy on foreign licensings led some local licensees to bargain in purchasing generally known mature technologies. The restrictive guidelines were significantly relaxed in the 1970s to allow the transfer of more sophisticated technologies. The policy was further relaxed in 1984, opening for all industries and for all terms and conditions. The government also used public R&D centers to assist the private sector in identifying particular foreign technologies and their suppliers and in strengthening bargaining power in transfer negotiations.

Table 12.2 also presents basic statistics of FL to Korea. It shows that, as with DFI, over 67 percent of FL was signed in the last period (1982–1986) and that the United States leads Japan in the receipt of royalty payments from the late 1970s, despite half the number of cases. These numbers indicate that the average royalty per case is far greater for the United States than for Japan, reflecting a significantly higher degree of sophistication in technology licensed from the United States. Kim's (1984) microeconomic study of 70 Korea firms confirms that American technologies are more capital-intensive, sophisticated, and complex than Japanese technologies.

Technical Consultancy

Table 12.2 shows that compared with other modes of technology transfer, technical consultancy is not significant in terms of value. The last period (1982–1986) accounts for over 78 percent of the total, and the United States leads Japan in supplying engineering consultancy services to Korea. The U. S. lead is attributed to the sharp increase of its share in the last period.

Turnkey Plants and Machinery

While Korea was restrictive on DFI and FL through the 1970s, it relied heavily on turnkey plants and made-to-order machinery for technology transfer. Firms in the process-based industries established in the 1960s and early 1970s, such as chemicals, cement, steel, and paper, resorted to the turnkey mode. In these industries, investment size was relatively large and proprietary engineering know-how was critical, although equipment was generally known. For these reasons, the best alternative for local firms without engineering capabilities was to rely completely on experienced foreign firms, to minimize the risks involved in a large investment and the time required to achieve normal operations. However, no quantifiable data is available to assess the quantity of technology transfer associated with turnkey plants' transfers.

Technology Transfer in Cell 2

The Korean government played a crucial role in transferring foreign technology embodied in standard serial machinery. The rapid growth of the Korean economy has called for paramount investment in production facilities. For example, the index of gross domestic fixed capital formation has risen rapidly from 50.7 in 1953 to 662.7 in 1970 and to 3,546.2 in 1984, with 1960 set equal to 100. Capital formation as a percentage of gross national product has risen from 5.5 percent to 25.3 percent to 33.4 percent during the same period. However, government policy has been biased in favor of foreign capital goods as a way to strengthen the international competitiveness of capital goods user industries. Such a policy led to massive imports of foreign capital goods, transferring new foreign technologies embodied therein, at the cost of retarding the development of the local capital goods industry (Kim, 1987a). The import liberalization rate in the machinery industry was relatively high until the first half of 1971, giving capital-goods users almost free access to foreign capital goods. Moreover, the slight overvaluation of the local currency, the tariff exemptions on imported capital goods, and the financing of purchases by supplier's credits, which carried low interest rates relative to those on the domestic market, all worked to increase the attractiveness of capital goods imports (Rhee and Westphal, 1977).

Table 12.2 also present data on capital goods imports. Japan leads the United States and the other countries in supplying capital goods to Korea. The U.S. proportion has steadily increased over time, but its share remained about half of the Japanese share in the whole period. Furthermore, of the four categories of technology transfer listed in Table 12.2, capital goods imports far surpass other means of technology transfers in terms of value. Capital goods imports were worth 34 times the value of DFI, 72 times the value of FL, and almost 300 times the value of technical consultancies. In sum, the total value of capital goods imports is 21 times that of all other categories combined. The trend is similar for individual source countries. For example, the total value of capital goods imports from the United States is 10.3 times that of all other categories combined from the United States. Thus, Korea may have acquired more technology from DCs through the importation of capital goods than through any other means. Compared to NICs, such as Argentina, Brazil, India, and Mexico, Korea has relied more on the import of capital goods for foreign technology transfer than on DFI and FL (Westphal et al., 1985).

Technology Transfer in Cell 3

Technology transfers that take place in cell 3 are nonmarket mediated, in which foreign suppliers play a relatively passive role. Reverse engineering done by local firms for their product and process development is the most important mode in this cell; both producers and users take advantage of this mode. Reverse engineering by public R&D centers for localization of technology beyond the capacity of local firms and technical information services provided by various public agencies may also be good examples. Since technology transfers in this cell cannot be quantified, one has to be satisfied with fragmented pieces of evidence from empirical studies and other anecdotes.

Reverse Engineering by Private Firms

The Korean government also has measures to facilitate the transfer of foreign technologies through the mode in cell 3. For example, in 1979 the Korean government introduced a scheme to designate locally developed innovative products and offered preferential treatment, tax incentives, and 2-year protection from entry by foreign technology or local imitation as a way to foster local development efforts. In the case of the machinery industry, preferential financing is offered even to the purchaser of such products.

There appear to be four types of firms that undertake reverse engineering. The first type comprises producers. Kim's (1980) study of consumer electronics firms reveals that of 15 black/white TV assemblers in 1975, 11 entered the industry by reverse engineering done by experienced engineers poached from existing firms. A study of 42 innovative capital goods producers shows that these firms primarily deployed the forms and channels to technology transfer in cell 3 (see Kim and Kim, 1985). Bae and Lee's (1986) study of small and medium-sized firms in Korea also shows that reverse engineering was the major means of product development for these firms. A recent study on the transfer of factory automation (F) to Korea shows that the majority of 28 firms doing business in CAD/CAM, 11 in automatic warehousing, and 22 in robotics, used reverse engineering as a way to get FA technology (Kim, 1988a).

The second type of firm is users. As in von Hippel's (1976) concept of user-paradigm, FA users first developed equipment related to FA in Korea. As mentioned previously, they imported the first batch of FA equipment to improve their productivity, but they soon developed FA equipment by assimilating imported technology on the basis of their experience in using foreign equipment and their own R&D efforts to meet subsequent needs and needs within their *chaebol* (Korean version of Japanese zaibatsu) group. An electronics firm has reportedly developed 2,500 units of 45 different pieces of FA equipment ranging from part-inserting robotics and automatic printed circuit board inspectors to automatic wrapping and unmanned vehicles. Many chemical, cement, paper, and steel makers studied by Kim (1987b) largely resorted to turnkey plants for the initial setup, but used reverse engineering for subsequent expansions. All of these firms have progressively sequenced from the importation of foreign equipment and systems to the imitative production of their own models for import-substitution. These firms later became equipment producers to capitalize on their capabilities, as the local market slowly took shape.

The third type includes firms that entered their manufacturing business first as sales and service agents for foreign exporters. Such experience provided local agents with opportunities to assimilate foreign technologies. For example, most of the 28 firms in the CAD/CAM business started as local sales/after-service agents for foreign suppliers. Many of them are now investing for their own R&D for assimilation and import-substitution of foreign systems. A similar pattern is also observed in Korea's entry into the computer industry (Kim et al., 1987).

The fourth type of firm includes new technology-based small producers that are started by technical entrepreneurs who have recently spun-off from local universities, R&D centers, or existing firms. Given the initial capability in innovation, they began developing innovative equipment and systems through reverse engineering of sophisticated foreign products (see Kim, 1988b).

Reverse Engineering by Public R&D Centers

Public R&D centers, 16 in number in 1981 and then reduced to 8 by mergers, have played a major role in developing new technologies through reverse engineering. Public R&D centers undertake joint research with the private sector to help local firms acquire new technology without collaborating with foreign sources or to help them gain better bargaining power in technology transfer negotiations. An example of the former would be the Korean reaction to the Japanese refusal to license technology for polyester film production to Korea, in fear of losing its market in Korea; a public R&D center in collaboration with a local chemical firm successfully undertook a reverse engineering task to develop the technology. Korea now is the world's major supplier for audio and video cassette tapes.

Public R&D centers also play an important role in developing new technologies that have large economic externalities. For example, the Korean government invested about $300 million in developing design and production capabilities for semiconductors and computers. The government established a public R&D institute several years before the private sector's entry into computers and semiconductors in an attempt to gain first-stage experience in R&D in the new technologies and to generate experienced researchers and production workers. This R&D center has been the spearhead and backbone of R&D in computer and semiconductor design.

In short, the major role of public R&D centers in a developing country, as discussed by Utterback (1975), is to facilitate and lubricate foreign technology transfer by assisting in the private sector's acquisition of foreign technology, formally or informally; to solve immediate or short-term problems; and to undertake their own R&D activities to pave the road for the private sector to have an advantageous position at a later point in time in acquiring newer technologies.

Technical Information Service

The government also exerts efforts to facilitate the international transfer of scientific and technical (S&T) knowledge through its technical information services provided by various public agencies. Through several monthly periodicals and on-line computer systems, these agencies collect, process, and disseminate S&T information on a nonprofit basis.

Technology Transfer in Cell 4

Technology transfer takes place in cell 4 where technology transfer per se is not negotiated and priced in the market, but foreign partners play a relatively active role in transferring technological know-how. Like those in cell 3, qualitative assessments have to be made, because no quantifiable information is available for the modes in cell 4.

There are at least two distinct cases. First, foreign buyers of locally produced goods under OEM arrangements deliberately provide technical know-how to ensure that locally manufactured products meet buyers' stringent specifications. Second, foreign vendors of components and equipment provide local buyers with important technical services indirectly related to a system, for which they sell their products. The first mode of technology transfer, which was mentioned repeatedly by local firms in field interviews (e.g., Kim, 1987b; Westphal et al., 1981; Kim, 1980) is a by-product of the export-oriented industrialization strategy in Korea. Therefore, public policy for export promotion has had an important impact on foreign technology transfer.

In conclusion, the government has played an important role in managing and facilitating the transfer of foreign technology by regulating collaborative agreements concerning direct foreign investment and foreign licensing and by providing incentives and preferential financing to those who acquire foreign technologies through means other than collaborative agreements. The government has also contributed significantly to technology transfer through the development of an R&D infrastructure such as public R&D institutes and technical information centers, which have played an important role in helping local firms acquire better bargaining power in technology transfer negotiations and also in the reverse engineering of foreign technologies.

IMPLICATIONS FOR DEVELOPED COUNTRIES

The conceptual framework and empirical evidence in Korea lead to several questions that DCs need to address to gain a better understanding of the pros and cons of technology transfer to LDCs. Should DCs try to stop transferring technology to LDCs in fear of boomerang effects? If yes, then can DCs stop transferring technology to LDCs? The evidence presented above suggests that the answer to both questions is "no."

Any attempt to restrict technology transfer to LDCs through the modes in cell 1 will jeopardize economic growth and yet cannot prevent LDCs from obtaining technology. The restriction of DFI to LDCs will jeopardize the global strategy of multinational firms in DCs, while that of FL will shorten the economic life cycle of their technologies and products. If one DC refuses to transfer a technology, a sophisticated technology buyer in the LDCs can turn to an alternative source. Examples abound. When the Japanese refused to license peroxide technology to Korea in fear of losing its market in the country (Korea imported 100 percent of its peroxide from Japan), Koreans turned to America, who was willing to license the technology to enter the new market. When large semiconductor firms in Japan and the United States were reluctant to transfer semiconductor technology to Korea, Korean firms were able to negotiate a dozen licensing agreements with small semiconductor firms in the United States between 1983 and 1985. These small firms were willing to sell the technology for a quick infusion of cash during the business slump in semiconductors (Kim, 1987c).

Alternatively, a sophisticated technology buyer can turn to another mode of technology transfer. Examples are again plentiful. When the Japanese refused to license video cassette recorder (VCR) technology to Korea, Korean firms employed reverse engineering (the mode in cell 3) of Japanese products (the mode in cell 2), augmented by technical consultancy (a mode in cell 1) provided by foreign engineers recruited on a short-term basis by the Korean firms. Now Korea challenges Japan in the world market.

DCs cannot stop transferring technology to LDCs through the mode in cell 2, because the transfer of standardized machinery is merely a pure form of commodity trade. Any restriction on trade will hamper economic growth of the individual firms and, in turn, of the entire nation. The empirical data (the value of Korea's imports of capital goods was 21 times those of DFI, FL, and TC combined) and impressions gained in field interviews with Korean firms suggest that Koreans appear to have learned more from imported capital goods than from other modes of technology transfer. Kim and Kim's (1985) study offers useful insights as to how Koreans innovate by taking advantage of locally available foreign products.

DCs can do little to stop technology transfer through the modes in cell 3. Rather, it is the outcome of the absorptive capacity and entrepreneurship of firms and R&D centers in LDCs that take advantage of these modes. Foreign technologies transferred through other means serve as important inputs for reverse engineering. The most innovative and profitable papermaker in Korea, for example, never entered collaborative agreements with foreign partners in the form of either DFI or FL but progressively reverse-engineered foreign models in developing the most sophisticated, computerized paper-making line (Kim, 1987b).

Technology transfer modes in cell 4 are also important means of economic activity for multinationals from DCs. OEM manufacturing in LDCs is a strategy of international sourcing of components and end-products by firms in DCs to sustain price competitiveness in both domestic and international markets. Informal technical assistance provided by foreign component suppliers is simply an extra service needed to conclude sales and to enable successful implementation of their components by the buyer.

None of the technology transfer modes in the four cells can be restricted by DCs to reduce the boomerang effects from LDCs. All modes, except for those in cell 3, about which DCs can do little, are, in fact, vital economic means for the growth of firms in DCs.

A second question arises: If technology transfer to LDCs cannot and should not be restricted, then does technology transfer from DCs to LDCs directly result in boomerang effects in DCs? Data show otherwise. Figure 12.1 presents a market-mediated total technology transfer to Korea in dollar value from Japan and the United States, together with the two sets of trade data between Korea and these two countries. The figure also shows an inverse relation between technology transfer to and exports from Korea. The total value of technology transfer from Japan is almost double that from the United States. Korea's exports to the United States, however, are almost double those to Japan. Furthermore, in 1986, for example, the

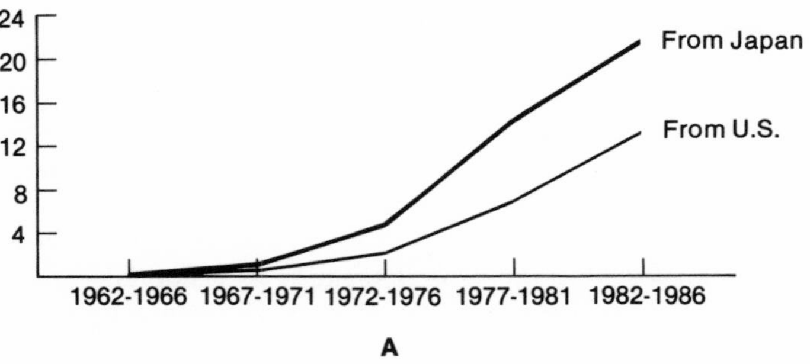

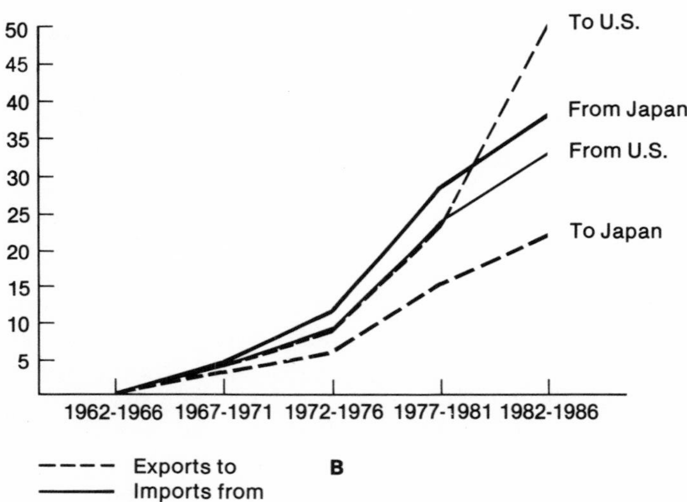

Figure 12.1 Technology and commodity trade between Korea and its two leading partners (1962–1986).

trade imbalance with the United States was almost $7 billion in favor of Korea, whereas that with Japan is $5.5 billion in favor of Japan. That is, Korea obtained foreign technology primarily from Japan but exported its products mainly to the United States. Therefore, Korea's export performance to the United States is not the direct outcome of the U. S. technology transfer to Korea. An Organization for Economic Cooperation and Development (OECD) study (1981) also concluded that trade competition came from countries that were not the biggest customers for technology and capital goods. Then, what is the source of the trade competitiveness of the fast growing LDCs? The international competitiveness of LDCs vis-à-vis a particular DC stemmed not so much from that DC's technology transfer to the country as from its absorptive capacity to assimilate, adapt, and improve foreign technologies. The internal weaknesses of DCs in industrial structure and innovation also account for the rapid export expansion of LDCs. Japan's postwar industrial history and the recent growth of Asian NICs (e.g., Taiwan, Korea, Hong Kong, and Singapore) demonstrate this point.

The third question emerges: What then is the net effect of the technology transfer of DCs to LDCs? Technology transfer definitely benefits recipient countries because it can be a vital source of technological change, leading to productivity improvement or to new products, processes and industries (see Kim, 1980). Technology transfer also benefits supplier countries. The OECD study (1981) concluded that the net return from technology transfers by DCs has been positive overall in terms of trade, employment, and consumer benefits in DCs. However, gross effects have fallen unequally on different industries. Engineering and machinery industries have benefited from increasing demand in LDCs during the period of low demand in other DCs. Some light manufacturing industries, however, had their problems compounded by the increased competition from LDCs. Kim's (1985) study of the United States–Korea link in technology transfer also concluded that although technology transfers from the United States to Korea have been accompanied by an increase in the volume of light commodity exports from Korea, its capital goods imports from the United States have increased dramatically to $6.2 billion in the 1977–81 period and doubled again to $12.4 billion in the 1982–1986 period. One might argue that the United States also faces increasing capital goods imports from Korea. American multinational corporations, however, comprise a significant part of the machinery industry in Korea. Helleiner (1979) shows that 64.2 percent of Korean general machinery exports and 67.3 percent of its electrical machinery exports to the United States were from American multinational corporations with production facilities in Korea.

Finally, what should DCs do to maintain technological leadership? No nation can maintain technological leadership through stringent controls of technology outflows: Witness the United Kingdom in the nineteenth century. Transfers are likely to continue at a significant rate, because on the supply side alternative sources of technology are increasing and the firms in possession of the technology may have to transfer it, as discussed previously, to expand sales and to extend the economic life of their technologies and products, maximizing the return from the technologies they possess. On the demand side, industries in some LDCs have developed increasing capabilities to master received technologies, to exert strong bargaining power in acquiring foreign technologies, and to undertake R&D to create their own innovations. Only through continuous innovation can DCs maintain their current position in technology leadership.

IMPLICATIONS FOR LESS DEVELOPED COUNTRIES

The conceptual framework and Korea's experience as presented above also offer useful implications for other LDCs that attempt to maximize benefits from technologies available in DCs. Three issues may be addressed in discussing the implications. The first issue is related to market-mediated technology transfers in cells 1 and 2. That is, LDCs should not view technology transfer from DCs to be a source of their foreign dependency and for this reason restrict it. The experiences of LDCs, like India, that adopted restrictive policies on foreign technology transfer and that stuck to policies of self-reliance, like the People's Republic of China in the 1960s and 1970s, have demonstrated that the preclusion of foreign technology can retard long-term economic growth. Rather, they should view technology transfer as a catalytic source of technological change, leading to the international competitiveness and economic growth of their countries. The experiences of other countries, like the Asian NICs, demonstrate that it is not technology transfer that leads to technological dependency on multinationals. Rather, it is the lack of local absorptive capacity to assimilate, adapt, and improve imported technologies that leads to dependency on foreign suppliers.

Nevertheless, heavy reliance on DFI as a means of technology transfer may, to some extent, lead to foreign dependency. DFI definitely transfers production capability (capability to operate and maintain a production system) but hardly investment capability (capability to set up or expand new production systems) or innovation capability (capability to innovate new products and processes), particularly when the parent company undertakes DFI to exploit the local market in LDCs. Kim's (1987c) study of microelectronics in Korea concluded that semiconductor manufacturing by multinational firms in Korea before 1984 only transferred simple packaging technology but fostered neither the skills, knowledge, and learning capabilities of the production workers nor the engineering capabilities of the domestic economy. Ernst (1985) reached a similar conclusion in his study of automation and the Third World. Amsden and Kim's (1985) comparative study of Hyundai and Daewoo (a joint venture with GM) in the automobile industry in Korea shows that the local firm outperformed the multinational subsidiary in product development and market performance, as the parent company constrained the latter's investment in R&D and GM was inactive in transferring technology transfer to its subsidiary.

The second issue is related to nonmarket-mediated technology transfer modes in cells 3 and 4. That is, LDCs can benefit greatly from informal technology transfers. It cannot be said in precise quantitative terms how important informal technology transfers have been in Korea, but earlier discussions, together with other studies (e.g., Kim, 1982; Kim and Kim, 1985) clearly indicate that they have been very important in Korea's acquisition of technological capabilities. This mode of technology transfer has clearly prevailed in innovative small firms and for a long time has been significant in broadening all exporters' capabilities (Westphal et al. 1985). In short, Korea's experience indicates that the majority of important or crucial information needed to solve technical problems can be obtained, free of charge, through nonmarket-mediated mechanisms, if LDCs have the local capability to undertake reverse engineering tasks.

The final issue concerns the views on foreign technology transfer and indigenous efforts in LDCs. Foreign technology transfer should not be viewed as a substitute for indigenous technological efforts or vice versa. Rather, they should be viewed as complementary. By providing new dimensions in technology, foreign technology transfer enables LDCs to make a quantum jump in indigenous technological efforts. Similarly, indigenous technological efforts lead to local ability to identify appropriate technology and to bargain better in technology transfer negotiations. Once imported, capabilities accumulated through indigenous efforts enable local firms to quickly assimilate, adapt, and improve transferred foreign technology.

SUMMARY AND CONCLUSIONS

The process of technology transfer is so diverse and complex that it defies a simple analysis. But the conceptal framework presented here enables one to identify various mechanisms of international technology transfer and to examine Korea's public policies promoting the inflow of foreign technologies and Korea's actual experience in the international transfer of foreign technology. The analysis led to the conclusion that informal mechanisms (i.e., those in cells 2, 3, and 4) are as important, if not more, as formal mechanisms (i.e., DFIs, FLs) in international technology transfer, particularly when the recipient country has absorptive capacity. This chapter then discussed the various implications of the conceptual framework and Korea's experience for both DCs and LDCs.

Table 12.3 schematically presents the discussions so far and their conclusions. In quadrant 2, where DCs transfer technologies but LDCs do not have absorptive capacity, DCs will enjoy their technological monopoly power and LDCs will suffer from the syndromes of technological dependency, a

Table 12.3 Assessment of Pros and Cons of International Technology Transfer

		The Existence of Absorptive Capacity in LDCs: Yes	The Existence of Absorptive Capacity in LDCs: No
Willingness of DC to transfer technologies through formal mechanisms to LDCs	Yes	Transfer takes place. Both DCs and LDCs gain (1)	Transfer takes place. DCs gain but LDCs become dependent (2)
	No	Transfer takes place. DCs lose but LDCs gain (3)	Transfer does not take place. Both DCs and LDCs gain little (4)

typical outcome of a zero-sum game. Neither DCs nor LDCs gain in quadrant 3, where DCs are not willing to transfer their technology LDCs and LDCs do not have the capability to benefit from existing technology in DCs. It is in quadrants 1 and 4, where LDCs have absorptive capacity, that DCs worry about the boomerang effects of technology transfer. But regardless of whether or not a particular DC is willing to transfer technologies through formal mechanisms, LDCs in quadrants 1 and 4 would be able to acquire foreign technologies, either through alternative sources or through alternative (informal) mechanisms. Why, then, do DCs not take advantage of opportunities to expand their market through DFI or to extend the economic life of technologies through FL (quadrant 1)? It is also in this quadrant 1 that LDCs will not end up being technologically dependent on DCs. That is, quadrant 1 is the best alternative for both DCs and LDCs. Here international technology transfer benefits both the supplier and recipient countries.

REFERENCES

Amsden, Alice H., and Kim, Linsu. (1985). "The role of transnational corporation in the Republic of Korea's production and exports of automobile," HBS Working Paper Cambridge, Mass.: Harvard Business School.

Bae, Zong-tae, and Lee, Jinjoo. (1986). "Technology development patterns of small and medium sized companies in the Korean machinery industry," *Technovation,* 4:279–296.

Baranson, Jack, and Roark, Robin. (1985). "Trends in north–south transfer of high technology," in Nathan Rosenberg and Claudio Frischtak (eds.), *International Technology Transfer: Concepts, Measures, and Comparisons,* New York: Praeger Press, pp. 24–42.

Cha, Dong-Se. (1983). *Weja Doipeo Hyogwa Boonsuk* (An analysis of the effects of direct foreign investment), Seoul: Korea Institute for Economics and Technology.

Ernst, Dieter. (1985). *Automation, Employment and the Third World - The Case of the Electronics Industry,* The Hague: IDPAD, Institute of Social Studies.

Helleiner, G. D. (1979). "Transnational corporations and trade structure," University of Toronto. Mimeo.

KEB (Korea Exchange Bank). (1987). "Direct foreign investment in Korea," *Monthly Review,* October, pp. 3–13.

Kim, Kee Young. (1984). "American technology and Korea's technological development" in Karl Moskowitz (ed.), *From Patron to Partner,* Lexington, Mass.: Lexington Book, D.C. Heath Co.

Kim, Linsu. (1980). "Stages of development of industrial technology in a LDC: A model," *Research Policy,* 9:254–277.

Kim, Linsu. (1982). "Technological innovation in the capital goods industry in Korea: A micro analysis," Working Paper, International Labor Office in Geneva.

Kim, Linsu. (1985). "Technology transfer and R&D in Korea: national policies and the U.S.–Korea Lin," *Korea's Economy,* 1(1): April.

Kim, Linsu. (1987a). *Technological Transformation in Korea: Progress Achieved and Problems Ahead,* a paper prepared for the World Institute for Development Economic Research, the United Nations University, Helsinki, Finland.

Kim, Linsu. (1987b). *Imitating and Apprentice: How Korea Acquired Technological Capability Fast,* College of Business Administration, Korea University.

Kim, Linsu. (1987c). *The Generation and Diffusion of Microelectronics: Local Capability, Employment Effects, and Public Policies in Korea,* a paper presented at a U.N. University New Technology Conference at the University of Limburg, Maastricht.

Kim, Linsu. (1988a). "The transfer of programmable automation to a rapidly developing country: An initial assessment," forthcoming in *International Economic Journal.*

Kim, Linsu. (1988b). "Entrepreneurship and innovation in a rapidly developing country," *Journal of Development Planning,* 18.

Kim, Linsu, and Kim, Youngbae. (1985). "Innovation in newly industrializing country: A multiple discriminant analysis," *Management Science,* 31(3):312–322.

Kim, Linsu, Lee, Jangwoo, and Lee, Jinjoo. (1987). "Korea's entry into the computer industry and its acquisition of technological capability," *Technovation,* 6:277–293.

OECD (Organization for Economic Cooperation and Development). (1981). *North/South Technology Transfer: The Adjustment Ahead,* Paris: OECD.

Rhee, Yung, W., and Westphal, Larry E. (September 1977). "A micro econometric investigation of choice of technology," *Journal of Development Economics,* 4:205–237.

Utterback, James M. (1975). "The role of applied research institutes in the transfer of technology in Latin America," *World Development,* 3(9):665–673.

Von Hippel, Eric. (1976). "The dominant role of users in the scientific instrument Iinovation process," *Research Policy,* 5 (3):212–239.

Westphal, Larry E., Kim, Linsu, and Dahlman, Carl J. (1985). "Reflections on the Republic of Korea's acquisition of technological capability" in Nathan Rosenberg and Claudio Frischtak (eds.) *International Technology Transfer: Concepts, Measures, and Comparisons,* New York: Praeger, pp. 167–221.

Westphal, Larry E., Rhee, Yung W., and Pursell, Garry (1981). "Korean industrial competence: Where it came from," World Bank Staff, Working Paper No. 469, Washington, D.C.: World Bank.

13

Improving the Pattern of Technology Transfers and Trade Between the United States and Japan

BELA GOLD

To analyze meaningfully past and prospective patterns of technology transfer between the United States and Japan, they must be considered within the larger framework of the international trade adjustments to which they are responsive. Substantial transfers of technology from the United States to Japan after 1950 have been largely replaced since the mid-1970s by large Japanese exports to the United States of industrial products that benefited from the previously imported technologies. The resulting huge net import balances have generated increasing friction that is likely to be eased only if substantial adjustments are made on both sides.

Before discussing potential ameliorative policies, some helpful analytical perspective may be provided by briefly summarizing Japan's industrial development strategy and then reviewing actual technology and trade movements before and after the mid-1970s.

JAPAN'S INDUSTRIAL DEVELOPMENT STRATEGY

Japan's largely destroyed industrial plant and its limited resources in the late 1940s led its government to take the lead in formulating an industrial redevelopment plan instead of waiting for the prospective initiatives of emerging independent entrepreneurs.

Highlights of this plan included: (1) early development of the basic industrial materials industries, such as aluminum, steel, and power; (2) construction of machine building industries to support conversion of such materials into manufacturing capacity; (3) organization of a shipbuilding industry to ensure the availability at reasonable cost of the coal, oil, ores, and other foreign raw materials whose domestic supplies were inadequate—and to provide the means of eventually exporting the manufactured products that would pay for the imported materials and help support the domestic economy; and (4) thereafter, progressive refurbishing of other industries, such as textiles, along with the expansion and modernization of its automobile and consumer goods industries (Johnson, 1982).

What were considered to be the critical needs for effectuating such a far-reaching reconstruction of the industrial economy? In addition to broad political support for the program as a whole, key requirements included: access to advanced foreign technology; access to foreign raw materials; and the availability of very large amounts of capital to finance such foreign purchases as well as the construction of modern manufacturing facilities. Other important domestic requirements included upgrading managerial and technical capabilities as well as labor skills. In short, regarding technological competitiveness is certainly a necessary condition for achieving market competitiveness over any extended period of time, but it is not sufficient in itself. Such capabilities must be reinforced by appropriately adapted marketing and finance activities as well as personnel policies to effectuate management's basic objectives of growth and improved profitability (Gold, 1988, 1986c).

In reviewing the resulting stunning achievements of Japan's industries, it is interesting to note that they did indeed buy, license, and borrow the best available foreign technologies from the United States and some European countries, while also seeking raw material sources all over the world. However, foreign borrowing provided only a very limited proportion of its industrial capital requirements compared with domestic contributions derived from low wage rates, high savings rates, strong governmental guidance of the capital markets, and heavy reinvestment of earnings. Also extremely important was the virtually unstinting cooperation of its hard-working and highly disciplined labor force, along with the deep commitment of virtually all elements of the private sector, as well as the government, to hasten the reestablishment of Japan as a world economic power.

As a result of persistent and intensive efforts, Japan was able not only to reach and even exceed international levels of productivity and cost efficiency, but also to reverse the poor pre-war image of the quality of its products. The ensuing rapid growth in acceptance of their offerings in the United States and other foreign markets was sustained thereafter by the continuing pressure of Japanese firms' management to keep improving their products and also to keep modifying their service capabilities in accordance with the intensively probed preferences of foreign customers.

REVIEW OF ACTUAL TECHNOLOGY AND TRADE MOVEMENTS BETWEEN THE UNITED STATES AND JAPAN

1950 to Mid-1970s

During the period from 1950 to the mid-1970s, there was a substantial flow of industrial technologies from the United States and some European countries to Japan. Early beneficiaries included the steel, machinery, and electric power industries. Later, important infusions affected automobiles and contemporary models of consumer electronics and office equipment. In all such instances, the upgrading of products and production technologies was quickly followed by increased manufacturing capacity and the exploration and cultivation of export markets.

The extraordinary magnitude of these early achievements (Kawasaki, 1985) may be illustrated by reference to Japan's basic steel industry, one of the central foci of the initial development program. Contrary to much wishful foreign thinking, this involved reaching well beyond the initial copying of foreign technologies and practices to achieve successively superior levels of performance. As these emerged in an array of giant new steel mills, raw steel output rose from 24.4 to 131.5 million tons between 1960 and 1973. The technological upgrading of its plants was demonstrated by increases in the size of its blast furnaces to nearly five times the size in the United States and also by the doubling of their output per cubic foot of furnace volume; by the sharp increase in utilization of the advanced basic oxygen furnace beyond U.S. levels; by the reduction of energy requirements per ton of steel by 30 percent; by a substantial out-distancing of the United States in respect to the proportion of steel output accounted for by continuous casting; and by reduction of man-hour requirements per ton of capacity for the Japanese industry to less than one-half of the average for the U.S. industry, and to less than one-fourth of the U.S. average of the five leading Japanese plants. In short, by 1975, the Japanese steel industry was substantially superior to the United States by every important measure of efficiency, quality, and cost (Gold, 1978a).

Moreover, the intensive development of production capabilities was matched by aggressive market development efforts. For example, a senior official of Mitsui, the huge trading company, was first sent to the Harvard Business School to become familiar with the thinking and behavior patterns of American executives, after which he traveled to the major industrial centers of the United States to inquire about the primary foci of steel users' complaints about their domestic suppliers. His first major success was to alert his head office to the dissatisfactions of West Coast steel users with the quality, prices, and delivery delays associated with their dependence on distant U.S. producers. This was followed by progressive expansion of Japanese penetrations beyond this initial successful target into other steel markets, as well as into an increasing array of industries.

The intensity of such market development efforts is also exemplified by an extraordinary responsiveness to risky, innovative opportunities. For example, the Japanese undertook to supply the Norfolk and Western Railroad's demand for much heavier railroad track than had previously been produced to facilitate still larger shipments of coal from the Midwest to Virginia for export. They also agreed to supply the Alaskan pipeline with large amounts of wider-diameter pipes than previously had been built. In both cases, U.S. steel producers had declined to bid, on the assumption that such orders would never be repeated and hence would not warrant construction of special plants required—to their belated regret.

The notable imbalance in such exchanges is evidenced by the fact that U.S. commodity exports to Japan were kept to minor proportions as a result of direct and indirect governmental efforts to protect its farmers and its emerging industries as well as to husband foreign exchange for development purposes. At the same time, the establishment of U.S. manufacturing plants in Japan was largely restricted to a very few cases involving the use of advanced technologies that the Japanese were eager to have introduced, such as computer and other office equipment producers. In addition, some American manufacturers were permitted to make partial investments in a few Japanese industries to gain access both to the Americans' manufacturing methods and to their distribution systems in the United States, as illustrated the limited investment of Chrysler Corporation in Mitsubishi Motors.

Mid-1970s to Present

Imbalances in technology and trade transfers between the United States and Japan have intensified since the mid-1970s. There has been a continuing, although diminishing, transfer of important industrial technologies from the United States to Japan. These have included such frontier sectors as semiconductors, advanced electronics, computers, and telecommunications. Also, two quite different forms of technology transfers from the United States have grown substantially: increasing Japanese enrollments in American universities, especially in graduate technical and business programs; and increasing Japanese investments in academic and private U.S. research organizations to share in the benefits of their efforts.

On the other hand, U.S. exports of agricultural and manufactured goods to Japan have continued to be sharply restricted by formal and informal practices that have been instituted or condoned by the Japanese government.

Meanwhile, Japan continued to intensify efforts to strengthen the international competitiveness of its established industries, while adding a succession of new industries representing the advancing potentials of technology and markets (Gold, 1979). Its Kashima steel mill established new levels of achievement for computerization in steel mills (Gold, 1978b) Then the new Ohgishima steel mill in Tokyo Bay surpassed even its world-leading predecessors. In the early 1980s, the Kimitsu steel mill employed a staff of more than 250 for more than 3 years to achieve probably the most far-reaching computerization of a complex manufacturing plant achieved to date (Gold, 1986b). During these years, a succession of modern automobile plants set new standards for productivity, quality, and cost effectiveness in low-priced and medium-priced cars. The development of efficient plants to produce basic industrial materials and machine tools laid the foundation for a rapidly expanding array of industries ranging from agricultural equipment and various sectors of electronics to telecommunications and aircraft.

Turning to the resulting flow of exports from Japan to the United States, these may be divided into three categories. The largest throughout this period continued to be manufactured goods, supplementing heavier flows of steel, automobiles, and electronic goods with machine tolls and other machinery, robots, semiconductors, computers and other business equipment, telecommunications, and programmable manufacturing systems as well as sporting goods, women's clothing, cosmetics, and a seemingly endless array of other products.

A second sector, which is much smaller than commodity exports but growing more rapidly in recent years, involves the establishment of Japanese-owned manufacturing plants in the United States, including an increasing proportion of the industries in which they are also exporting products from Japan. Beginning with plants restricted to assembly parts shipped from Japan—ranging from radios, television sets, and other small consumer products to automobiles and even company airplanes—recent years have witnessed the transfer to the United States, or purchases in the United States, of increasingly complete manufacturing operations producing these same products as well as a variety of others including machinery, automobile tires, and even steel. This development seems to have been motivated not only by the desire to endure rapid and informed access to what is widely regarded as the largest, most attractive, and most dynamic market in the world, but also by a perceived necessity to provide at least partial safeguards against possible U.S. protectionist measures during an economic downturn. More recently, the expansion of Japanese operations in the United States has also been intensified by the threat to competitiveness generated by the sharply increased value of the yen relative to the dollar.

A third sector of competition-improving flows from Japan to the United States relates to certain advanced industrial management practices. These include: "just-in-time" inventory operations, "quality circles" to encourage labor involvement in improving the effectiveness of production, closer labor–management cooperation, and rotating technical and managerial assignments to develop broader skills as well as a more rounded understanding of all functions of the firm. But their widely recognized success in competition and in gaining the active cooperation of American employees is likely to encourage increasing imitation by American managers.

In short, it is important to recognize some of the fundamental sources of Japan's strengthened industrial competitiveness, not only to refute some self-justifying American complaints, but to clarify the necessary objectives of effective responsive measures. It is true that the Japanese commonly began by identifying and utilizing the best technologies and facilities being used by foreign producers as the basis for initiating their own entry into various industries. They then achieved their goal of "standing on the foreigners' shoulders" by developing significant improvements in the relevant technologies, production facilities, operating methods, and standards of product quality. The effects of such advances have been significantly enhanced by the unstinting cooperation of labor in efforts to maximize competitiveness.

However, the very large trade imbalances that have developed and are still continuing cannot be attributed solely to Japanese efforts. A powerful supporting factor has been the declining competitiveness of most of the U.S. industries that have been affected. In steel, automobiles, machine tools, consumer electronics, and other hard-hit industries, U.S. industries have generally failed to adopt the most advanced technologies and have relied on aging production facilities. The resulting lags in productivity combined with the continuation of relatively higher wage rates during 1980–1985 not only attracted aggressive Japanese and other foreign exporters, but also encouraged increasing reliance by American manufacturers on imports of components and even of finished products for sale under their domestic labels. Even more serious has been the increased interest of many large manufacturing firms in buying competitors and in investing in other industries—even in banking, securities, and other nonmanufacturing activities[1]—rather than seeking major investments to regain technological and cost competitiveness in their fields of established expertise.

SOME STRATEGIC PERSPECTIVES FOR THE NINETIES

Before considering possible means of shrinking Japan's huge net trade imbalance with the United States, it should be recognized that there has been strong resistance in Japan to all proposals seeking major reductions. This has been true even with respect to proposals for increasing agricultural imports from the United States, despite the sharply higher prices paid by Japanese consumers because of domestic protectionism. Their manufacturing industries are not sympathetic to eliminating barriers to imports from the very producers in the United States whose markets they have been allowed to invade. Indeed, Japanese producers have been making vigorous efforts to offset the corrective pressure on the trade imbalance of the recent sharp increase in the yen–dollar relationship by accepting reduced profit margins and by redoubling cost-cutting programs—with considerable success.

Although Japan has retained substantial formal, and especially informal, restrictions on imports from the United States despite years of often heated negotiations, the combination of a sharp increase in the U.S. foreign debt and a prospective slowdown in U.S. economic activity suggests that painful adaptive adjustments may have to be initiated without continued prolonged delays. U.S. experience in retaining protective measures and subsidies for over expanded and inadequately competitive industries has made us familiar with the political difficulties and economic costs of contemplating major reallocations of resources. Hence, needed corrective measures cannot be left to the Japanese alone.

Common Objectives and Disparate Needs

Both countries need to ensure the continuing international competitiveness of a wide array of industries to fulfill most, if not all, of the nation's essential needs, while also selling at least enough overseas to pay for needed imports.

In a number of basic industries, Japan's more recent expansion has yielded major competitive advantages with respect to productive efficiency, product quality, and costs in comparison with the United States, as has been reviewed. As a result, Japan has pressed for, and gained, major access to attractive U.S. markets. But the United States also has a variety of industries, agricultural as well as manufacturing, that have demonstrated effective competitiveness with, and even superiority to, Japanese capabilities. Yet these have been subjected to highly discriminatory import restrictions. Major American complaints have centered around a variety of crop and livestock products, construction opportunities, and a variety of manufacturing industries, including automobiles, electronics, and chemicals.

Both countries also require continuing development of new industries to pursue emerging domestic and foreign market potentials. The important difference here has been that the United States had made heavier commitments to, and has been much more successful in, generating major advances in industrial technologies and in developing advanced products. But the Japanese have been far more successful in gaining improvements generated by the United States. Examples include radios, television sets, video records, semiconductors, and various types of business machines. Aside from cases in which legally questionable factors have been charged, such experiences would seem to demonstrate the need for U.S. firms to increase the speed and effectiveness with which significant innovations are brought to market.

Another commonly recognized requirement is to develop and support needed defense capabilities.[2] To this objective, the Japanese have continued to allocate only a miniscule proportion of their resources, largely because they have been encouraged to rely on U.S. reinforcements. On the other hand, the United States has made very heavy resource commitments to international as well as domestic defense needs. This has tended to generate proportionately tighter restrictions in the United States on the availability of capital for investment in upgrading industrial capabilities.

Both countries also seek to expand their foreign trade by establishing plants abroad. This facilitates utilizing advantageous foreign resources and gaining access to additional markets, especially if such access is threatened by local protectionism. Whereas the United States has permitted the establishment of Japanese-owned production facilities in this country, in addition to allowing heavy imports, there has been very little reciprocity beyond the early establishment of American computer and office machinery plants, when Japan was eager to gain access to the new technologies involved. Nevertheless, the United States has continued to allow the expansion, in the United States, of Japanese-owned manufacturing operations seeking to offset the high dollar value of the yen. Nor is it irrelevant to note that similar disparities in access affect the flow of investments between the United States and Japan.

Some Distinctive Problems

However, the two countries also have certain distinctive problems. Because of its consistent postwar commitment to extremely low population growth (Economic Planning Agency, 1983), continuing expansion of Japan's economy and the resulting tightening of domestic manpower supplies reinforces the previously cited pressure for exporting some of its industrial production capabilities. At earlier stages of growth, these anticipated supply restrictions encouraged the more rapid adoption of mechanization, robotics, and increased automation. But the progressive decline of excess manpower in agriculture, and increasingly in distribution, necessitates facing the need to ease further increases in domestic labor requirements.

Resulting decisions reflect a need to weigh, as one alternative, the net advantages of shifting production to developing countries that offer ample unskilled labor, low wages, and cheap materials, but very limited local demand along with potential political uncertainties. The other choice, which would involve locating in the United States or some other advanced country, offers high levels of demand and ample managerial, technical, and labor skills, but also higher wage rates and material costs. It is hardly irrelevant to add that Japan's financial institutions, which are urgently in need of finding foreign outlets for the enormous capital accumulations that they have amassed, seem to prefer investments in large stable economies, even if returns are somewhat lower. Here again, another critical consideration is that other leading industrial countries, as well as the United States, are becoming increasingly intolerant of Japan's continuing domestic barriers to foreign imports, and may become hostile environments unless corrective measures are initiated.

Turning to American industry, its single most urgent problem is to regain the international competitiveness that it enjoyed for many decades before the 1980s (Gold, 1987). This will require very large investments in modernized as well as new facilities. Another requirement will be to upgrade the capabilities of significant sectors of management along with the unstinting cooperation of labor. A third important need will be for our government to deal more effectively in curtailing the continued dumping of foreign products on U.S. markets and also with helping to eliminate unfair foreign restrictions on U.S. imports.

PROSPECTIVE RESPONSIVE MEASURES

It is obviously easier to identify needed responsive measures on both sides than to achieve significant progress in implementing them—as has been demonstrated by very meager real gains that have been achieved by repeated negotiations between the United States and Japan in recent years. Progress may well resist acceleration until deteriorating production, employment, and trade prospects force Japan and other net exporting nations to face the major penalties likely to be borne by all unless reasonable, mutually supportive policies are effectuated. However, even recognition of the urgency of cooperative international adjustments is unlikely to be sufficient, for needed ameliorative measures within each country are bound to be more beneficial for some sectors than for others, thereby compounding conflicting international interests with equally forceful and politically even more influential domestic disagreements.

Although it might seem logical to deal with such complexities initially by seeking international agreements that merely specify key improvement policies along with aggregate import and export adjustment targets, the powerful interests within each country that are identified with particular sectors of the economy ensure that many such specific claims must be dealt with directly if any significant accomplishments are to be expected.

Possible Measures by Japan

Reducing Japan's net export balance with the United States would obviously require expanding domestic consumption and effecting some reductions in total exports while continuing to improve standards of living.

Increasing domestic consumption would help to absorb part of a reduction in manufactured exports as well as increases in imports of agricultural and manufactured products. Increased government investments in national defense capabilities as well as social capital facilities and associated services would generate increasing demands for domestic and imported manufactured products as well as manpower. In addition, easing international criticism would also require allowing foreigners to construct and operate more plants in Japan as well as to invest in other local enterprises.

More specifically, exports of manufactured products might be reduced not only through the already mentioned increase in domestic consumption, but also through permitting or facilitating reductions in the capacity of the less competitive industries and plants. Such contractions might be induced by encouraging increased imports of competitive products (Nomura, 1983; Moritari, 1982); by reducing governmental aids such as import restrictions, low interest loans, or special subsidies; and by outright governmental assistance in shifting to other excess shipbuilding capacity. In addition, exports from Japan have been, and could be further, reduced by shifting some production activities to the United States and other countries.

In short, the primary objectives of such industrial policies would be to improve domestic standards of living and defense capabilities as well as the productivity of Japanese resources by:

1. Utilizing only the most efficient domestic producers to supply national and overseas markets;

2. As well as those foreigner firms who prove to be the most efficient suppliers of imports or of locally produced goods and services; and
3. Adding returns from an expanding array of overseas subsidiaries utilizing largely foreign resources to serve additional markets.

Thus, the resources released from the contraction of some current agricultural and industrial operations would be absorbed by supplying higher levels of domestic consumption, including social services, by supporting substantially expanded defense capabilities, by manning growing foreign-owned operations within Japan and by significantly increasing industrial research and development programs.

Possible Measures by the United States

The most important means of strengthening the international competitiveness of U.S. industries seem to center around the need to:

1. Reestablish the competitiveness of our basic industries and continue advancing the capabilities of new expanding industries;
2. Increase the effectiveness of our industrial managements; and
3. Strengthen governmental support for improving the competitiveness of U.S. industries.

A wide array of major American industries have been declining in international competitiveness during the past decade. The single most important reason for this has probably been continued reliance on older technologies and production facilities in most of our older industries due to inadequate investments in upgrading of their capabilities (Gold, 1982a). Necessary increases in cost competitiveness are, therefore, likely to require not only the introduction of more advanced technologies, including programmable automation and flexible manufacturing systems (Gold, 1982b, c), but also higher quality standards, lower unit labor costs, and reduced inventories. To achieve such gains will probably require further reductions in marginal capacity, the progressive modernization of most remaining production facilities, and the construction of many new plants to facilitate utilization of newly emerging technologies and also to permit more economical servicing of expanding markets through the relocation of capacity (Gold, 1984).

Such efforts to regain effective competitiveness will obviously require overcoming past shortcomings in managerial performance. One of the most influential of these has been a widespread emphasis on maximizing short-term profitability at the expense of adequate allocations to upgrade capital facilities, to explore and develop future markets, and to support research and development seeking major rather than just incremental improvements in products and processes. Another widespread shortcoming concerns gaining the thorough cooperation of labor in improving productive efficiency, which is especially frustrating because of the marked success of a number of Japanese firms in working with American labor (including Honda, Matsushita, and Nissan). A third general shortcoming has been the superficiality and even the frequent nonexistence of efforts to integrate technological needs and potentials with prospective changes in procurement, production, marketing, and finance as the basis for strengthening programs to improve competitiveness. Such integrated thinking is fostered in Japanese firms through the widespread practice of transferring executives from function to function in the course of successful promotions instead of restricting them to vertical advances within their basic functional groupings.

Regaining international competitiveness also requires certain contributions from government even in an economy committed to dominance by private enterprise (Gold, 1986a). One such contribution would involve preventing the victimizing of American producers by foreign exports that have been involved in heavy government subsidies. Another would involve pressuring foreign governments to eliminate discriminatory barriers to American exports. Although the U.S. government has devoted considerable efforts to such objectives, one can hardly avoid concluding that the results have fallen far short of equivalent reciprocity with Japan as well as numerous other nations. Additional potential government contributions to improving the industrial competitiveness of domestic industries suggested by the efforts of other governments include: more comprehensive monitoring and reporting of industrial research developments abroad; more widespread and effective training programs to facilitate labor shifts to new industrial opportunities; and tax policies designed to encourage increased investment in research, plant modernization, and the construction of new plants.

CONCLUDING OBSERVATIONS

However logical proposed ameliorative measures might appear to be, realism requires recognition of the major difficulties in the way of achieving substantial progress in modifying foreign trade balances between the United States and Japan. Powerful economic and political interests are rooted in such flows. Even if promising agreements were reached concerning the general directions and magnitudes of such readjustments, considerable periods would probably be required to achieve them.

Of course, recognition of such a wide array of needed adjustments to regain U.S. strength in international trade does not mean that all of them can be effected simultaneously and within a few years. But it does seem important that the needs be recognized in their multiple dimensions and interconnections if effective responsive measures are to be developed. Such a comprehensive perspective may also be helpful in planning progressive advances instead of continuing to respond to momentary flare-ups while allowing the deeper and more serious problems to keep intensifying.

At any rate, allowing any progress toward sharply reducing recent imbalances to continue at the past glacial pace may prove costly to the interests of both nations. The threat of a significant economic recession in the United States and in the world economy within the next 2 years suggests that it may become more difficult to negotiate substantial concessions by either side under the pressures of rising unemployment.

NOTES

1. Prominent examples include General Motors, General Electric, Ford, U.S. Steel, DuPont, and others.
2. But opponents of such undertakings continue to press their views, see Miyazaki, I. (March 1982). "Economic prosperity or a strong military?" *Economic Eye* (Tokyo: Japan Institute of Social and Economic Affairs).

REFERENCES

Economic Planning Agency. (January 1983). *Japan in the Year 2000,* Tokyo: *Japan Times.*

Gold, B. (1988). "International competitiveness, technology transfer and R & D," in D. A. Gulley (ed.), *The Changing World Metal Industries,* New York: Columbia University Press. p. 265–301.

Gold, B. (December 1986). "On the potentials, requirements, and limitations of information technology in manufacturing," *Prometheus: The Journal of Issues in Technological Change and Science Policy* Australia. 4 (2):254–271.

Gold, B. (January 1986c). "Some international differences in approaches to industrial policy," *Contemporary Policy Issues,* IV (1):12–22.

Gold, B. (September 1984). "Integrating product innovational market development to strengthen long-term planning," *Journal of Product Innovation Management,* Vol. 1 (2): 173–181.

Gold, B. (1982a). "On the potentials and limitations of international licensing of technology," in C.H. Uyehara (ed.), *Technology Exchange: The U.S.–Japanese Experience*, Washington, D. C.: University Press of America. p 48–54.

Gold, B. (Nov.–Dec. 1982b). "Cam (Computer-Aided Manufacturing) sets new rules for production," *Harvard Business Review,* Vol. 60 No. 6 p. 88–94.

Gold, B. (November 1982c). "Robotic, programmable automation and international competitiveness," *Transactions in Engineering Management of the Institute of Electrical and Electronic Engineers.* Vol. EM 29, No. 4, p. 135–146.

Gold, B. (1979). "Factors stimulating technological progress: Some Japanese experience," in B. Gold (ed.), *Productivity, Technology, and Capital,* Lexington, Mass.: D. C. Heath-Lexington Books. p. 277–290.

Gold, B. (July 1978a). "Steel technologies and costs in the U.S. and Japan," *Iron and Steel Engineer.* apanese Translation in *Juho Shuho* (Tokyo) July 1978a. Vol. 55, No. 4, p. 32–37.

Gold, B. (Winter 1978b). "Technological progress in Japanese industries: Computerization in steel," *Quarterly Review of Economics and Business.* Vol. 18, No. 4, p. 7–22.

Kawasaki, T. (1985). *Japan's Steel Industry*, Tokyo: Tekko Shimbun Sha.

Johnson, C. (1982). *MITI and the Japanese Miracle*, Stanford, Calif.: Stanford University Press.

Miyazaki, I. (March 1982). "Economic prosperity or a strong military?," *Economic Eye*, Tokyo: Japan Institute of Social and Economic Affairs.

Moritari, M. (June 1982). "A technological strategy for import expansion," *Economic Eye*, Tokyo: Japan Institute of Social and Economic Affairs.

Nomura, N. (July 1983). *Changing Streams—Economy Toward Recovery Path Needs—Economic Forecast*, Tokyo: Nihor Krizai Shimbun Databank Bureau.

14

Industrial Buying Behavior in the Peoples Republic of China: The Yin and Yang of Buyer–Seller Relationships in a Centrally Planned Economy

WESLEY J. JOHNSTON

Since its "reopening" to trade with the West in 1979, the China market has seemed both tantalizing as the largest potential sales opportunity ever available and impenetrable as more and more industrial marketers have failed to realize any of that potential. With each step forward, the marketing goals of many companies seemed to become increasingly unattainable with the appearance of each new layer of bureaucratic procedure or government organization to be satisfied. Vacillation is another impediment in selling to Chinese enterprises due to a series of fluctuating policies first liberalizing, then restricting foreign trade. Foreign exchange currency was readily available in 1984, but severely limited after reserves plunged dramatically in 1985. Experimentation in special economic zones and open cities was labeled less than successful and cut back drastically because of corruption. In the first 9 months of 1985, more than 800 joint ventures were formed between U.S. companies and state enterprises, almost as many as had been formed in the previous 5 years. Real financial commitment, however, was slow in developing. Direct investment totaled only about $1 billion, and dwindles to $150 million when offshore oil exploration capital is excluded (Pye, 1986). This constant tension of the vacillation in business progress has also been manifested in China's politics. In 1986, another major readjustment period began with China's seventh "Five-Year Plan." This Plan detailed three basic economic tasks (Hong, 1987):

1. To maintain a balance between total social demand and total supply so that the reform will progress smoothly; and to lay a foundation for the building of a new unique Chinese socialist economy in 5 or more years.
2. To keep continuous and steady economic growth and forcefully strengthen key

construction, technical renovation, and intellectual development, preparing a reserve force in material, technology, and personnel for further economic and social development in the 1990s.
3. To raise people's living standards on the basis of production development and the promotion of economic benefits.

In 1987, however, warnings of the dangers of "bourgeois liberalization" began, along with calls to adhere to the key conservative doctrinal tenets of the "Four Basic Principles" (leadership of the party, the socialist road, the people's democratic dictatorship, and the guidance of Marxist–Leninist–Maoist thought) (Delfs, 1988). The party general secretary, Hu Yaobang, was forced to resign under the pressure of an antiliberal ideological campaign. However, in October, at the thirteenth party congress, there was a general rejection of the conservatives' policy objectives by the nearly 2,000 party leaders attending. Currently, "reading the newspapers, and talking to Chinese, it seems to be 1986 again" (Delfs, 1988). Political reform and the limits of traditional Marxist theory are again frequent subjects of newspaper articles. Also, ambitious economic goals are surfacing. With the high level of inflation and the significant lack of progress in factory reform, however, one gets the feeling that if progress is not soon forthcoming the reformers may lose momentum and the conservatives may regain influence.

This cyclical movement toward and then away from openness with the West and economic progress through freer market mechanisms has confused many outside observers, prompting significant questions. Where does China really stand on foreign trade? What opportunities will exist in the future for U.S. industrial marketers? The idea of cyclic patterns in the movement from one point to another along the "way" (Tao) is fundamental, however, to the Chinese view of progress. This motion of the Tao was given a definite structure by the introduction of the polar opposites "yin" and "yang." In the Chinese view, the dynamic interplay of these two forces is necessary to generate balanced progress. This chapter explores dealing with China and the problems inherent in their yin and yang philosophy by focusing on the opportunities andproblems facing American firms and presenting two roads to selling exports to China.

OPPORTUNITIES

The Need

Given the ambitious goals of the Seventh Five-Year Plan, selling industrial exports to China should be an easy task. The Plan requires the following to be accomplished (Hong, 1987):

1. Under the premise of the continuous increase of economic benefits, the total output of industrial and agricultural production in the 5 years ought to increase by 38 percent; gross national product, by 44 percent; and total investment in fixed assets in state-run enterprises by nearly 70 percent over the previous Plan's 5-year period.

2. Extension of foreign trade will be attempted. It is planned that the total business turnover from import and export in 1990 will be 40 percent higher than 1985; and the scale of foreign loan utilization and introduction of advanced technology will also be enlarged.
3. Production development will be synchronized with the improvement of the consumption level of both urban and rural residents.

The only way to accomplish these goals is to open up the market to freer trade and to import technology at a fairly rapid pace. Despite all the confusion and inconsistencies in policy, many analysts feel that opportunities for foreign companies are better now than they have ever been. The Seventh Five-Year Plan dampens the free-for-all atmosphere that characterized the China market in the last half of the previous plan. More importantly, however, it promotes a stable pro-growth policy.

Import Trends

The following represents a brief overview of the trends in the import of industrial products into China (Smith, 1985).

China has developed a vertical pattern of trade, typical among developing nations. It exports mostly primary goods, such as grain, coal, and other raw materials and natural resources. In general, Chinese manufactured products are not competitive in the world market.

Plant Technology

For several years, China has imported plant and equipment worth billions of dollars. Often included were complete turnkey operations. This rapid development of infrastructure is currently being blamed for foreign exchange shortages, and spending has been curtailed. While it is unlikely that this sector will revive any time in the near future, replacement parts, operating (MRO) equipment, maintenance, and repair will continue to be needed. A major exception to curtailed spending will be energy production plants, since power shortages are the most critical of China's infrastructure problems.

High Technology

Technology imports are shifting toward smaller items. Personal computer systems and related electronic equipment are targeted as growth areas. This area, in general, has always been important to the Chinese. Export controls imposed for political reasons by Western countries have limited the types of equipment that China can buy. Nonetheless, China is still quite willing to spend its foreign exchange currency on high technology products. So willing, in fact, that it results in poor purchasing decisions. For instance, China has imported millions of dollars worth of computers, while lacking the knowledge to operate or service them.

Another error the Chinese have made in buying advanced technology is to always prefer state of the art. However, it is often too advanced to interface with their other existing technology and is difficult to operate or maintain. China is still eager to purchase high technology, but the realization that merely possessing it is not enough is beginning to have an effect. The emphasis on the level of technology is also beginning to shift from "state of the art" to that which will fit in with existing operations. Special buying priorities include data processing, electronics, and fiberoptic technology.

Infrastructure
Infrastructure improvement will be a critical area for buying products and technology for the foreseeable future. China is expected to add between 5 and 6 million kilowatts of energy generating capacity per year. Rail, sea, and air transportation capacity will also be rapidly expanded. Aviation passenger capacity is to be doubled by 1990, and rail freight and passenger capacity by the year 2000.

PROBLEMS

Bureaucratic Structure

Perhaps for many industrial marketers, the most difficult aspect of selling to China is understanding the numerous layers of bureaucratic structure and dealing effectively with them. The most important point to remember in selling to Chinese enterprises is that all are state owned. Thus, all enterprises have both professional management and government bureaucrats involved in decision making. In addition, various levels of government become involved in business decision making, from local trade offices to the Ministry of Foreign Economic Relations and Trade (MOFERT).

Since 1980, when Premier Zhou Ziyang took office, central directives have aimed at increasing the coordination of policy between the regional trade offices. These regional trade offices present a unified foreign trade policy and act as a regulatory liaison between the central authorities and local trade offices. In addition, import/export licensing requirements have been tightened and the Customs Office is now an independent body with augmented powers.

In addition to MOFERT, the central government agencies that administer and promote foreign trade are the foreign trade corporations (FTCs) under MOFERT and the related local and specialized trade offices. Less of a central link, but often crucial as a liaison between foreign business and the FTCs, is the China Council for the Promotion of International Trade (CCPIT).

The following presents a brief description of the key agencies and their responsibilities in regulating trade:

MOFERT
The Ministry of Foreign Economic Relations and Trade is the principal coordinator of foreign trade. Its responsibilities include: Implementation

of state principles and policies on foreign economics and trade; importation of advanced technologies; and coordination of the activities of the regional and local foreign trade offices in accordance with its other responsibilities.

FTCs

China's foreign trade corporations were created to balance local and central authority. They are the primary link between foreign business and end-users. The FTCs also act as liaisons between foreign business and the central government. FTCs are divided along product lines into ten organizations. They are often the first point of contact for foreign firms trying to enter the China market. The duties of the FTCs include: The implementation of the directives of MOFERT concerning the development of the import and export of their respective commodities; the signing of purchase and sales contracts with foreign enterprises and the arrangement of financial settlements; and monitoring of foreign exchange settlements. The central importance of the FTCs has been reduced in several ways. Ministerial and local trading corporations have begun to appear and some individual enterprises have the authority to compete with the FTCs. FTC branch offices, located in the major industrial cities, act as minioffices for trade promotion, issue some specialized import and export licenses, and conduct market research. The branches are under the control of the head office but are supervised by local authorities. They are gradually becoming the center of China's import business.

The CCPIT

The China Council for the Promotion of International Trade is an independent organization under the jurisdiction of MOFERT. The duties of the CCPIT include: Promoting foreign economic and trade ties; concluding nongovernmental trade agreements with foreign firms; and arbitrating economic, trade, and maritime disputes.

Others

Other political subdivisions of the local government are authorized to supervise auxiliary trade services. These offices handle transportation, shipping, packaging, advertising, and other issues. In addition, an increasing number of separate national agencies may provide trade assistance. Some, like the CCPIT, are under the jurisdiction of MOFERT. Others are independent or related to other ministries. In special cases, large industrial enterprises and designated special projects may be authorized to conduct business within the boundaries of an approved plan, usually limited to a certain value. These exemptions may bypass the FTCs and local trade offices altogether.

Since China's formal trade structure is still evolving, it is not always clear who the appropriate contact is, or whether contracts have been properly approved and signed by the correct legal and governmental agencies.

The two best sources for contract decisions are the treaty and law department of MOFERT and the legal department of the CCPIT.

Required Commitment

Traditionally, the Chinese have emphasized the importance of a developed business relationship. Even so, a Chinese company will prefer to do business with a company it has dealt with successfully in the past. It is also important to establish this relationship by entering through the proper channels when initially approaching the market. While there are more direct methods of entry than struggling with the many layers of bureaucracy, using such an approach too early runs the risk of leaving out someone with veto power. Taking the more complex approach implies sincerity and commitment in dealing with a Chinese enterprise and the trade organizations that represent it.

Long-term commitment to the market is also important. This includes providing the necessary capital for what may be a lengthy period of minimal or nonexistent profits. Some companies already doing business in China feel the formula "2 + 2 = ½" is symbolic of the typical business relationship. It costs twice as much and takes twice as long in China to make half the normal profits made elsewhere. Entering the market is expensive and the costs of maintaining an office there are quite high (Kraar, 1987). Presenting the image that a company is a large and well-established firm seeking a long-term relationship in China is a key to success.

The company's product is also a critical variable. While most countries have restrictions on some imports, the list in China is extremely long and detailed. Even products within categories the Chinese want to import have problems. Shortages in the power supply and other infrastructure shortcomings can prevent the sale of some desired products. Product life cycles appear to have relatively long introductory stages with high learning curve requirements. Thus, the acceptance of even the strongest products can take a while. The same loyalty that controls business relationships also applies to brand names. However, heavy promotion can help overcome the lack of a previous presence in the market.

Transaction Details

In making an industrial sale, finding a buyer is probably not the most difficult aspect of the transaction. There are, however, several hurdles the industrial marketer must negotiate once a potential buyer has been located. First, an import license must be secured. The end-user must then sign a contract that is submitted to MOFERT for approval. Payment will depend on the availability and approval of the expenditure of foreign exchange currency. Before shipping the goods, the industrial marketer needs to resolve a number of issues, such as trademark and patent protection, political insurance, and legal arbitrations, should any problems develop.

Then, the actual logistics issues have to be resolved, for instance, how to ship and deliver the goods, where to submit the imports for commodities inspection, and how much to set aside for customs duties. All of these details must be settled before delivery is attempted.

Negotiating through these levels of bureaucracy can be time consuming, confusing, and frustrating. It is a process that requires following the proper sequence of procedures. Leaving out one step of the process or one of the administrative offices responsible for reviewing the contract, or approaching the end-user too early in the process can lead to problems that may be difficult, if not impossible, to resolve.

Summary of Problems

This section presents a summary of the main problems industrial marketers have to resolve when selling to Chinese enterprises. The points come from the preceding material and personal knowledge of the Chinese market. The following obstacles are often encountered in developing business relationships with China:

1. Confusion caused by the overlapping bureaucratic organizations: The same transaction can be handled by different Chinese sectors whether it be government-level bureaucracy or local business. At this point, an inside-information provider is vital.
2. Chinese process-oriented buying behavior versus U.S. action-oriented selling behavior: When a U.S. company does business with a government-owned business, or more accurately, a public bureaucracy, Americans find they have to sacrifice their action orientation for process orientation, which usually tries their patience. Chinese process-oriented buying behavior often involves a hierarchical project evaluation, collective decision making on project approval, and other unusual delays, which all contribute to low efficiency.
3. Chinese indirect, nonverbal cues in negotiations versus Americans' straightforward yes or no style: This is one of the biggest culture shocks in many business negotiations. The problem is exacerbated when more than one level of management on the Chinese side participates in the negotiations and Americans fail to read whose nonverbal cues play a decisive role and whose verbal participation is insignificant.
4. Overdependence on a translator: In some cases, selecting a translator from a third party can be wise. But, overrelying upon the abilities of a translator to bridge the culture gap as well as the language gap can be a mistake. A successful translator must be trusted by one side, while the other side can "read" some information from the way the translator behaves. To judge the reliability of the information provided by the translator, the other side needs to see how well his advice and suggestions are accepted by the decision makers.
5. Lack of skills in developing human relationships: Clusters of interpersonal relationships often are beyond the recognition of the Americans, as well as the translator. Japanese are good at picking up various group dynamics occurring in the other negotiating team. When the Japanese begin doing business with a Chinese enterprise, they like to have the buyers around them in a social setting before conducting business. Americans are often tempted to conduct business

first, and then celebrate a successful negotiation. Presenting a "gift" is the norm of the Japanese (also a norm of the Chinese). This does not mean to suggest that Americans should "bribe" Chinese officials/managers. On the contrary, if Chinese officials/managers later find out that those gifts are "ear-marked," or conditional, the givers lose their credibility. The point here is that the Japanese appear to be better at using personal relations to establish a business relationship.

To understand effectively Chinese buying behavior, one has to learn how to cope with China's bureaucracy, which frustrates and/or confuses many companies. One way to approach the market is directly. This involves selling to and/or through a local enterprise. This model is covered in the next section, and is described as the "Buying Group" model. It requires an understanding of the Chinese bureaucracy and the patience to fulfill carefully its requirements. The "Agency" model, also presented in the next section, is a case of using a local Chinese organization to help navigate the red tape. Therefore, apart from understanding the official organizational bureaucracy, it is beneficial to a U.S. company to find a key public sector organization and, more crucially, a very responsible key figure, to handle its case.

TWO ALTERNATIVE APPROACHES TO THE YIN AND YANG OF BUYER–SELLER RELATIONSHIPS IN CHINA

The "Buying Group" Model

The Benxi Iron & Steel Import & Export Corporation (BISCIEC) is an example of selling directly to Chinese enterprises in the form of an authorized buying bureaucracy (see Appendix 1). BISCIEC, one of the major iron and steel import/export corporations in China, is a subordinate branch of the China Ministry of Metallurgical Industry of Beijing. Normally, any import transactions should be conducted through the Beijing bureaucracy; however, local corporations, such as BISCIEC, have certain purchasing authority depending on the total cost of the goods to be imported. The following illustrates how the buying group model works in various situations.[1]

Buying and Importing Mining Equipment Through the Ministry

China, or more specifically, the Ministry of Metallurgical Industry of China started buying mining equipment from America, Japan, and West Germany in 1977, a year before the Economic Reform. Import priority was given to heavy industrial technology and equipment. One issue in China's doing business with other countries is the availability of foreign exchange currency. This is especially prominent in large capital equipment purchases. China is determined not to become burdened by a large foreign debt and seriously limits its budgeting of foreign currency. Before a buying group can enter into any negotiation, a local corporation like BISCIEC must be allocated foreign currency by the Beijing Ministry. Therefore, it is natural for the direct buyer to be extremely price sensitive and focus on the amount of foreign currency budgeted. Here is a case to illustrate the issue:

In 1983, through the Beijing Ministry, a negotiation was conducted by the Benxi Corporation for equipment urgently needed to modify their hot-strip mill, built in the early 1970s. The plant was constructed by the Chinese, but some technical issues still remained unsolved. Plant technicians pleaded for the right to import foreign technology. The foreign currency allocation was made before the suppliers' bids were received and negotiations started, but after the technicians had set the criteria for the proposed product. Thus, the buying group was limited during the negotiation to meeting the technical specification with a budget of $50 million for the project.

Three American enterprises were the first to provide bids. The president of one of the three visited China five times during 2 years and conducted dozens of negotiations, but failed to win the bid. Instead, a West German business won the contract. Japanese businesses also provided bids, but Benxi Corporation did not even enter into negotiations with them. The Chinese wanted to do this transaction with the Americans because of their trustworthy reputation and technical knowledge, as well as their open and straightforward negotiating style. The Chinese, however, were unable to accept the American bid due to foreign exchange constraints. No one from the Chinese side could release the information about the $50 million appropriation. Therefore, negotiating became guesswork for the Americans. Also, the American side could not lower the price because of higher labor costs. The American firms were without government subsidies such as those provided to the Japanese and German businesses. The result was that the German business took the bid at $40 million, covering all the technical services offered by the Americans. Benxi Corporation was disappointed that the American firms could not realize the Chinese preference to do business with them.

This case shows how important it is for U.S. industrial marketers to have "inside information" while not violating the Chinese norms. Several bureaucratic restrictions that the Chinese could not admit, but that were influencing the decision, prevented the American firms from getting the project. All the Chinese could do was to try to cooperate on aspects other than price. The Chinese feel that negotiation is compromise. In this case there was less possibility of making a compromise between the American businesses and Benxi Corp. Benxi could not get any more money allocated, although they had the right to choose from whomever met the specifications within the budgeted limit and they could sign the contract. The American businesses were not government subsidized and thus were not able to set their prices below the cost.

Another example involving the buying group occurred in 1977 when Benxi Corporation, through the ministry in Beijing, bought ten sets of 120-ton trucks from an American enterprise. This was the first mining equipment transaction between China and the United States. The American side and Benxi Corporation had a harmonious business relationship and strong interpersonal relationships developed. The American technicians sent to China were successful in establishing close relations with their Chinese colleagues. During the contracted term, from 1977 to 1981, the American side provided quality technical services and, most importantly, sent experts to do valuable on-the-job training at the work site. This training permitted the Chinese technicians to be independent from the Americans in the future.

The American truck supplier was assiduous in carrying out the contract and never had any difficulties with the negotiations. They made every item clear in the contract and were flexible on some changes such as providing some spare parts and handling damage claims.

This first transaction established an important relationship for the American enterprise and produced tremendous influence with other Chinese mining companies. Benxi Corporation in effect became an advertiser for American businesses because the American seller established an excellent relationship with the Chinese buyer. Since then, many Chinese mining companies have visited Benxi Corporation and learned how the Americans trained their people.

This successful transaction brought, directly and indirectly, more exports from the United States to China. Later on, Benxi Corporation bought more 120-ton trucks, the Shanxi mining corporation imported 300 sets, the biggest water dam project imported 100 to 150 sets of 50-ton and 80-ton trucks, and mining corporations from other parts of China also followed suit. Thus, through a successful initial sale, the United States gained a large share of the Chinese market for mining equipment. This early success even prevented competitors from entering the market. For instance, a Japanese company offered more favorable terms for a transaction than the American side. The Japanese were willing to provide one 120-ton truck free of charge for 1 year's use before the Chinese had to decide whether they would buy from them. Moreover, they would provide 1 year of free service. Benxi Corporation did try the truck for 1 year and three Japanese technicians were sent to train their people. Comparing the Japanese to the American technicians, the three Japanese men worked harder. They also lived on the worksite for an entire year. This was not done by the Americans, although the Americans did provide quality service regularly and called when something went wrong.

A year later, the president of this Japanese company came to Benxi Corporation to get feedback on the trucks and offered a price 20 percent cheaper than the American side offered with the same equipment. The truck was $1 million/set. Benxi Corporation bought the one they had tried but their technicians rejected importing trucks from Japan.

A local enterprise like Benxi does have the right to make some direct buying decisions. While the previous examples have examined buying from foreign countries through the head office—Ministry of Metallurgical Industry in Beijing—there are cases where Benxi Corporation made the buying decision independently.

One of the cases is the import of a direct-reading spectrometer that costs \$2 million. The reason for its purchase was technical superiority over the existing one. The new model had multifunctions and could experiment on more than 40 elements, far better than the one the Chinese currently had. The buying motive was improving technical equipment. Benxi technicians learned that other iron and steel enterprises had recently imported this improved spectrometer, and they requested that they also be allowed to import one. In a case like this, the importing procedures are much simpler and efficient than those required to be processed through the Beijing bureaucracy.

The first significant difference is the authorization level required based on the product cost. If it is less than \$3 million for the project or the product, then a local enterprise is granted the buying and decision-making authority. This, however, is dependent on the previously mentioned availability of foreign exchange currency. At the beginning of every budget year, normally the Chinese calendar year, each enterprise is appropriated a certain amount of foreign currency. Later during the year purchasing needs may be identified and buying procedures initiated to acquire the desired item. The following illustrates the buying procedures for a direct-reading spectrometer bought at the local level:

The technicians of a subordinate factory of the corporation first fill out a report form describing the function of the product, the necessity of having it, a feasibility study, and other reports. Then they present their proposal to their factory's technology department. After being technically approved there, the technology department presents the proposal to the factory general manager who brings it to a collective decision-making session (composed of several top managers). Finally, the subordinate factory sends its request for the import to the import/export corporation.

Upon receiving the report from the local factory, the corporation proceeds as follows: the equipment department managers hold an extended meeting with staff from the planning department, technology department, and finance department of the subordinate factory and the corporation. At the meeting there is a technical defense of the proposed import project. A vote is taken with the majority making the decision. Finally, a formal document is developed. If, by this time, the corporation has foreign currency available, the corporation could start inquiries. If no money is available, the corporation sends the formal report to Beijing Ministry of Metallurgical Industry for allocation of foreign exchange currency.

If the corporation has a sum of appropriated foreign exchange currency, the general manager has the final decision-making power after the board of directors has made the decision. Benxi Corporation has nine managers, but the general manager has the final say, although in theory the decision should be made by majority rule.

The decision procedures are different for projects greater than \$3 million. If started from a local enterprise, such as a subordinate factory, it would provide the import/export corporation with all the relevant technical data. Next, the import/export corporation presents it, after any necessary modifications, to the Beijing Ministry of Metallurgical Industry. The Ministry then presents the project report to the National Planning Committee for budget appropriation. After the National Committee has approved and allocated the foreign currency, an inquiry is conducted by another public sector organization in Beijing, the China National Technology Import & Export Company (CNTI&EC is a national public enterprise overseeing all the large import transactions of technology and industrial equipment). The CNTI&EC invites bids from foreign countries through the Ministry of Metallurgical Industry. The Ministry informs the local enterprise when the bid is received. During the business negotiation, which is conducted by CNTI&EC, the local enterprise or the ultimate user has the right to reject some contract terms, reject the whole contract, or accept the transaction, although it is the CNTI&EC that signs the contract. Any transactions over $10 million have to go through the CNTI&EC bureaucracy.

Summary of the Buying Group Model

Selling directly to China can be a difficult process. The larger the potential sale, the more numerous the levels of bureaucracy encountered. In the Buying Group model, certain corporations are established as import/export enterprises and are empowered to deal directly with foreign industrial marketers. This power is contingent, however, upon a number of factors: Technological feasibility studies, group consensus votes, availability of foreign exchange currency, and other, perhaps even unseen, factors. The question exists as to whether the profit is worth the effort.

The "Agency" Model

In this section a model is presented offering an approach different than the buying group model for industrial selling in the China market: the agency model. An example of selling to Chinese enterprises through an agency involves the Tianjin Scientific and Technical Exchange Center with Foreign Countries (TSTECFC) (see Appendix 2). TSTECFC is playing an increasing role in helping foreign businesses market their technology and products to Tianjin, one of the largest industrial cities in China.

A U.S. industrial marketer was looking for technical representation in China.[2] The process required successful accomplishment of three distinct phases. The following illustrates the use of the agency model:

Phase One: Getting to Know the Buyers and Seller

In 1984, a three-member group from TSTECFC visited several cities in the United States. In one city, the group visited a university and its science center, the city's business association, and some industrial manufacturers.

When the group returned to Tianjin, after a 1-month trip, several business representatives from the United States then visited Tianjin and were received by the Tianjin center. The Tianjin center arranged for them to meet with the relevant manufacturers and businesses in Tianjin. Since then, some business negotiations have been conducted and transactions reached.

A Chinese–American living in the United States has been the liaison between the center and the businesses in the United States. He visits Tianjin twice a year, bringing business information about the United States and has established a relationship with the center. He is also a consultant for U. S. industrial sellers. In one case, while the Tianjin center group was in the United States, its members visited the plant of an industrial seller and were greatly impressed by the technology and services possessed by the factory. The highest ranking officials of the factory met with the group and presented them with catalogues of its products. On returning to Tianjin, the center distributed the catalogues to the interested factories in Tianjin and, thus, found potential buyers. The center further learned that this kind of product, special bearings, were demanded by several customers. These were electrical machinery plants producing different kinds of motor-driven products into which these special bearings are incorporated.

Phase Two: Establishing a Relationship

TSTECFC began by examining what means could be used to introduce and market the products of the industrial seller in Tianjin. After several rounds of letters and telecommunications, plus person-to-person discussions with this overseas representative, the center began cooperating with the industrial seller in the following ways:

First, the center held conferences to introduce the company to the local business community. Present at the conference were representatives from the city's industrial manufacturers, technology centers, and colleges. Thus, through the center, the industrial sellers were introduced to potential buyers.

Second, the center presented its proposal for further business cooperation between buyers and sellers. The points addressed in the proposal were:

1. The center was responsible for advertising the company's technology and products in China. The company benefits because it does not have to send representatives or establish an office in China. Also, the center has far more influence than the company's representatives could generate, because a public bureaucracy like the center has formal relationships with city bureaucracies such as the planning committee, different bureaus (like local departments or committees), and government-owned factories. Moreover, the center is able to get accurate information regarding foreign currency appropriation, approvals from superior management, and other government information.
2. The products provided by the company must be of advanced quality.
3. The seller provided catalogues and samples periodically to help promotion.
4. The center was responsible for screening two engineers to be the representatives of the company in Tianjin. Candidates were to be interviewed by the company in Tianjin. The company made the final decision on the candidates.

5. The company was responsible for covering all the expenses for the two representatives' 30-day on-the-job training in the U.S. company's facilities.
6. After their return from training in the United States, the center provided the two representatives with an office and office facilities such as telex and other equipment.
7. The company was to pay $5,000 to the center for opening the agency, and $10,000 every year to the center for business activities.
8. The center was responsible for providing a written report to the company in the United States including: names of the customers visited; their interests in the company's products; the probability of potential transactions; postsale services required; and sales support.

Based on the above suggestions, the American side had a lawyer prepare a formal "Technical Sales Representative Agreement." The follow-up decision is mainly made by the manager of the center. The manager coordinates every party involved in this cooperative program and is responsible for the quarterly report to the company. His management superiors depend totally on him; therefore, his suggestions play an important role. Having a manager who is familiar with every procedure, is responsible and possesses a key office position is crucial to the establishment of an effective program.

Phase Three: Continuing Operations

The two sales engineers are responsible for any technical and maintenance problems of the products (equipment). If the problems are beyond their control, the two representatives report to the company in the United States.

For Chinese enterprises to make purchases from the U.S. company, the required foreign currency must be approved by the national level bureaucracy. A relevant technical feasibility study is a prerequisite for the appropriation of the foreign currency. The Tianjin Science & Technology Committee is responsible for the feasibility study and approval, and the center is a direct subordinate sector of it. The implication here is that the center can provide better guidance to a prospective customer who then has a much greater chance than other organizations of having the appropriation granted.

Another channel to get foreign currency appropriated is through a bank, via a loan. This is much more complicated. The center, in this situation, has to provide data to show that the buyer is reliable with respect to payback, that is, the buyer must have the capability to export something to earn foreign currency. This is beyond the business scope of many Chinese enterprises. Moreover, greater bureaucracy is involved for bank loans. The foreign trade corporations are responsible for signing the contract, and any foreign trade business has to be reported to the national level corporations. Due to the existing overlapping foreign trade corporations, deciding which corporation one should approach is confusing. Also, competition sometimes occurs between the FTCs. For example, the import of bearings can be done through Machinery Import & Export Corporation, or by China

Technology Import & Export Co., or by a Foreign Trade Corporation and other related ministries.

Buying procedures are often very complicated and almost impossible to list. Even with the listed steps at hand, all the contingent approaches and changing situations are still confusing. Going through a public agency like the center and having a responsible subordinate manager may be a more efficient and effective way to enter the China market. A drawback is that some control is given to the agency by the industrial seller.

Other Examples of the Agency Model

For national level projects, projects planned by the national government and given priority, bids are invited from different countries. Some of the important local projects involve bid invitation as well. The procedures are as follows: First, the individual sector (either a factory or a bureau) presents a project report to the authorities. The report includes scientific proof of the need for the proposed import of equipment or technology; the development of the product; and the primary screening of one to three potential manufacturers of the project (here referring to the sellers in the international market). To complete such a project report, the individual enterprise has to contact potential buyers before the enterprise receives final approval.

Second, the concerned bureaucracies above the individual enterprise approve the projects proposed by their respective enterprises. The fact is, not all projects are approved at this level, and only those that provide a very strong argument and scientific data, and also show sophisticated knowledge of the products and the manufacturers (foreign sellers), are likely to be approved. The dilemma is that potential sellers are reluctant to enter into any business negotiations until the Chinese side has appropriated the money or until the project proposal is approved. By then it is too late, however, as the individual enterprise has to know enough about the manufacturer to convince the government to appropriate funds. Sending salesmen or consultants to China for promotion before the project is set is risky and expensive for foreign businesses; however, it is necessary to do so if one wants to sell technology and equipment in China. The agency model helps to minimize this risk and uncertainty.

If the seller is interested in developing a marketing project, including joint-venture, technology transfer, or selling industrial equipment, he can send his catalogue and other related materials to the center, that will send the materials to selected enterprises that may be interested in the program. Next, the center will require a written report from the Chinese enterprises that should state whether this program can be developed; evaluate the technology of the potential seller's product; determine possibilities for establishing a cooperative relationship; establish relevant qualifications of their enterprise; and detail their requirements for the program. If both parties are interested, the center will help send a letter of invitation and visas for the potential sellers to come to China and meet with the individual enterprise. If both parties have reached a better understanding of each other after face-to-face communication, and they believe that there are good possibilities for cooperation, the center will use its influence to promote and facilitate the business.

Another approach to developing buyer–seller relations is for the center to hold a technology exchange conference for the foreign businesses whose products are needed by Chinese enterprises. The center will invite all the potential buyers from the entire country to the conference. This a more efficient and effective way for some larger industrial marketers and could not be done by foreign businesses themselves, nor by their offices (if they have any) in China. The foreign businesses pay an advertising fee and the administrative expenses for the advertising. Since the center has access to many types of home businesses, as well as Chinese technicians and other experts, it generates more information and buyer reaction than would the foreigners by themselves. Chinese technicians are invited to the conference to evaluate the foreigners' technology, and the center may release the news to local or even national mass media. Some orders, such as maintenance equipment for gas pipe lines, have been placed through this channel.

Seller-Directed Cooperation

One medical apparatus and instruments manufacturer in the United States hoped to promote its surgical apparatus in China. The center located a first-rate orthopedics hospital to be the sample show-room. The manufacturer equipped the operating room with its advertised products and trained two Chinese surgeons to use them. Since this hospital periodically trains surgeons from all over the country, the American equipment receives high professional exposure.

Buyer-Directed Cooperation.

Introducing business opportunities to outside firms is another function of the center. The center provides business information to the outside world through formal or informal channels. For example, one American was amazed at the Chinese "dragon boat." Thus, the center made an inquiry to a business in Chicago asking whether a sightseeing boat could be produced. Tianjin will produce the wooden shell and the United States will provide the operating equipment.

Summary of the Agency Model

The agency model approach to marketing in China has several advantages for industrial marketers. It permits both direct and indirect representation for sellers. It also provides buyer and seller-directed facilitation. However, the performance ability of the agency and its representatives is a key factor. In examining some of the issues the Tianjin center faced and solved, it becomes clear that the agency model can be a powerful tool for U.S.

industrial marketers if the Chinese representatives involved are effective business facilitators.

CONCLUSION

China's industry is focusing on modification or replacement of existing industrial equipment and technology. The need to purchase this technology from the West exists in several product categories including plant equipment, high technology, transportation, communications, and other infrastructures. If American sellers can be made aware of these needs and begin to develop products that meet China's demand, a large potential market exists for American industrial products manufacturers.

The problem to date, however, has been how to penetrate the layers of bureaucracy and satisfy the requirements of the Chinese government. Because of organizational systems that are not as efficient as those of other free enterprise-oriented countries, many uncertainties and difficulties exist in doing business with China. Some observers feel that the "Eldorado"-like promise of China has dimmed in recent years, and it is time to begin to look elsewhere for potential partners/buyers of technology (Fischer, 1988). On the other hand, the Chinese feel that in comparison with business people from other countries (e.g., Japan), the American businessmen are less persistent, patient, and culturally flexible. To some extent, the Chinese believe that their primary suppliers, currently the Japanese, are more process-oriented while Americans are more action-oriented in doing business. The Chinese, apparently, would often prefer doing business with U.S. companies over others but are left with no choice. This chapter shows how complicated the Chinese industrial buying process is, but also presents potential solutions to the problem of selling to China—the Buying Group model and the Agency Model.

APPENDIX 1

BISCIEC handles the import of equipment, spare parts, instruments, meters, and some special raw and semifinished materials for technical revamp and renewal of equipment to meet the needs for the production and scientific research of Benxi Iron & Steel Co.

It handles the negotiation and the signing of a contract concerning cooperative production, cooperative investment and management, compensatory trade, and processing of imported materials.

It handles the export of the metallurgical products and by-products produced by Benxi Iron & Steel Co. and also technical transfer.

ORGANIZATION OF BISCIEC

Board of Directors
General Manager
Vice General Manager
Export Department handling the export of products, equipment produced by Benxi Iron & Steel Co. and technical transfer.
Import Department handling the import of equipment, spare parts, instruments, and qualified experts for Benxi Iron and Steel Co.
Department of Foreign Economic Affairs engaging in technical exchange, use of foreign investment, cooperative investment and management, processing of imported materials, compensatory trade, labor export, contracting foreign projects of Benxi Iron & Steel Co. and also handling the business in special economic and developing zones of China.
Comprehensive Planning Department engaging in the business of statistical tables and reports.
Finance Department responsible for the setting of foreign exchange and for the payment of foreign insurance, freight incidentals, and internal current accounts.
Transport and Store Department responsible for the business of transport concerning the import and export of BISCIEC.
Market Conditions Dept. responsible for collecting international Market conditions information.

APPENDIX 2
A Brief Introduction to the China Tianjin Scientific and Technical Exchange Center with Foreign Countries (TSTEC)

China Tianjin Scientific and Technical Exchange Center with Foreign Countries is an organization for science and technology exchange and cooperation with foreign countries on a nongovernmental level. It was established in 1980 with the aim to organize and promote exchange and cooperation between the scientific and technological circles in Tianjin and their counterparts in various countries on the basis of friendship, equality, and mutual benefit. Its goal is to promote science and technology, economic and social developments, and the mutual understanding and friendship between the Chinese people and peoples of all other countries.

THE MAIN ACTIVITIES OF TSTEC

1. Building an international bridge between scientific research institutes, academic societies, higher educational institutions, medical circles, factories, mines, and other enterprises in Tianjin and various countries, to establish relations or exchange and cooperation in these fields.
2. Exchanging scientific and technical personnel with foreign countries for joint research and technology development.
3. Handling the business of technical cooperation including joint design research and development, and handling the business of technical trade, including the transfer of techniques, know-how, and patent licenses.
4. Handling joint venture affairs, cooperative production, and compensatory trade.
5. Inviting foreign specialists and scholars to give lectures and conduct technical symposia in Tianjin.
6. Organizing and conducting bilateral and multilateral international science and technology conferences and public lectures and seminars.
7. Organizing specific or comprehensive international exhibitions for exchange of science and technology.

8. Organizing overseas visits, study tours, short-term advanced studies, and other academic exchanges by scientific and technical personnel in Tianjin.
9. Collecting and displaying catalogues and samples of new products from foreign countries.
10. Promoting exchanges of scientific and technical information between science and technology institutions in Tianjin and their foreign counterparts.
11. Receiving financial and material support provided by science and technology communities in various countries for personnel training and scientific and technical activities for Tianjin.
12. Facilitating communication and cooperation between the China science and technology exchange center and other organizations and foreign countries in various provinces and municipalities in China in scientific and technical exchange and in carrying out scientific and technical activities.

NOTES

1. The following information was obtained through an interview with a manager from the corporation, and is based on his personal experiences. This manager had significant involvement in several business negotiations and transactions between China and the United States, as well as China and Japan, regarding mining equipment bought by his corporation.
2. The following information was provided by a manager of the center based on his own experiences.

REFERENCES

Delfs, Robert. (1988). "Ideological liberation creeps in to Zhao Ziyang's China with cat-like tread," *Far Eastern Economic Review*, 24 March, pp. 49–55.

Fischer, William, A. (1988). "China and the opportunities for economic development through technology transfer," presentation at the Second Annual IBEAR Research Conference, Los Angeles, Calif., April 7–9.

Hong, Jiahe. (1987). "The development of chinese economy," *Proceedings of the Third World Advertising Congress*, Beijing: Third World Advertising Congress, pp. 17–18.

Kraar, Louis. (1987). "The China bubble bursts," *Fortune*, July 6, pp. 86–89.

Pye, Lucian W. (1986). "The China trade: Making the deal," *Harvard Business Review*, July–August, pp. 74–80.

Smith, Charles R. (1985). *Advertising and Marketing in China*, Hong Kong: The Asia Letter Ltd.

Conclusion

TAMIR AGMON AND MARY ANN VON GLINOW

The main message of this book is to bring technology transfer and international business together. There is no process of international business without a technology transfer, particularly the process-embodied kind. As the focus in the research and the practice of technology transfer is on the transfer that takes place across borders, understanding the environment of international business is essential for those who research or practice technology transfer.

Historically, international business and technology transfer have been treated as distinctly different fields of inquiry. Due to this different treatment and the way that it is expressed in the arena of management research and teaching, the natural interrelationship between them became murky.

The traditional approach to international business grew out of an extension of the functional fields of management. A more complete view of international business is beginning to emerge out of international marketing, international finance, international human resource management, and international aspects of operations research. Yet, in business schools the functional areas of management rarely overlap, and the interdisciplinary approach to the study of international business is generally viewed with some suspicion by academic researchers.

On the other hand, the study of technology transfer has generally been accomplished through particular case studies that owe no allegiance to a discipline or a functional field. They often make use of more than one functional field of management, but in some other cases the functional fields of management are totally ignored.

In this book, we have integrated the two fields. More precisely, we have placed technology transfer as a process that takes place within, while creating the environment of international business at the same time. This is a complex structure and it requires a complex and multidimensional approach. We have achieved it by designing a multiauthor volume. Each one of the contributing authors did his or her own work relating it to a certain topic, a specific case, or a specific country. The complex and wholistic approach is accomplished by taking the book as a whole and regarding the different chapters as related links in one purposeful chain of events.

The book provides a cohesive story line. The story begins with the major environmental elements in Part I, moves through some functional fields in Part II, and then moves on to the major arena of the international business activities in the 1980s—the transfer of technology between the Asian and the American shores of the Pacific in Part III.

In a way the message of the book can be described as a concerto in three movements: the first introduces the background basic themes, the second introduces some ideas, which are picked up and developed against rich contextuality in the third, and the final movement.

We believe that the integration of technology transfer and international business provided by this book is necessary in order to make both topics better understood. A better understanding of the nature of the process of technology transfer will make those researchers and practitioners who are dealing with issues of international business better equipped to carry out their mission. Understanding the complex environment of international business, and the realization that technology transfer is a necessary, and integral part of international business may bring technology transfer to the center stage of international management where it belongs.

Author Index

Subject Index